Programmer's Supplement for Release 5

Books That Help People Get More Out of Computers

X Protocol Reference Manual, R-4 Release, 500 pages

Describes the X Network Protocol which underlies all software for Version 11 of the X Window System.

Xlib Programming Manual, R-4 Release, 672 pages
Xlib Reference Manual, R-4 Release, 792 pages

Complete programming and reference guides to the X library (Xlib), the lowest level of programming interface to X.

X Window System User's Guide, R-4 Release

Orients the new user to window system concepts, provides detailed tutorials for many client programs, and explains how to customize the X environment.

Standard Edition, 752 pages
Motif Edition, 734 pages

X Toolkit Intrinsics Programming Manual, R-4 Release

Complete guide to programming with Xt Intrinsics, the library of C language routines that facilitate the design of user interfaces, with reusable components called widgets.

Standard Edition, 624 pages
Motif Edition, 666 pages

X Toolkit Intrinsics Reference Manual, R-4 Release, 776 pages

Complete programmer's reference for the X Toolkit.

Motif Programming Manual, Motif 1.1, 1032 pages

Complete guide to programming for the Motif graphical user interface.

XView Programming Manual, XView Version 3.0, 768 pages
XView Reference Manual, 266 pages

Complete information on programming with XView, an easy-to-use toolkit that is widely available.

The X Window System in a Nutshell, R-3 and R-4 Release, 380 pages

A single-volume quick reference that is an indispensable companion to the series.

Contact us for a catalog of our books, for orders, or for more information.

O'Reilly & Associates, Inc.

103 Morris Street, Sebastopol CA 95472
(800) 338-6887 US/Canada   707-829-0515 overseas/local   707-829-0104 Fax

R5 Update

Programmer's Supplement for Release 5

of the X Window System,
Version 11

by David Flanagan

O'Reilly & Associates, Inc.

Programmer's Supplement for Release 5
by David Flanagan

Copyright © 1991 O'Reilly & Associates, Inc. All rights reserved.
Printed in the United States of America.

Editor: Adrian Nye

Printing History:

November 1991: First printing.

This book is based in part on *Xlib—C Language X Interface*, by Jim Gettys, Ron Newman, and Robert Scheifler, which is copyright © 1985, 1986, 1987, 1988, 1989, 1990, 1991 by the Massachusetts Institute of Technology, Cambridge, Massachusetts, and Digital Equipment Corporation, Maynard, Massachusetts. Portions of that document are copyright © 1990, 1991 by Tektronix, Inc. Appendix A is based on *X Window System, Version 11, Release 5 Release Notes* which is copyright © 1991 by MIT. Appendix B is based on the *Inter-Client Communication Conventions Manual* by David Rosenthal, which is copyright © 1988 Sun Microsystems, Inc. Appendix C is based on the *X Logical Font Description Conventions* by Jim Flowers, which is copyright © 1988, 1989 by MIT and Digital.

We have used this material under the terms of its copyright, which grants free use, subject to the following conditions:

"Permission to use, copy, modify and distribute this documentation (*i.e., the original MIT, DEC, Tektronix and Sun material*) for any purpose and without fee is hereby granted, provided that the above copyright notice appears in all copies and that both that copyright notice and this permission notice appear in all copies, and that the names of MIT, Digital, Tektronix, and Sun Microsystems not be used in advertising or publicity pertaining to this documentation without specific, written prior permission. MIT, Digital, Tektronix and Sun Microsystems make no representations about the suitability of this documentation for any purpose. It is provided 'as is' without express or implied warranty."

Note, however, that those portions of this document that are based on the original X11 documentation and other source material have been significantly revised and that all such revisions are copyright © 1991 O'Reilly & Associates, Inc. Inasmuch as the proprietary revisions cannot be separated from the freely copyable MIT source material, the net result is that copying of this document is not allowed. Sorry for the doublespeak!

Many of the designations used by manufacturers and sellers to distinguish their products are claimed as trademarks. Where those designations appear in this book, and O'Reilly and Associates, Inc. was aware of a trademark claim, the designations have been printed in caps or initial caps.

While every precaution has been taken in the preparation of this book, the publisher assumes no responsibility for errors or omissions, or for damages resulting from the use of the information contained herein.

This book is printed on acid-free paper with 50% recycled content, 10-15% post-consumer waste. O'Reilly & Associates is committed to using paper with the highest recycled content available consistent with high quality.

ISBN 0-937175-86-2

Table of Contents

4 Internationalization 39

5 Internationalized Text Input 73

Figures

Examples

Tables

Preface

By convention, a preface introduces the book itself, while the introduction describes the subject matter. You should read through the preface to get an idea of how the book is organized, the conventions it follows, and so on.

In This Chapter:

Preface

About This Manual

Release 5 of the X Window System is notable for the major new functionality it adds, particularly at the Xlib level: font service, scalable fonts, device-independent color, and internationalized text input and output. Chapters 1 through 7 of this book explain the major (and the miscellaneous) changes to both Xlib and the X Toolkit for Release 5. Chapter 1 is an introduction that provides an overview of X11R5 and a "roadmap" to the remaining chapters, which are largely independent of one another and can be read in any order desired. These "programmer's manual" chapters are followed by a reference manual section which contains reference pages for each of the new Xlib, Xt, and Xmu functions, new Xaw widgets, and new X clients which are of interest to programmers. Together, these parts form a complete Release 5 update to Volumes One, Two, Four, and Five, the O'Reilly & Associates programmer's manuals and reference manuals for Xlib and the X Toolkit. All the material in this book will be included in future editions of those manuals.

Assumptions

This book is a supplement to other manuals. It is not meant to stand alone, and while it does provide complete coverage of topics such as scalable fonts and device-independent color, it does not explain basic X concepts such as font naming and the use of colormaps. It assumes that the reader is at least somewhat familiar with Xlib and Xt programming in the C programming language. Some of the changes described are to obscure areas of X; if you are not familiar with those areas, chances are that the changes will not affect you.

Related Documents

Nine other books on the X Window System are available from O'Reilly & Associates, Inc.:

> Volume Zero—*X Protocol Reference Manual*
> Volume One—*Xlib Programming Manual*
> Volume Two—*Xlib Reference Manual*
> Volume Three—*X Window System User's Guide*
> Volume Four—*X Toolkit Intrinsics Programming Manual*
> Volume Five—*X Toolkit Intrinsics Reference Manual*
> Volume Six—*Motif Programming Manual*
> Volume Seven—*XView Programming Manual*
> Quick Reference—*The X Window System in a Nutshell*

In addition, the following books, forthcoming from O'Reilly & Associates, document the X Color Management System and the PHIGS-SI three-dimensional graphics library, both of which are new in X11R5:

> *The X Color Management System*, by Al Tabayoyon, Joann Taylor, and Chuck Adams.
> *PHIGS Programming Manual* by Tom Gaskins

The *PHIGS Programming Manual* will be available in early 1992, and *The X Color Management System* will be available in April 1992. Another forthcoming O'Reilly & Associates book will explain X system administration.

The following documents are included on the X11 source tape and are new or have had major changes since X11R4:

> *Xlib—C Language X Interface*, by Jim Gettys, Ron Newman, and Robert Scheifler
> *The X Font Service Protocol*, by Jim Fulton
> *PEX-SI User Guide*, by Marty Hess, Cheryl Huntington, *et al*
> *PEX Protocol Specification*, by Sally C. Barry *et al*
> *X11 Input Extension Library Specification*, by Mark Patrick and George Sachs
> *X11 Input Extension Protocol Specification*, by Mark Patrick and George Sachs

Font Conventions Used in This Manual

Italic is used for:

- UNIX pathnames, filenames, program names, user command names, and options for user commands.

- New terms where they are defined.

`Typewriter Font` is used for:

- Anything that would be typed verbatim into code, such as examples of source code and text on the screen.

- The contents of include files, such as structure types, structure members, symbols (defined constants and bit flags), and macros.

- Xt, Xaw, and Xlib functions.

- Names of subroutines in the example programs.

Italic Typewriter Font is used for:

- Arguments to functions, which could be typed in code as shown but are arbitrary.

Helvetica Italics are used for:

- Titles of examples, figures, and tables.

Boldface is used for:

- Chapter and section headings.

Requests for Comments

To help us provide you with the best documentation possible, please write to tell us about any flaws you find in this manual or how you think it could be improved.

Our U.S. mail address, e-mail address, and phone numbers are as follows:

O'Reilly & Associates, Inc.
103 Morris Street
Sebastopol, CA 95472
800-338-6887
international +1 707-829-0515

UUCP: uunet!ora!bookquestions   Internet: bookquestions@ora.com

Bulk Sales Information

This manual can be resold by workstation manufacturers as their official X Window System documentation. For information on volume discounts for bulk purchase, call O'Reilly and Associates, Inc., at 800-338-6887 or send e-mail to linda@ora.com (uunet!ora!linda).

For companies requiring extensive customization of the book, source licensing terms are also available.

Obtaining Release 5 of the X Window System

The X Window System is copyrighted but freely distributed. The only restriction this places on its use is that the copyright notice identifying the author and the terms of use must accompany all copies of the software or documentation. Thanks to this policy, the software is available for nominal cost from a variety of sources, some of which are listed below. Note that some of this detailed information may become dated rather quickly. The best source of current information is the *comp.windows.x* network news group.

You can get the X software directly from MIT on 6250 bpi 9-track or QIC-24 magnetic tapes written in UNIX *tar* format, along with printed copies of the X documentation, by sending a check in U.S. currency for $450 to:

> MIT Software Distribution Center
> Technology Licensing Office
> MIT Bldg. E32-300
> 32 Carlton Street
> Cambridge, MA 02142

Their telephone number is (617) 253-6966, and the "X Ordering Hotline" is (617) 258-8330. If you want the tapes and manuals shipped overseas, the price is $550. The software and manuals may also be ordered separately.

Sites that have access to the Internet can retrieve the distribution from a number of machines using anonymous *ftp*. Here are a few of the current sites:

Location	Hostname	Address	Directory
Western USA	*gatekeeper.dec.com*	16.1.0.2	*pub/X11/R5*
Central USA	*mordred.cs.purdue.edu*	128.10.2.2	*pub/X11/R5*
Central USA	*giza.cis.ohio-state.edu*	128.146.8.61	*pub/X.V11R5*
Southeast USA	*uunet.uu.net*	192.48.96.2	*X/R5*
Northeast USA	*crl.dec.com*	192.58.206.2	*pub/X11/R5*
UK JANET	*src.doc.ic.ac.uk*	129.31.81.36	*graphics/X.V11R5*
Australia	*munnari.oz.au*	128.250.1.21	*X.V11/R5*

DO NOT do anonymous *ftp* during normal business hours, and please use the machine nearest you.

The distribution is also available by UUCP from UUNET, for sites without Internet access. The files are split up to be small enough for UUCP distribution. See the next section for instructions on getting files from UUNET if you are not a UUNET subscriber.

Example Programs

The examples in this book appear in the *contrib* section of the X11R5 distribution, in the directory *contrib/examples/OReilly/R5suppl*. They are also available free from UUNET (that is, free except for UUNET's usual connect-time charges). If you have access to UUNET, you can retrieve the source code using *uucp* or *ftp*. For *uucp*, find a machine with direct access to UUNET, and type the following command:

```
cp uunet\!~/nutshell/xlib/r5update.tar.Z yourhost\!~/yourname/
```

The backslashes can be omitted if you use the Bourne shell (*sh*) instead of *csh*. The file should appear some time later (up to a day or more) in the directory */usr/spool/uucppub-lic/yourname*.

You don't need to have opened an account to UUNET to be able to access their archives via UUCP from within the United States of America. By calling 1-900-468-7727 and using the login "uucp" with no password, anyone may uucp any of UUNET's online source collection. (You may wish to start by copying *uunet!/usr/spool/ftp/ls-lR.Z*, which is a compressed index of every file in the archives.) As of this writing, the cost is 40 cents per minute. The charges will appear on your next telephone bill.

You don't need to subscribe to UUNET to be able to access its archives by *ftp* either. However, you need to use a machine connected to the internet. To use *ftp*, *ftp* to *uunet.uu.net* and use *anonymous* as your user name and *guest* as your password. Then type the following:

```
cd nutshell/xlib
binary (you must specify binary transfer for compressed files)
get r5update.tar.Z
bye
```

The file is a compressed tar archive. To restore files after retrieving the archive, type:

```
uncompress r5update.tar.Z
tar xf r5update.tar
```

Four example programs, plus an *Imakefile* and a *README* file, will be installed in the current directory.

Acknowledgments

The information in this book was obtained in large part from documents by Chuck Adams, Vania Joloboff, Bill McMahon, Al Tabayoyon and Glenn Widener. These documents later became part of the X Consortium standard Xlib specification *Xlib—C Language X Interface*, and the X Consortium standard *X Logical Font Description Conventions*. Most of the reference pages in this book are edited and reformatted versions of those shipped with the X11R5 distribution. The reference pages for the new Xaw widgets are adapted from *Athena Widget Set—C Language Interface* by Chris Peterson, and the reference pages for the Xmu functions are adapted from the document *Xmu Library*.

I'd like to thank Adrian Nye for his editing and good advice while I was writing this book. More than once he kept me from panicking over schedule and details. Jim Fulton of NCD reviewed the chapter on font service and scalable fonts, and Al Tabayoyon of Tektronix reviewed the chapter on device independent color. Both had knowledgeable comments and helped clarify some of the important concepts in those chapters. Bob Scheifler of the X Consortium and Bill McMahon of Hewlett Packard reviewed both chapters on internationalization, and straightened out a lot of my misconceptions on this confusing topic. Bob Scheifler also took time out of his busy release schedule to answer a long list of my internationalization questions and was always quick to respond to e-mail on any topic. David Lewis went above and beyond the call of duty and provided useful comments on just about everything I wrote. Tim O'Reilly also reviewed and edited the chapters as I wrote them. Other reviewers were Beth Harvey and Cindy Starks of ICS, Ian Darwin of SoftQuad, and Ellis Cohen of the Open Software Foundation. Though much credit goes to these reviewers, I alone am responsible for any remaining errors.

The final form of this book is the work of the staff of O'Reilly & Associates. Eileen Kramer, Kismet McDonough, and Ellie Cutler did a great job of copyediting and final production. Ellie Cutler wrote the index and Daniel Gilly helped with the onerous task of reformatting the reference pages. Lenny Muellner was always happy and quick to answer my *troff* questions, and Donna Woonteiler helped me to understand the production process, and put up with my questions and lack of a realistic timetable.

— David Flanagan

1

Introduction to X11R5

This chapter provides a brief introduction to each of the major new compo-nents of X11R5, and provides a roadmap to the rest of this book. You can use it to decide which of the following chapters to read first.

In This Chapter:

1
Introduction to X11R5

Although Release 5 of the X Window System contains enough new material to fill a book, X11R4 applications should port to X11R5 with few, if any, difficulties. The most significant new features of X11R5 are font service, scalable fonts, device-independent color, internationalization, and 3-D structured graphics. They are all powerful and exciting additions to X, but thankfully, are optional. Programmers may be eager to incorporate these features into their programs, but they are not in any way required to do so in order to use X11R5: the introduction of scalable fonts does not disrupt the use of non-scalable fonts, and the introduction of device-independent color does not make an application that uses device-dependent colors obsolete.

The major new components of X11R5 each satisfy a specialized need. Scalable fonts will probably be of primary interest to developers of formatted text previewers and WYSIWYG word processors. Device-independent color will be most useful in data visualization and other applications that require precise control over allocated colors, and also in artistic and design applications that require colors that are reproducible across devices. The new internationalization features of X11R5 cater to developers who plan to market their programs in more than one country, and 3-D graphics is of interest for computer-aided design and similar applications. These new, specialized components of X11R5 are independent of one another. The decision to upgrade a program to take advantage of device-independent color does not tie you into using 3-D graphics, for example.

Because the new capabilities of X11R5 are independent of one another you may read about them in any order you wish. I have tried to order the chapters by significance and likely frequency of use, but of course cannot second guess everyone's needs. Because the new features of X11R5 are optional and don't interfere with the use of pre-X11R5 X functions, you may skip some chapters entirely. Bear in mind, though, that material is chosen for inclusion in a release of X11 based on industry demand and maturity of concept. Device-independent color, internationalization, and 3-D structured graphics are technologies that have been around for several years and have been proven in small, specialized niches. Their sudden wide availability through X may lead to an explosion in interest and new applications. The new features of X11R5 are, almost by definition, state-of-the-art. Even if you will not be programming directly with them, you may want to be familiar with the concepts behind them.

The sections that follow provide an overview of X11R5 and the structure of this book.

1.1 Font Service and Scalable Fonts

Before X11R5, font handling by X was perhaps adequate, but not outstanding. The availability of fonts was limited by the small number of supported font file formats and by the amount of disk space available to each X server. Font scaling was not feasible because the computation time it would require would overload the X server, and interoperability was compromised because font files were not compatible across architectures. The natural solution to many of these problems in a networked window system is a networked font server. In X11R5, a single machine at a site can be configured to provide font service to all the X servers on a local network (and potentially to the printer servers as well). Because the fonts do not need to be duplicated at each server, many more can be made available without running out of hard-disk space. Because there is a separate process dedicated to font service, scaled fonts can be computed without affecting the performance of the X server, and can be cached for later use by other X servers. Because the font server protocol defines a single standard format for font data, interoperability is much easier. Because more than one server or server process can provide font service, adding a new font file format is simply a matter of running a new font server that reads and exports that format. Because fonts are exported from a single location, font vendors can easily implement access control and license service in the font servers they provide for their fonts.

Scalable fonts have always been possible with the X protocol, but no implementations before X11R5 have supported them, in part because, as indicated above, having the X server perform font scaling can lead to long delays and poor response time, particularly in current single-threaded servers. The X11R5 server from MIT can scale bitmap fonts, and the font server shipped by MIT can export scaled outline fonts. To support font scaling, a convention is required for naming fonts that are scalable—applications must be able to recognize these fonts as scalable in order to take special advantage of them. The X Logical Font Description (XLFD) standard has been updated to address font scaling. Chapter 2, *Font Service and Scalable Fonts*, covers the architecture of font service, and the programming issues behind using scalable fonts.

1.2 Device-independent Color

Until X11R5, color support in X has been intrinsically device-dependent: a triplet of red, green, and blue values that appear orange on one display may appear substantially different on another. Furthermore, with a device-dependent color space, there is no way of choosing colors that will be at fixed perceptual intervals from one another. There are a growing number of applications for which device-dependent color is simply not adequate: scientific visualization applications may use color and shading in precise ways for data representation, and drawing and design applications may use colors for aesthetic impact, colors that must be reproducible on other computers and must be tied to international color standards so they are reproducible in paint, ink, laser printer toner, and so on. X11R5 introduces the X Color Management System (Xcms) to support the precise description of device-independent colors in a variety of internationally standardized color spaces, and the precise control over the allocation and display of those colors and over the conversion of color specifications from one color space to another.

Color theory or colorimetry is a surprisingly complex field of study, and the theory and practice of Xcms is the subject of a book of its own, *The X Color Management System*, from O'Reilly & Associates. Chapter 3, *Device-independent Color and Xcms*, presents the most common and useful features of Xcms but leaves discussion of the more difficult areas to the forthcoming definitive book.

1.3 Internationalization

Recent years have seen amazing growth in the global economy, in communications technology, and in international cooperation and competition. The industrialized world has been networked, but software technology has had a hard time keeping up. Historically, computers have been pretty good at manipulating English text, awkward at handling European text with accented, non-ASCII characters, and hopeless with Japanese and other (often ideographic) Asian languages. The difficulties are at the foundations of our notions about text representation and manipulation: how do you represent text when a language has more than 256 characters? How do you display text that switches between English, phonetic Japanese, and ideographic Japanese? How does a user input ideographic text from a standard keyboard? These and many similar questions have been resolved in Europe and in Asia, but the next, more ambitious goal is interoperability: the same piece of software should run, unmodified, in any language desired by the user. A lucrative global marketplace awaits the developers of such "internationalized" applications, and X11R5 provides the first comprehensive and standard framework within which to write them.

Internationalization occupies a large part of this book. Chapter 4, *Internationalization*, provides an overview of the issues and problems of internationalization and covers all X11R5 internationalization except for internationalized text input. This last is a large topic on its own and is the subject of Chapter 5, *Internationalized Text Input*.

1.4 Three-dimensional Structured Graphics

X11R5 supports 3-D graphics through a library known as PHIGS-SI. PHIGS is an internationally standardized API for high-level, 3-D structured graphics: *high-level* because some of the graphics "primitives" in PHIGS are far from primitive and can define quite complex 3-D solids; *structured* because PHIGS is based on a fundamentally different model than Xlib. Xlib drawing primitives simply draw the requested line, ellipse, text string, or whatever, and then return. PHIGS primitives don't actually perform any drawing; instead they define "structures" that may be combined with other primitives and structures to form nested structures of arbitrary complexity. These structures are stored in a database of sorts and are retrieved and drawn as needed during the course of the program. A number of attributes, such as color, shading, and line style control the rendering of each structure. These attributes are part of the structure itself, but may be changed independently of the drawing primitives in the structure.

Note that PHIGS is the name of the standard API, and PHIGS-SI is the name of the X11R5 implementation of that standard. (The "SI" stands for "sample implementation.") PHIGS-SI is probably the most complete implementation of the PHIGS standard and the still-evolving PHIGS PLUS extension to that standard.

PHIGS-SI could have been implemented directly on top of Xlib, but because PHIGS primitives are so much more complex than Xlib primitives, this would be very inefficient. For this reason, X11R5 contains a server extension known as PEX that supports 3-D graphics primitives directly, and allows the server to take advantage of special hardware, if any exists, when implementing those primitives. PEX stands for "PHIGS Extension to X," but this name is misleading, because the PEX protocol supports general 3-D graphics primitives. PHIGS-SI is the only library in X11R5 that uses the PEX extension, but there is talk of a lower-level "PEXlib" library in the future.

The PHIGS standard defines a large, high-level API, and the PHIGS-SI library contains over 600 functions. Since it is clearly not feasible to document such a huge library in this slim volume, PHIGS-SI is not covered here at all. Two books on PHIGS are forthcoming from O'Reilly & Associates: *PHIGS Programming Manual* and *PHIGS Reference Manual*. These books document PHIGS (and PHIGS PLUS) thoroughly, and pay special attention to the PHIGS-SI implementation.

1.5 Resource Management in X11R5

There are a number of changes in Xlib and Xt resource management for X11R5. Though not as dramatic as the other new features of Release 5, these changes may be more important, simply because they are less specialized. Only some programmers will ever need to use the new internationalization functions in X11R5 but most will want to take advantage of the new resource management features.

The most notable changes to resource management are all designed to make application customization even more flexible for users, particularly users who have multiple-screen displays or who frequently switch between monochrome and color displays. The new features include a ? wildcard in resource files, inclusion of resource files from other resource files, user defaults specified separately for each screen of a display, and the ability for the user to easily specify which of several customized app-defaults files should be read by an application. These features and others are documented in Chapter 6, which is devoted entirely to resource management.

1.6 Other Changes in X11R5

There are a number of miscellaneous changes in X11R5, including new header files that aid in writing portable applications, new widgets in the Xaw widget library, a client and protocol for editing widget resources while an application is running, new secure mechanisms for X server access control, and a newly standardized extension that supports input devices other than the mouse and keyboard. These and other miscellaneous changes are described in Chapter 7, *Other Changes in X11R5*.

1.7 Reference Pages and Appendices

The second half of this book is the reference section. It contains UNIX-style manual pages for all of the new X11R5 Xlib and Xt functions, except the more obscure Xcms functions. It also contains man pages for new and changed X11R5 clients of interest to programmers, and pages for the new widgets in the Athena widget set and the new functions in the Xmu "miscellaneous utilities" library. Appendix A, *Release Notes*, contains excerpts from the X Consortium release notes for X11R5. It contains information about building the X11R5 release and provides details about bug fixes and other minor changes in clients, widgets, and so on. Appendix B, *ICCCM Changes*, documents changes made to the Inter-client Communication Conventions Manual (ICCCM) to accomodate device-independent color. Appendix C, *XLFD Changes*, documents the changes made to the X Logical Font Description (XLFD) standard to accommodate scalable fonts.

2

Font Service and Scalable Fonts

This chapter explains the new font service architecture and the use of the scalable fonts. Font service is entirely transparent to the X programmer—it is impossible for the programmer to tell whether a given font came from a font server or from a font file read by the X server. Although there are no new functions or datatypes related to font service, the architecture overview and font server configuration information in this chapter may be of interest.

In This Chapter:

Fonts

2
Font Service and Scalable Fonts

If you have worked with X at a site with workstations from several vendors, you may have encountered frustrating problems with the use of fonts. If fonts have different names on one host than they do on another, you may have found that an application that performs normally on one display will abort with a "Can't load font" error on another. Or you may have had to maintain separate defaults files for use on different displays.

Ideally, the site administrator could simply place fonts in a directory of a networked file system that is accessible to all hosts at the site. Unfortunately, no binary format for font data has been standardized, and the X servers supplied by different vendors sometimes expect data in mutually incompatible formats. If a vendor wishes to support several font formats, the server must include code to parse each one.

X11R5 provides an elegant solution to these problems in the form of a networked font service. Under this new model, an X server can obtain font data in a simple bitmap format from a *font server* process running somewhere on the network. The font server does the work of parsing font files for any supported format and exports font data in a bitmap format standardized by the X Font Service Protocol. X servers that take advantage of font service no longer need to do the work of parsing fonts themselves. In the near future, however, it is likely that workstation-based X servers and X terminals will continue to support file-based fonts along with their support for font servers.

The Font Service Protocol was designed by Jim Fulton of Network Computing Devices. The font server in the MIT distribution was implemented primarily by Dave Lemke, also of NCD. In addition, Apple Computer has donated a font server (which runs only on the Apple Macintosh computer) to export the Apple bitmap fonts, and, if available, the Apple TrueType fonts as well.

Another new feature in X11R5 is font scaling. In previous releases, each font was available only in a limited number of standard point sizes and resolutions. In the MIT distribution of X11R5, both the X server and the font server implement a simple bitmap font-scaling algorithm that allows fonts to be obtained at any desired point size and resolution. Bitmap fonts are easily scalable, but the resulting scaled font is generally jagged and difficult to read. Fortunately, X11R5 also provides a set of outline fonts. Outline fonts scale nicely, but the scaling process requires significant computation, and an X server, particularly a single-threaded server, might freeze for several seconds each time it scaled a font. This is one of the problems that font servers are intended to address, and it is the font server in the MIT release, rather than the X server, that contains the scaling algorithm for these outline fonts. The fonts and the scaling code were donated by Bitstream, Inc.

X11R5 font service and scalable font support consists of the following components:

- The X Font Service Protocol, a standardized, extensible protocol for communication between a font server and font clients, such as an X display server. This protocol also standardizes the format used for the communication of font data between font server and font client.

- Additions to the X server to allow it to participate in the font service protocol.

- A convention for the naming and inclusion of font servers in the X server font path.

- A bitmap font-scaling algorithm in the X server.

- A set of scalable outline fonts (in Charter and Courier typefaces) from Bitstream, Inc.

- A font server capable of scaling and exporting the new outline fonts as well as the standard X bitmap fonts.

- A font server that runs on an Apple Macintosh computer to export the Apple bitmap fonts and, if available, scaled Apple TrueType fonts to any X servers on the network.

- A respecification of the X server's handling of **XListFonts**, **XLoadFont**, and **XLoadQueryFont** to allow pattern matching for scalable fonts.

- An addition to the *X Logical Font Description Conventions* (XLFD) to handle pattern matching for scalable fonts.

There are no new or changed Xlib functions for the support of font service or scalable fonts. There are new conventions for naming and listing scalable fonts, however, and applications that want to make explicit use of scalable fonts will have to follow these conventions. Note that X11R5 defines a new abstraction, the **XFontSet**, which is used in internationalized applications, but that this has nothing whatsoever to do with font service.

2.1 Font Service

Typically, a font server will run on one host per site and will export all the fonts available at the site, but there are a variety of other ways that font service can be configured. A large site may choose to have multiple font servers to prevent overloading of a single server or to protect against service outages caused by network trouble or server crashes. A font server could export fonts parsed from a variety of formats, or a separate server could be used for each format. A vendor of fonts with a custom format might provide a special font server to export those fonts, and might use the special server to implement licensing policies—restricting the maximum number of simultaneous users of a font, for example. Finally, note that in the terminology of X font service, the X server is a *font client*, and that it is perfectly legal to have other font clients such as printer drivers. Figure 2-1 shows a font server providing service to a workstation, an X terminal, and a printer driver.

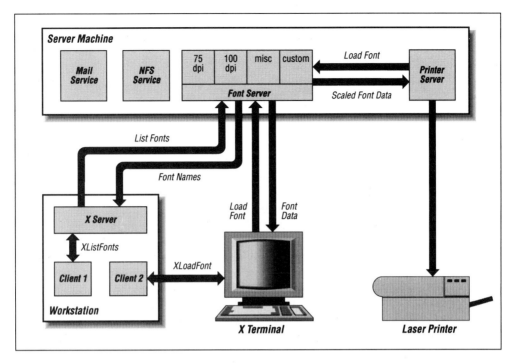

Figure 2-1. A typical font server configuration

Font servers will often group the fonts they export into *catalogues*. Catalogues serve the same purpose as do the subdirectories of */usr/lib/X11/fonts*, which is to divide a large number of fonts into related groups so that they can be specified separately in a font path. So if your font server exports fonts tuned for 75-dpi and 100-dpi screen resolutions, for example, it may group them into catalogues named "75dpi" and "100dpi." Or if your site has purchased fonts from several font vendors, your font server might group them into catalogues by vendor name.

2.1.1 Font Server Naming

To the X server, a font server is just another element in a font path—a place to look when searching for fonts. If a font server is running at your site, you can use it by adding its name (if it is not already there) to your font path with **xset fp**. A font server that runs on a TCP/IP network is named as follows:

> tcp/*hostname*:*port-number*[/*catalogue-list*]

where the optional *catalogue-list* is a list of catalogue names separated with plus signs.

A font server that runs on a DECnet network is named as follows:

decnet/*nodename*::font$*objname*[/*catalogue-list*]

Example 2-1 shows various font paths that might be set in order to use a font server running on the host "ora-server."

Example 2-1. X font paths containing font servers

```
tcp/ora-server:7000

tcp/ora-server:7000/75dpi, /usr/lib/X11/fonts/misc

tcp/ora-server:7000/100dpi+misc, /usr/lib/X11/fonts/misc

tcp/ora-server:7000/100dpi+misc, tcp/ora-server:7001/new-fonts
```

Naming a font server is conceptually the same as naming an X display, but obviously the naming schemes used are very different. When naming an X server, a TCP/IP connection is distinguished from a DECnet connection solely by the number of colons that separate the hostname from the display number, and this scheme is not elegantly extensible to other network technologies in the future. Furthermore, an X server communicates over a port which is a relative offset (the display number) from a "hardcoded" base port number, but base port numbers cannot simply be allocated; they must be assigned by the powers that be in the network world. Font server names specify an absolute port number, rather than a relative number. The default is 7000 as in Example 2-1, but this can easily be overridden (it is a command-line option) if it conflicts with other services or even other font servers. If X were rewritten today, display names would probably be just like font server names: they would explicitly specify the network type and absolute port number.

2.1.2 Font Server Configuration

The font server shipped as part of the MIT X11R5 distribution is named **fs**. Generally it is started up automatically on reboot of whatever server machine it is running on. For standalone machines, it may be appropriate to have **xdm** start up the font server when a user logs in. On startup, **fs** reads a configuration file named on the command line, or the default file */usr/lib/X11/fs/config*. This configuration file lists the directories of fonts that the server should export, and controls such things as the maximum number of clients allowed to connect to the server, and the default point size the server should return when a font name does not specify a size. The format of this file is documented in the **fs** man page in the reference section of this book, and the default config file is a good example. Note that this configuration file is not installed by default when X11R5 is built. Unless you plan to always use the command-line configuration option to **fs**, you should install the configuration file by hand, or add this line at the end of *mit/config/site.def* to have it installed automatically by the build process:

```
#define InstallFSConfig YES
```

The forthcoming O'Reilly & Associates book on X administration will cover font server configuration in more detail.

The X11R5 distribution from MIT also includes a font server for the Apple Macintosh which will export Apple bitmap fonts (and Apple TrueType fonts if they are available) to X servers on the network. The source code for this server is in *mit/fonts/server/MacFS* and will only build on a Macintosh running A/UX. The *README* file in this directory provides minimal documentation on building and configuring the server. Note that the fonts themselves are not part of the X11R5 distribution; these must exist on the Macintosh that will be exporting them.

2.2 Scalable Fonts

Until Release 5, X relied exclusively on non-scalable bitmap fonts. If there was no installed font in the point size and resolution you wanted, then you were out of luck—it is obviously not feasible to provide every font in every point size and for every possible resolution. Bitmap fonts do not scale well, because their pixel-by-pixel specification can only be made smaller by omitting pixels or made larger by making pixels bigger, resulting in a jagged, low-resolution font. The fonts shipped by MIT for Release 5 include several "outline fonts" which describe characters by their component curves rather than by individual pixels. This description allows for successful scaling to any desired point size and resolution. The font server shipped by MIT in Release 5 has the capability to read and scale these outline fonts, and therefore the number of fonts available to the user is greatly increased. (Note, however, that a good bitmap font that is "hand-tuned" to a particular point size and screen resolution will generally be better looking than an outline font scaled to that size and resolution. Font design is an art, and the human touch is still important.)

Scaled outline fonts are only available through the font server, but the R5 X server itself implements a simple bitmap font-scaling algorithm. The following two sections apply equally to all scalable and scaled fonts, whether outline or bitmap, from the X server or the font server.

2.2.1 Finding Scalable Fonts

Supporting scalable fonts raises some important questions about the behavior of the Xlib function **XListFonts**. First, since there are (theoretically) an infinite number of point sizes and resolutions that a font could be scaled to, it is no longer possible to list all available fonts in *all* available sizes. So some special syntax is needed to indicate that a font is scalable and is available in any desired size, even if that size is not listed. But backwards compatibility is also an issue—the new point sizes provided by scalable fonts should not be hidden from existing pre-X11R5 applications.

These seemingly contradictory goals are resolved by changing the semantics of the call to **XListFonts** and by extending the *X Logical Font Description Conventions* slightly.* In

---

*The XLFD Conventions are printed as Appendix M of *X Protocol Reference Manual*, Volume 0 of the O'Reilly & Associates series of X books. The new material covering scalable fonts appears in Appendix C, *XLFD Changes*, of this book.

X11R5, scalable fonts are returned by **XListFonts** with the string "0" in the PIXEL_SIZE, POINT_SIZE, and AVERAGE_WIDTH fields (the seventh, eighth, and twelfth fields of the 14-field XLFD font name). Non-scalable fonts will never have these three fields zero, and therefore these fields are sufficient to distinguish scalable from non-scalable fonts. Most font servers will list a few specific *derived instances* of each scalable font at standard sizes and resolutions for the benefit of older X applications that expect to find font names in this form.

The X server and font server are only required to match scalable fonts when the font name pattern they are passed is a *well-formed* one. A well-formed font name is one that contains all 14 hyphens specified in the XLFD convention. Wildcards are permitted for any field, but may not replace multiple fields—all fields must be present in the name. For example,

```
*-helvetica-bold-o-*-*-*-120-*
```

is not a well-formed name, but

```
-*-helvetica-bold-o-*-*-*-120-75-75-*-*-iso8859-1
```

is well-formed. Shortcut names specified as in the first example have come into common use, but with the increasing variety of display resolutions and fonts with non-standard charsets, it is good practice to specify these extra fields, even if you are not interested in using scaled fonts. If **XListFonts** is passed a pattern that is not well-formed, it may not include scalable fonts in the search at all.

To list scalable fonts, call **XListFonts** with a well-formed pattern with "0" or "*" in its PIXEL_SIZE, POINT_SIZE, and AVERAGE_WIDTH fields. Example 2-2 shows some queries that will return scalable fonts. You can quickly try them out by replacing the call to **XList-Fonts** with the client **xlsfonts**.

Example 2-2. Listing scalable fonts

```
/* List all Latin-1 fonts.  Returned names of scalable fonts will have
 * "0" for pixel size, point size, and average width
 */
fonts = XListFonts(dpy, "-*-*-*-*-*-*-*-*-*-*-*-*-iso8859-1", 1000, &count);

/* List all scalable courier fonts.  Non-scalable fonts will
 * not be listed.
 */
list = XListFonts(dpy,"-*-courier-*-*-*-*-0-0-*-*-*-0-*-*", 200, &count);
```

2.2.2 Finding Derived Instances of Scalable Fonts

A scalable font name with a point size (and pixel size and average width) of zero is not very useful by itself. If you call **XLoadFont** on this font name without a size, you will get some implementation-defined default size. Instead of listing scalable Helvetica fonts, for example, you will more often want to list all Helvetica fonts at some particular point size. The list you get may contain non-scaled bitmap fonts as well as derived instances of scalable fonts. In order to include derived instances of scalable fonts in a search, it is necessary to specify some of the size fields explicitly. There are five *scalable fields* in an XLFD font name: PIXEL_SIZE, POINT_SIZE, RESOLUTION_X, RESOLUTION_Y, and AVERAGE_WIDTH (fields 7, 8, 9, 10, and 12.) In order for **XListFonts** to list a particular scaled size of a scalable font, enough of these scalable fields must be specified so that the font name pattern matches exactly one derived instance of the font. If too few of the scalable fields are specified, there will be no unique match, and if too many are specified, there may not be any possible scaling that meets all of those specified criteria.

When searching for fonts at a particular size, you will typically wildcard the pixel size and average width by setting those fields to "*" and explicitly specify the point size you want along with the x- and y-resolutions of your screen. (You can calculate screen resolutions with macros like `DisplayWidth` and `DisplayWidthMM`, as shown in a later example.) These three fields specify all that is needed to correctly scale the font. You need not (and should not) specify the pixel size, because the point size and y-resolution of the screen determine the desired pixel size. You need not specify the average width because the point size and x-resolution of the screen, together with the height to width ratio implicit to the font, determine the desired width. It is also possible to name a single derived instance of a scalable font by specifying a pixel size plus x- and y-resolutions. There are also other combinations of fields that will work, but none particularly useful in practice. Example 2-3 shows font name patterns that will match derived instances of scalable fonts.

Example 2-3. Finding derived instances of scalable fonts

```
/* Load a 12-point bold helvetica font defined at a 100x100 dpi
 * resolution.  The actual font loaded might be a derived instance of a
 * scalable font, or it might be a bitmap font--there is no way to
 * distinguish them.
 */
font = XLoadFont(dpy, "-*-helvetica-bold-r-*-*-*-120-100-100-*-*-iso8859-1");

/* Load a 20 pixel high helvetica font defined at 100x100 dpi */
font2 = XLoadFont(dpy, "-*-helvetica-medium-r-*-*-20-*-100-100-*-*-iso8859-1");

/* List all 13-point Latin-1 helvetica fonts defined at a 106x97 dpi
 * resolution.  This pattern will match derived instances of scalable
 * fonts, and will probably only match derived instances of scalable
 * fonts, because there are not likely to be bitmap fonts defined at this
 * particular size and resolution.
 */
list = XListFonts(dpy,"-*-helvetica-*-*-*-*-*-130-106-97-*-*-iso8859-1",
                  50, &count);
```

There are a number of reasons that a font name pattern could fail to match derived instances of scalable fonts. It is difficult to devise an algorithm that will correctly match scalable fonts against any font name pattern. For this reason, the X server or font server is not required to include scalable fonts in its search if the pattern it is given is not well-formed. A well-formed pattern must contain 14 hyphens. Note in particular that the first character in a well-formed name must be a hyphen.

An underspecified font name will not match any derived instances of scalable fonts. This is because your font name could match any number of derived instances, and it is not possible to list them all. When only the point size and pixel size are specified, for example, they are enough together to determine the desired y-resolution for the font, but any x-resolution (and therefore any average width) is still possible. To uniquely match a derived instance, you'd have to specify the x-resolution of your screen or a desired average width for the font. The MIT implementation, however, makes reasonable guesses for unspecified resolution values, so underspecified font names do not occur. If only point size is specified, then default resolutions (75 or 100 dpi) are used. If both point and pixel size are specified as above, then the y-resolution they specify is used for both x- and y-resolution fields.

Similarly, an overspecified font name, one with point size, pixel size, and x- and y-resolutions, for example, may not match any derived instances of scalable fonts: if the specified y-resolution is different from the y-resolution implicitly defined by the combination of point size and pixel size, then there is no way that the font can be scaled to satisfy your request. Example 2-4 shows font name patterns that will fail to match any derived instances of scalable fonts.

Example 2-4. Font name patterns that don't match scaled fonts.

```
/* List 15-point bold oblique helvetica fonts.  Derived instances of
 * scalable fonts will probably not be included in the list because the
 * pattern does not have all 14 fields.
 */
helvbold15 = XListFonts(dpy,"*-helvetica-bold-o-*-*-*-150-*", 50, &count);

/* List all 17-point, 17-pixel bold oblique helvetica fonts defined at
 * 100dpi x- and y-resolutions.  This pattern will not match any derived
 * instances of scalable fonts (nor any font) because a 17 point font
 * at 100dpi is not 17 pixels high.
 */
helvbold17 = XListFonts(dpy,"-*-helvetica-bold-o-*-*-17-170-100-100-*-*-
                        iso8859-1",50, &count);
```

2.2.3 Using Scalable Fonts

Many applications use only a small number of fonts, that are opened at startup and never changed. These applications may leave the choice of fonts to the user. If the user overrides the default with a font that doesn't exist, the application may simply print an error message and exit. Applications such as this need no modification to work with scalable fonts. Users who want to take advantage of scalable fonts, must provide a well-formed and correctly specified font name. Other applications, such as word processors or presentation graphics packages, may allow the user to select fonts from a menu or list at runtime. This kind of application will have to be modified to recognize and make use of scalable fonts. Example 2-5 and Example 2-6 demonstrate one approach.

Example 2-5 shows a procedure that determines whether or not a given font name represents a scalable font. This procedure is intended to be called once for each font returned by XListFonts.

Example 2-5. Determining if a font is scalable

```
/*
 * This routine returns True if the passed name is a well-formed
 * XLFD style font name with a pixel size, point size, and average
 * width (fields 7,8, and 12) of "0".
 */
Bool IsScalableFont(name)
char *name;
```

Programmer's Supplement for Release 5

Example 2-5. Determining if a font is scalable (continued)

```
{
    int i, field;

    if ((name == NULL) || (name[0] != '-')) return False;

    for(i = field = 0; name[i] != '\0'; i++) {
        if (name[i] == '-') {
            field++;
            if ((field == 7) || (field == 8) || (field == 12))
                if ((name[i+1] != '0') || (name[i+2] != '-'))
                    return False;
        }
    }
    if (field != 14) return False;
    else return True;
}
```

Example 2-6 shows a procedure that takes a scalable font name and a desired point size and loads the derived instance of that font at the requested size and at the precise resolution of the screen. It is intended to be called with a scalable font name as returned by **XListFonts**.

Example 2-6. Loading a derived instance of a scalable font

```
/*
 * This routine is passed a scalable font name and a point size.  It returns
 * an XFontStruct for the given font scaled to the specified size and the
 * exact resolution of the screen.  The font name is assumed to be a
 * well-formed XLFD name, and to have pixel size, point size, and average
 * width fields of "0" and arbitrary x-resolution and y-resolution fields.
 * Size is specified in tenths of points.  Returns NULL if the name is
 * malformed or no such font exists.
 */
XFontStruct *LoadQueryScalableFont(dpy, screen, name, size)
Display *dpy;
int screen;
char *name;
int size;
{
    int i,j, field;
    char newname[500];     /* big enough for a long font name */
    int res_x, res_y;      /* resolution values for this screen */

    /* catch obvious errors */
    if ((name == NULL) || (name[0] != '-')) return NULL;

    /* calculate our screen resolution in dots per inch. 25.4mm = 1 inch */
    res_x = DisplayWidth(dpy, screen)/(DisplayWidthMM(dpy, screen)/25.4);
    res_y = DisplayHeight(dpy, screen)/(DisplayHeightMM(dpy, screen)/25.4);

    /* copy the font name, changing the scalable fields as we do so */
    for(i = j = field = 0; name[i] != '\0' && field <= 14; i++) {
        newname[j++] = name[i];
        if (name[i] == '-') {
            field++;
            switch(field) {
            case 7:  /* pixel size */
            case 12: /* average width */
```

Example 2-6. Loading a derived instance of a scalable font (continued)

```
                    /* change from "-0-" to "-*-" */
                    newname[j] = '*';
                    j++;
                    if (name[i+1] != '\0') i++;
                    break;
            case 8:  /* point size */
                    /* change from "-0-" to "-<size>-" */
                    sprintf(&newname[j], "%d", size);
                    while (newname[j] != '\0') j++;
                    if (name[i+1] != '\0') i++;
                    break;
            case 9:  /* x-resolution */
            case 10: /* y-resolution */
                    /* change from an unspecified resolution to res_x or res_y */
                    sprintf(&newname[j], "%d", (field == 9) ? res_x : res_y);
                    while(newname[j] != '\0') j++;
                    while((name[i+1] != '-') && (name[i+1] != '\0')) i++;
                    break;
            }
        }
    }
    newname[j] = '\0';

    /* if there aren't 14 hyphens, it isn't a well formed name */
    if (field != 14) return NULL;

    return XLoadQueryFont(dpy, newname);
}
```

3

Device-independent Color and Xcms

The X Color Management System (Xcms) supports device-independent color specifications. It defines a new syntax for the color strings used throughout Xlib, and provides a programming interface that allows extremely precise control over the allocation of colors. Many applications use color purely as decoration and can leave the choice of specific color to the whim of the user. Writers of this sort of application should be aware of the new color specification format, but may skip the rest of the chapter. Programmers who need precise and consistent control over color, for data visualization or artistic applications, should read the entire chapter.

In This Chapter:

3
Device-independent Color and Xcms

The X server supports a color name database in order to translate textual color names into intensity values for the red, green, and blue primaries. This is a convenience for users and a simple attempt at device-independent color—if server vendors tune the database to the particular displays they support, then applications that use the standard named colors can be confident that those colors will appear the same across all displays.

In practice, however, the color database has not been tuned for most displays. Furthermore, there are a growing number of visualization and other applications that use color and shading to display data and convey information rather than simply as decoration. These applications need the ability to precisely specify device-independent colors and often to divide a range of colors into perceptually equal intervals. A small number of hand-tuned named colors in a database is simply not adequate. X11R5 addresses these needs with Xcms, the X Color Management System, which was developed primarily by Tektronix for the X Consortium.

What's New

The following components of X11R5 are relevant to device-independent color and Xcms:

- A new standard textual representation for device-independent color strings.

- Modifications to several existing Xlib functions to support this new standard representation.

- The provision for a database that maps color names to device-independent color specifications. This database is read by Xlib rather than by the X server.

- The Xcms API—a new set of Xlib functions that allow the allocation of device-independent colors and provide extremely precise control over conversions between device-independent color representations. Several of these functions are device-independent analogs to the device-dependent X11R4 color allocation and lookup functions.

- The X Device Color Characterization Conventions (XDCCC), a standard format for new root window properties that contains the information about the physical characteristics of the screen necessary to support the conversion of device-independent color specifications into device-dependent values. A new client, *xcmsdb*, is provided to set the values of these properties.

No changes to the X protocol or the X server are required.

3.1 The Fundamentals of Color Representation

Colorimetry is an involved science, and this book can only scratch its surface. This chapter documents the most useful and commonly used Xcms functions, but because a complete understanding of Xcms requires a deeper introduction to colorimetry than is presented here, some of the more obscure functions will be glossed over and left undocumented. The reference section of this book contains man pages for all the functions described in this chapter, but does not document the remaining Xcms functions. If you are curious about colorimetry or need or want to know all the details of Xcms, O'Reilly & Associates will be publishing a book on Xcms, *The X Color Management System*, by Al Tabayoyon, Joann Taylor, and Chuck Adams of Tektronix. It gives a more thorough treatment of colorimetry, provides complete documentation of Xcms, and describes how to make effective use of color in your applications. It should be available in March, 1992.

Until Release 5, X provided only an RGB system for describing colors. In this scheme, the color of a pixel is described by three numbers which represent the intensity of the electrical signal sent to the electron guns that excite the red, green, and blue phosphors in a monitor. This model is simple from the standpoint of a systems programmer because it is so closely tied to the physical hardware. Unfortunately, our eyes do not perceive color proportionally to the voltage applied to the electron guns, so equal voltage changes over a range of red, green, or blue intensities do not produce an equal perceptual change. At low intensities, a change of many voltage steps may be required before any perceptual difference is produced. In addition, selecting a desired color by additive mixing of each of the primaries is not as simple as it sounds. Fine-tuning a color by this method is essentially a process of trial and error. The RGB color model is a device-dependent color model because it is tied directly to the physical characteristics of a given screen—the electrical response of the electron guns, the precise composition of the phosphors used, and so on. If the same RGB color specification is displayed on two different monitors, the resulting colors will be noticeably different.

By definition, a device-independent color specification will result in identical displayed colors regardless of the device that is used. The device-independent color representations supported by X11R5 are all based on an international standard color representation model known informally as CIEXYZ. In CIEXYZ and related color spaces, a color is described by the value of three coordinates (as is the case with RGB), and the color space itself is commonly referred to by the names of its coordinates. X11R5 supports the CIEXYZ color space, related spaces known as CIExyY, CIExyY, CIEuvY, CIELuv, CIELab, and a color space designed by Tektronix known as TekHVC. The interpretation of the coordinates of all but the last of these spaces is not particularly intuitive and requires some knowledge of colorimetry. These spaces will not be described here; instead all discussion and examples in this chapter will use the TekHVC color space. This is a perceptually uniform color space designed to be intuitive. It is mathematically related to the CIE spaces, but is easier to describe and to understand. In this model, a color is characterized by Hue, Value, and Chroma. The Hue of a color is what distinguishes it from colors of other color families—the blues are of different hues from the greens, for example. Value describes the lightness or darkness of a color, and Chroma describes the saturation or "vibrancy" of a color. The range of possible values for these three coordinates define the HVC "color solid." It is an irregular solid defined in cylindrical coordinates with Hue as the angle, Chroma the radius, and Value the z-coordinate of a point. The model is designed to make it intuitive to find a desired color. Because the space is perceptually uniform, uniform increments in the value of any of the coordinates of a color result in uniform perceptual differences in displayed colors. Figure 3-1 shows a diagram of the TekHVC "color solid," and a "hue leaf," the cross section of the solid for a single Hue.

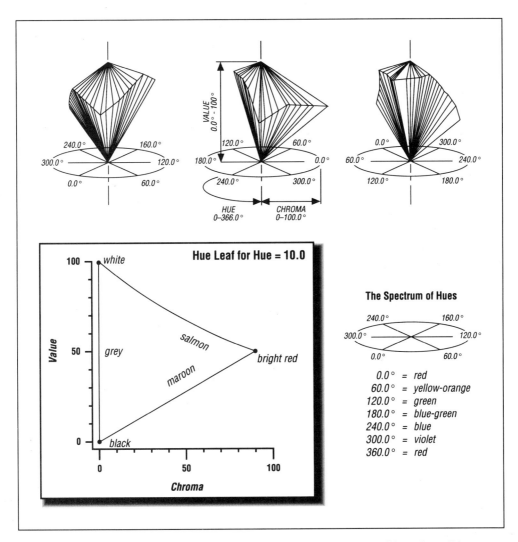

Figure 3-1. Three views of the TekHVC color solid and a single hue leaf from the solid

In the TekHVC space, Hues near 0.0 are reds, Hues near 60.0 are oranges and yellows, Hues near 120.0 are greens, Hues near 180.0 are blue-greens, Hues near 240.0 are blues, and Hues near 300.0 are violets. Because the Hue coordinate is an angle, the reds near 0.0 "wrap around" to Hues near 360.0. At any given Hue, the legal values of Value and Chroma define an approximately triangular area, sometimes called a *hue leaf*. For example, for the red Hues around 10.0, colors with Chromas near 0.0 are almost grey, and as the Chroma increases, the range of legal Values decreases, and the colors redden, passing through various reddish-brown shades, until around the maximum Chroma (near 90.0) there are only a few legal Values (near 50.0), and the colors are all bright "sports car" red. At the same Hue of 10.0, a Chroma of 55.0 and the minimum legal Value (near 30.0), the color is a deep maroon, and it lightens as the Value increases until at the maximum Value (near 65.0) it is a salmon pink.*

Any color that is visible to the human eye can be described by three coordinates in a device-independent color space, but no given device can display all possible colors. Stated in another way, all colors visible to the human eye lie within the TekHVC color solid, but the colors that can be generated by any particular device lie within some subset of that solid. Each monitor type has a *device gamut* which is the set of colors it can display. When a color is requested that is outside of the gamut for a device, some form of *gamut compression* must be used to map the requested color into a displayable color in a sensible way. When an Xcms function attempts to convert a device-independent color that is outside of the device gamut to a device-dependent color, Xlib automatically performs gamut compression on that color, and the function returns a special value that indicates that compression occurred.

3.2 Color Specification and Naming in X11R5

Several existing Xlib functions and several new Xcms functions allow the specification of colors in string form. Prior to X11R5, two types of color strings were supported: numeric RGB specifications beginning with the special character #, and color names to be passed to the X server and looked up by the server in a color name database. In X11R5, two new types of color strings are supported as well: a new numeric color specification syntax, and color names from a database searched by the client rather than the server. Both the new Xcms functions and the pre-X11R5 color functions support the new formats.

When the functions **XAllocNamedColor**, **XLookupColor**, **XParseColor**, **XStoreNamedColor**, or their device-independent Xcms analogs are passed a color string, they first attempt to parse it as a new-style specification for one of the supported color spaces. If this fails, they attempt to look up the color in the client-side color name database. If both approaches fail, they fall back on the pre-X11R5 behavior and attempt to parse the string in the old-style numeric format or pass the string to the X server to be looked up in the server database. Because the new X11R5 formats are supported by the pre-X11R5 Xlib functions, all X Toolkit widgets and type converters will work correctly with device-independent color specifications without change.

The sections below describe the new format for color strings and explain how the client-side database of device-independent color names is used.

---

*A good way to become familiar with the TekHVC color space is to use the TekColor Editor from Tektronix. It allows a user to interactively and graphically select TekHVC colors. It is not part of the MIT X11R5 distribution, but is available for anonymous ftp from the host *export.lcs.mit.edu* in the compressed *tar* file *xtici.tar.Z*.

3.2.1 Numeric Color Specification

Prior to X11R5, a color string of the form # followed by a string of hexadecimal digits could be used to describe a device-dependent RGB color. For example:

#ab17d6

describes a color for which the 8 most significant bits of the red value are the hexadecimal number ab, the 8 most significant bits of the green value are hex 17, and so on. This format continues to be supported in X11R5, but its use is discouraged.

In X11R5, a device-dependent RGB value is represented as follows:

RGB:*<red>*/*<green>*/*<blue>*

where *<red>*, *<green>*, and *<blue>* are each between 1 and 4 hexadecimal digits. Different primaries may be specified with different numbers of digits. If fewer than 4 digits are specified, they do not simply represent the most significant bits of the value; instead they represent a fraction of the maximum value. So the single digit 0xA does not mean 0xA000, but 10/15ths of 0xFFFF, or 0xAAAA.

X11R5 supports an additional device-dependent color space, called RGBi, in which each red, green, and blue integer *value* is replaced with a floating-point *intensity* between 0.0 and 1.0. In this model, the range of possible color values are simply mapped onto the real numbers between zero and one. So, for example, 0.5 always represents half intensity of a color. Note that these values represent the physical intensity of a color, which is not linearly proportional to the perceptual intensity of that color. A color specification for RGBi has the following form:

RGBi:*<red>*/*<green>*/*<blue>*

where *<red>*, *<green>*, and *<blue>* are floating-point numbers between 0.0 and 1.0, inclusive.

Device-independent color specifications follow the same syntax—a color space name followed by a colon and slash-separated color space values. The following forms are recognized:

CIEXYZ:*<X>*/*<Y>*/*<Z>*
CIEuvY:*<u>*/*<v>*/*<Y>*
CIExyY:*<x>*/*<y>*/*<Y>*
CIELab:*<L>*/*<a>*/*<b>*
CIELuv:*<L>*/*<u>*/*<v>*
TekHVC:*<H>*/*<V>*/*<C>*

Each of the values in these device-independent color spaces is a floating-point number. Note that different color spaces have different ranges of legal values for each parameter. For example, the *u* parameter of the CIEuvY color space must have a value between 0.0 and approximately 0.6, while the *H* parameter of the TekHVC color space represents an angle and thus varies between 0.0 and 360.0. Also, the valid values for one parameter often depend on the values of the others. In general, you will need to be familiar with the colorimetric theory behind a particular color space before attempting to specify colors in that space. See *The X Color Management System* for more information about these color spaces.

Example 3-1 shows this new style of color specification used in a resource file. Notice that color space names are case-insensitive.

Example 3-1. Specifying device-independent colors from a resource file

```
*Background: TekHVC:72.0/50.0/44.0
*Command.background: CIELab:75.0/.38/.71
*quit_button.background: rgbi:1.0/0.0/0.0
```

3.2.2 The Client-side Color Name Database

Support for device-independent colors in X11R5 is, by design, kept entirely on the client side. The X protocol and the X server itself still use device-dependent RGB colors exclusively, so it is not possible to use the new device-independent color specifications in the color name database read by the server. Because it is sometimes useful to give symbolic names to device-independent colors, X11R5 supports a client-side color database that maps names to device-independent or device-dependent color specifications.

Note that while X11R5 supports such a color database, the MIT release does not provide one, other than as an example to system administrators or users who want to define one of their own. The client-side color database should be thought of as a place for site-specific customizations, and useful, if non-standard, shortcuts for naming colors in user resource files. In particular, since the contents of the database are not standardized, application defaults files should not rely on any particular colors to be in the database.

X clients (on most UNIX systems) look for the client-side database in the file */usr/lib/X11/Xcms.txt* by default, but the MIT sample implementation allows a different file to be specified with the XCMSDB environment variable. The format of the database is implementation-dependent. Example 3-2 shows an example database in the format supported by the MIT distribution.

Example 3-2. Example entries from a client color database

```
XCMS_COLORDB_START 0.1
device red     RGBi:1.0/0/0
device blue    RGB:00/00/ff
navy blue      CIEXYZ:0.0671/0.0337/0.3130
gray0          CIELab:0.0/0.0/0.0
gray50         CIELuv:50.0/0.0/0.0
grey100        TekHVC:0.0/100.0/0.0
rouge          red
roja           rouge
XCMS_COLORDB_END
```

Note that any device-dependent or device-independent color format may be used, and that color *aliases* are allowed to provide alternate names for colors defined elsewhere in the client database or even in the server database. Color names may contain spaces, and the tab character is used to separate color names from color specifications. The first and last lines shown in the example are required before the first and after the last entry of the database. Any text before the first line shown in the example is treated as a comment. Comments may not appear elsewhere in the file.

3.3 Screen Characterization and the XDCCC

In order for Xcms to convert from device-independent color used by X clients to the device-dependent colors used by the X server, it must know the characteristics of the screen or screens connected to the server. What is needed is a 3 × 3 matrix to convert between the CIEXYZ and RGBi color spaces, and a lookup table to convert from RGBi intensities to RGB integer values. The X server stores this data in properties of the root window of each screen so that the Xcms functions have access to it without the necessity of extending the X Protocol. The names and formats of these root window properties are specified in the X Device Color Characterization Conventions (or XDCCC) which has been added to the *Inter-Client Communication Conventions Manual* (or ICCCM). The ICCCM is printed as Appendix L of Volume Zero, and Appendix B, *ICCCM Changes*, of this book contains the new section on the XDCCC.

X11R5 provides a new client, *xcmsdb*, which reads screen characterization data from a file and sets the data on the appropriate properties. System administrators may configure *xdm* to automatically invoke *xcmsdb* for every screen of a display, or users who make use of device-independent color may invoke it themselves. The source code for *xcmsdb* in the MIT distribution includes two sample screen characterization data files, but the distribution does not attempt to provide data for all possible screen types. If screen characterization data is not specified on root window properties, Xlib will fall back on default data. This means that you can experiment with the new Xcms features, but because the default data will almost certainly not match your display, the colors you see will not actually be the device-independent colors you request. Vendors may make screen characterization data available in the contributed section of the X11R5 release, but even these will not get you truly device-independent color: the physical characteristics of a monitor change as it ages, so for accurate color reproduction, you will have to have your monitor calibrated.

3.4 The Xcms Programming Interface

The Xcms programming interface is part of Xlib and contains many new functions and a number of new datatypes, all of which begin with the prefix "Xcms" (X Color Management System). Some of these new functions are close analogs to the pre-X11R5 color functions that allocate cells in colormaps and that store and query colors in colormap cells. Where the existing Xlib functions operate on an **XColor** structure, the analogous Xcms colormap functions operate on an **XcmsColor** structure that allows colors to be specified in a device-independent fashion. These are the functions that will be most frequently used by programmers.

There is a group of Xcms functions used to manipulate an Xcms datatype known as a "color conversion context" or CCC. In X11R5, every colormap has an associated CCC which contains attributes that control the details of the conversion of colors from one color space to another. Default CCCs are automatically handled by Xcms, and many programmers will never have to use them explicitly. The theory behind color conversions is complicated, and so only the simplest and most useful of the CCC functions are documented here.

Xcms also provides a number of functions to query the boundaries of the device gamut. This means that programmers can ensure that allocated colors will be displayable (without gamut compression) on a given screen. Or it means that programmers can query the most vibrant shade of a color displayable on a particular device. The gamut-querying functions that operate with the TekHVC color model are fully documented in this book. Because other color spaces have not been described in any detail in this chapter, those gamut-querying functions that operate in color spaces other than TekHVC are not documented here.

Finally, Xcms provides functions that allow the extension of Xcms by adding new color spaces and support for new types of display devices. These functions are not documented here. See *The X Color Management System* for full documentation of these functions as well as all the color conversion context functions and the gamut-querying functions.

Note that Xcms functions require significantly more computation that their device-dependent analogs. In particular, they require trigonometric and other floating-point operations. In the MIT distribution, the standard math library is not used. Instead, the floating-point operations are implemented in Xlib directly. Because these functions cannot take advantage of floating-point hardware and do not have the efficiency of a highly optimized math library, they are relatively slow. As a result, adding Xcms functions to a program can add noticeable delays, particularly when gamut compression occurs. You can force the Xcms functions to use the standard math library by editing the macros defined in *mit/lib/X/Xcmsint.h* and rebuilding Xlib.

3.4.1 Color and Colormap Functions

Xcms provides the following functions for setting or querying colormap cells. They are close analogs to pre-X11R5 color allocation functions, but use the **XcmsColor** structure to specify device-independent colors rather than the **XColor** structure, which can only specify RGB colors. These functions are fully documented in the reference section of this book.

XcmsAllocColor

> Allocates a read-only color cell with the specified color. Returns the color specification of the color actually allocated (i.e., the closest color the hardware could support). Analogous to **XAllocColor**, but with an additional argument that specifies the desired color space for the return value. If the requested color is outside of the gamut of the screen, gamut compression is performed.

XcmsAllocNamedColor

> Allocates a read-only color cell with the color specified in the passed color string. Returns the exact color specification for the color string, as well as the color specification and pixel value for the color actually allocated. If the requested color is outside of the gamut of the screen, gamut compression is performed. Analogous to **XAllocNamedColor**, but with an additional argument that specifies the desired color space of the return values. Any color string that can be allocated by **XcmsAllocNamedColor** can also be allocated by **XAllocNamedColor**. The difference is only that the Xcms function returns a device-independent specification of the color.

XcmsLookupColor

Converts a color string into an **XcmsColor** specification, but does not store that color in a color map. Returns the exact color specification of the color string as well as the closest color that could actually be produced on the screen. If the requested color is outside the gamut of the screen, gamut compression is performed. Analogous to **XLookupColor**, but with an additional argument that specifies the desired color space for the return values. Any color string that can be looked up by **XcmsLookupColor** can also be looked up by **XLookupColor**. The difference is only that the Xcms function returns a device-independent specification of the color.

XcmsQueryColor

Given a pixel value, returns the color of that pixel in the given colormap. Analogous to **XQueryColor**, but with an additional argument that specifies which color space the queried color should be represented in.

XcmsQueryColors

Returns the colors associated with a set of pixels in a given colormap. Analogous to **XQueryColors**, but with an additional argument that specifies the desired color space for the returned colors.

XcmsStoreColor

Sets the color of a read/write color cell in the specified colormap. Analogous to **XStoreColor**, but has a return value that indicates whether the conversion from device-independent color specification to RGB values was successful. If the requested color is outside the gamut of the screen, gamut compression is performed.

XcmsStoreColors

Sets the colors of multiple read/write color cells in the specified colormap. Analogous to **XStoreColors**, but has return values that indicate whether the conversions from device-independent specifications to RGB values were successful. If any of the requested colors are outside the gamut of the screen, gamut compression is performed.

The **XcmsColor** structure is the device-independent analog to the **XColor** structure, and is used by all of the Xcms functions described above. It contains a pixel value, a format value which specifies the device-dependent or device-independent color space used to describe the color, and a union of structures that specify the parameters for each of the supported formats. The structure is shown in Example 3-3.

Example 3-3. The XcmsColor strucuture

```
typedef struct {
    union {
        XcmsRGB RGB;
        XcmsRGBi RGBi;
        XcmsCIEXYZ CIEXYZ;
        XcmsCIEuvY CIEuvY;
        XcmsCIExyY CIExyY;
        XcmsCIELab CIELab;
        XcmsCIELuv CIELuv;
        XcmsTekHVC TekHVC;
```

Example 3-3. The XcmsColor strucuture (continued)

```
        XcmsPad Pad;
    } spec;                         /* the color specification     */
    unsigned long pixel;            /* pixel value (as needed)     */
    XcmsColorFormat format;         /* the specification format    */
} XcmsColor;
```

The legal values for the format field are: **XcmsUndefinedFormat, XcmsCIEXYZ-Format, XcmsCIEuvYFormat, XcmsCIExyYFormat, XcmsCIELabFormat, XcmsCIELuvFormat, XcmsTekHVCFormat, XcmsRGBFormat,** and **XcmsRGBi-Format.** The RGB substructure within the union **spec** consists of three unsigned 16-bit integers. All the other color space structures consist of three doubles, and the **XcmsPad** structure reserves four doubles for possible extensions. Example 3-4 shows these structures.

Example 3-4. Selected XcmsColor sub-structures

```
typedef unsigned int XcmsColorFormat;    /* Color Space Format ID */
typedef double XcmsFloat;

typedef struct {                 /* Device RGB */
    unsigned short red;          /* scaled from 0x0000 to 0xffff */
    unsigned short green;        /* scaled from 0x0000 to 0xffff */
    unsigned short blue;         /* scaled from 0x0000 to 0xffff */
} XcmsRGB;

typedef struct {                 /* RGB intensity */
    XcmsFloat red;               /* 0.0 - 1.0 */
    XcmsFloat green;             /* 0.0 - 1.0 */
    XcmsFloat blue;              /* 0.0 - 1.0 */
} XcmsRGBi;

    .
    .                            /* structures for other color spaces omitted */
    .

typedef struct {                 /* TekHVC */
    XcmsFloat H;                 /* 0.0 - 360.0 */
    XcmsFloat V;                 /* 0.0 - 100.0 */
    XcmsFloat C;                 /* 0.0 - 100.0 */
} XcmsTekHVC;

typedef struct {                 /* 4 doubles of pad */
    XcmsFloat pad0;              /* for use by Xcms extensions */
    XcmsFloat pad1;
    XcmsFloat pad2;
    XcmsFloat pad3;
} XcmsPad;
```

Example 3-5 shows a procedure that uses the TekHVC color space and **XcmsAllocColor** to allocate a number of colors with a given Hue and Chroma, and with perceptually uniform steps between a given maximum and a given minimum Value.

Example 3-5. Allocating device-independent colors

```
/*
 * This procedure allocates n colors with the given Hue and Chroma, and
 * with Values equally spaced between minv and maxv.  The pixels values
```

Example 3-5. Allocating device-independent colors (continued)

```
 * are returned in the passed array of pixels, which is assumed to be
 * large enough to hold them.  Returns XcmsFailure if one of the calls
 * to XcmsAllocColor returned XcmsFailure, otherwise XcmsSuccess.
 */
Status AllocShades(dpy, cmap, hue, chroma, minv, maxv, pixels, n)
Display *dpy;
Colormap cmap;
double hue, chroma, minv, maxv;
long *pixels;              /* RETURN */
int n;
{
    XcmsColor color;
    double value, deltav;
    int i;

    if (n > 1) deltav = (maxv - minv)/(n-1);
    else deltav = (maxv-minv);

    color.format = XcmsTekHVCFormat;
    color.spec.TekHVC.H = hue;
    color.spec.TekHVC.C = chroma;
    for(i = 0; i < n; i++) {
        color.spec.TekHVC.V = minv + i*deltav;
        if (XcmsAllocColor(dpy, cmap, &color, XcmsTekHVCFormat) == XcmsFailure)
            return XcmsFailure;
        pixels[i] = color.pixel;
    }
    return XcmsSuccess;
}
```

Example 3-5 has one serious weakness: no checking is performed to ensure that the minimum and maximum Values passed to the procedure are valid. This is particularly important because the range of valid Values depends on both Hue and Chroma. If either of the specifed Values is outside the boundaries of the TekHVC color space, or outside the gamut of the device being used, gamut compression will occur on the allocated colors. Later in this chapter, we develop a refinement to this example that allocates shades, all of which are within the gamut of the device.

3.4.2 Color Conversion

In X11R5, each colormap has a *color conversion context* automatically associated with it. A color conversion context, or CCC, is an opaque structure of type **XcmsCCC**. It contains the attributes that control the details of color conversion from one color space to another. These attributes include the procedure that is called to perform gamut compression when a device-independent color specification is outside the range of displayable colors for a particular device.

Xlib contains functions to create and destroy CCCs, set and get CCC attribute values, and associate a CCC with a colormap. Because the colorimetric theory behind these CCC attributes is beyond the scope of this chapter, these functions will not be described here. Many programmers will never have to use CCCs at all. Others may use CCCs, but will never use anything but the default CCC. This section describes the CCC functions that are useful to this second category of programmer.

Because every colormap has a CCC associated with it, all of the Xcms functions described so far have had an implicit CCC argument. The functions that will be described in the next section, however, do not require a colormap argument but are passed a CCC directly. For these functions, you may obtain the CCC of a colormap with the function **Xcms-CCCOfColormap**, or you may obtain the default CCC of a screen with **XcmsDefault-CCC**.

The color conversion context controls the details of color conversions performed by other Xcms functions. It can also be used to control the explicit conversion of colors with the function **XcmsConvertColors**. This function takes a CCC as an argument, along with an array of **XcmsColor** structures and converts those colors to a single specified target format.

The functions **XcmsCCCOfColormap**, **XcmsDefaultCCC**, and **XcmsConvert-Colors** are documented in the reference section of this book. The remaining CCC functions are listed in Table 3-1. For information on these functions and an explanation of the CCC attributes, see *The X Color Management System*.

Table 3-1. Other Color Conversion Context Functions

XcmsClientWhitePointOfCCC	XcmsScreenWhitePointOfCCC
XcmsCreateCCC	XcmsSetCCCOfColormap
XcmsDisplayOfCCC	XcmsSetCompressionProc
XcmsFreeCCC	XcmsSetWhiteAdjustProc
XcmsScreenNumberOfCCC	XcmsSetWhitePoint

3.4.3 Gamut-querying Functions

To make full use of a screen's color capability, some applications will want to explicitly query the gamut of a screen. Even programs that are not concerned with the precise boundaries of a screen's gamut may need to query the boundaries of an irregular color space to ensure that requested color specifications are legal for that space. In the TekHVC space, for example, the maximum value of Chroma varies with Hue, and the maximum and minimum legal Value varies with both Hue and Chroma. The functions described here can be used to verify that requested colors are legal for the color space, are within the device gamut, and can therefore be displayed as requested, without gamut compression.

The functions **XcmsQueryBlack**, **XcmsQueryWhite**, **XcmsQueryRed**, **Xcms-QueryGreen**, and **XcmsQueryBlue** return the device-independent color specification, in the desired format, of pure black, white, red, green, and blue. That is, they convert from the device-dependent colors RGBi:0.0/0.0/0.0, RGBi:1.0/1.0/1.0, RGBi:1.0/0.0/0.0, RGBi:0.0/1.0/0.0, and RGBi:0.0/0.0/1.0 to the specified color space. These functions are fully documented in the reference section at the end of this book.

The following functions are used to query the screen gamut in terms of the TekHVC color space:

`XcmsTekHVCQueryMaxC`

Determines the maximum displayable Chroma for a given Hue and Value.

`XcmsTekHVCQueryMaxV`

Determines the maximum displayable Value for a given Hue and Chroma.

`XcmsTekHVCQueryMinV`

Determines the minimum displayable Value for a given Hue and Chroma.

`XcmsTekHVCQueryMaxVC`

For a given Hue, determines the maximum displayable Chroma and the Value at which that Chroma is reached.

`XcmsTekHVCQueryMaxVSamples`

For a given Hue, partitions the displayable values of Chroma into a specified number of sampling intervals and determines the maximum value for each interval. This can be used to plot the boundaries of a screen's gamut at a given Hue.

These functions are fully documented in the reference section at the end of this book. Similar query functions exist for the CIELab and CIELuv color spaces, and are listed in Table 3-2. Because CIELab and CIELuv are less intuitive than the TekHVC space, those functions are not documented here. See *The X Color Management System* for complete information.

Table 3-2. Gamut-querying Functions for the CIELab and CIELuv Color Spaces

CIELab Queries	CIELuv Queries
`XcmsCIELabQueryMaxC`	`XcmsCIELuvQueryMaxC`
`XcmsCIELabQueryMaxL`	`XcmsCIELuvQueryMaxL`
`XcmsCIELabQueryMaxLC`	`XcmsCIELuvQueryMaxLC`
`XcmsCIELabQueryMinL`	`XcmsCIELuvQueryMinL`

Example 3-6 is a refinement to Example 3-5. It queries the screen's gamut to determine the minimum and maximum displayable Values for the given Hue and Chroma and allocates a specified number of colors spaced at perceptually equal intervals between that minimum and maximum. If the specified Hue and Chroma are within the screen's gamut, this function will only allocate colors that do not require gamut compression.

Example 3-6. Querying the screen gamut and allocating colors

```
/*
 * This routine allocates n shades of the color with specified Hue and
 * Chroma.  The shades will be at perceptually equal intervals between
 * the minimum and maximum Values of the device gamut for the given Hue
 * and Chroma.
 */
Status AllocShades(dpy, cmap, hue, chroma, pixels, n)
Display *dpy;
```

Example 3-6. Querying the screen gamut and allocating colors (continued)

```
Colormap cmap;
double hue, chroma;
long *pixels;            /* RETURN */
int n;
{
    XcmsColor color;
    XcmsCCC ccc;
    int i;
    double minv, maxv;
    double deltav;

    ccc = XcmsCCCOfColormap(dpy, cmap);

    if (XcmsTekHVCQueryMinV(ccc, hue, chroma, &color) == XcmsFailure)
        return XcmsFailure;
    else
        minv = color.spec.TekHVC.V;

    if (XcmsTekHVCQueryMaxV(ccc, hue, chroma, &color) == XcmsFailure)
        return XcmsFailure;
    else
        maxv = color.spec.TekHVC.V;

    if (n > 1) deltav = (maxv - minv)/(n-1);
    else deltav = maxv - minv;

    for(i=0; i < n; i++) {
        color.format = XcmsTekHVCFormat;
        color.spec.TekHVC.H = hue;
        color.spec.TekHVC.C = chroma;
        color.spec.TekHVC.V = minv + i*deltav;
        if (XcmsAllocColor(dpy, cmap, &color, XcmsRGBFormat) == XcmsFailure)
            return XcmsFailure;
        pixels[i] = color.pixel;
    }
    return XcmsSuccess;
}
```

4

Internationalization

There are several good reasons to internationalize your applications, including sales to foreign markets and simple courtesy to users who would prefer
to run those applications in different languages. Because internationalization
does involve some confusing concepts, this and the following chapter are
thicker than any others in the book. If there is any chance, however, that you
will someday have to port your applications to run in a different country or
language, you should at least be familiar with the concepts and techniques
introduced in these chapters. If you know what is involved in internationalization, you can avoid writing applications that will be difficult to internationalize
later on.

In This Chapter:

4
Internationalization

The largest new part of X11R5 is the support for writing *internationalized* programs. An internationalized application is one that runs, without changes to the binary, in any given "locale." Among other things, this means that a program must display all text in the user's language, accept input of all text in that same language, and display times, dates, and numbers in the user's accustomed format.

The internationalization of terminal-based programs is a problem that has been satisfactorily solved where terminals exist that can display and accept input for a particular language. The ANSI-C library contains mechanisms for this terminal-based internationalization, and X11R5 internationalization is based on these mechanisms. This chapter begins with a detailed overview of the goals, concepts, and techniques of internationalization, starting with ANSI-C internationalization and progressing to the new X11R5 internationalization features. After the overview, each section covers an individual topic in X internationalization. Internationalized text input with X11R5 is a large subject and is given its own chapter following this one.

Before beginning, note that the internationalization features of X11R5 are not self contained, and therefore may not work on all systems. If you do not have the ANSI-C internationalization features, you may be able to make do with alternatives provided by Xlib and by contributed libraries, but these have not been thoroughly tested and you may encounter difficulties. In ANSI-C internationalization, the C library reads a "localization database" customized for each locale. Many systems (systems sold in the U.S., at least) support ANSI-C internationalization, but do not ship databases for any but a default locale.*

A final point of interest: the word "internationalization" contains 20 letters. In the MIT X documentation and elsewhere, you may find it abbreviated as *i18n*—the letter "i" followed by 18 letters and the letter "n."

---

*If you have a system like this, but would like to experiment with X internationalization, add **–DX_LOCALE** to the **StandardDefines** definition in the *.cf* file for your system (in the directory *mit/config/*) before you build the release. This variable should allow X internationalization to work without the ANSI-C locale databases. It will not, of course, make ANSI-C internationalization itself work. If your system does not have any of the ANSI-C internationalization support, and in particular does not define the type **wchar_t** (a "wide character" used for text in some locales), you will also need to add **–DX_WCHAR** to the **StandardDefines** variable. Finally, your programs should include the file *<X11/Xlocale.h>* instead of the standard *<locale.h>* and be compiled with **–DX_LOCALE**; this will replace the ANSI-C **setlocale** with an X version of the function.

What's New

X11R5 provides the following components to support the writing of internationalized applications:

- Simple locale management functions.

- Routines for internationalized text-drawing.
  - Font set handling functions.
  - Font set metric and string measuring functions.
  - String drawing functions.

- Respecification of many Xlib functions to clarify their handling of strings in internationalized applications.

- New functions to support internationalized window manager and text properties for inter-client communication.

- New resource manager functions to support localized databases.

- Respecifications of many resource manager functions to make their behavior in internationalized applications clear.

- A change in the initialization sequence for the X Toolkit to allow a localized resource database to be read, and other minor changes to the Xt specification.

- New support for internationalized text input through input methods. (See Chapter 5, *Internationalized Text Input*.)

- Two sample implementations of all the new Xlib internationalization functions.

The X11R5 distribution is unusual in that it provides two different implementations of the new internationalization functions. The default implementation is named "Xsi" and is from the OMRON Corporation; the MIT distribution builds Xsi by default on all but Sony machines. Sony systems build the "Ximp" implementation from Fujitsu Limited, Sony Corporation, Fuji Xerox Co., Ltd, Oki Technosystems Laboratory, Inc., Toshiba Corporation, and Nihon Sun Microsystems, K.K. Both "Xsi" and "Ximp" implement the same specification,* but are mutually incompatible. In particular, the localization files they read are in very different formats.

---

*These names probably stand for "X sample implementation" and "X input method protocol."

4.1 An Overview of Internationalization

If you are a native English speaker, particularly an American, you may never have thought much about what is required for the internationalization of programs for the simple reason that all the programs you use already speak your language. There are four general areas that require attention when writing an internationalized application:

- An internationalized application must display all text in the user's native or preferred language. This includes prompts, error messages, and text displayed by buttons, menus, and other widgets. The obvious approach to this sort of internationalization is to remove all strings that will be displayed from the source code of the application and put them instead in a file that will be read in when the application starts up. Then it is a relatively simple matter to translate the file of strings to other languages and have the application read the appropriate one at startup. Many X applications that use the X resource manager to provide an app-defaults file are already internationalized in this way, though some still have non-internationalized error messages. Another approach to the internationalization of strings is the message catalog facility defined by the *X/Open Portability Guide, Issue 3* (often known as XPG3).* The three functions `catopen`, `catgets`, and `catclose`, provide a simple mechanism for retrieving numbered strings from a plain text file. These functions are available on some systems, but are not part of any formal standard, and are not universally available.

- An internationalized application must display times, dates, numbers, etc. in the format that the user is accustomed to. Where an American user sees a date in the form *month/day/year*, an English user should see *day/month/year*, and a German user should see *day.month.year*. And where an American user sees the number 1,234.56, a French user should see 1.234,56. The definition of "alphabetical order" is a similar customary usage that varies from country to country. In Spain, for example, the string "ch" is treated as a single letter that comes after "c." So while the strings "Chile" and "Colombia" are in alphabetical order for an American user, they are out of order for a Spanish user. These and related problems of local customs are resolved with the ANSI-C `setlocale` mechanism. Calling this function causes the ANSI-C library to read a database of localization information. Other functions in the C library (such as `printf` for displaying numbers and `strcoll` for comparing strings) use the information in this database so that they can behave correctly in the current locale. The X11R5 internationalization mechanisms are built upon this `setlocale` mechanism. It is described in more detail in the next section.

- An internationalized program must be capable of displaying all the characters used in the user's language, and must allow the user to generate all these characters as input. For terminal-based applications, this can be thought of as a hardware issue: a French user's terminal must be capable of displaying the accented characters used in French, and there must be some way to generate those characters from the keyboard. With X and bit-mapped displays, character display is not a problem—simply a matter of finding the required font or fonts. For languages like Chinese, fonts with many characters are

---

*X/Open is an influential international group working to encourage computer inter-operability. It is not related to the X Consortium or the X Window System.

required, but X supports 16-bit fonts, which is large enough for almost all languages. Keyboard input for Chinese and other ideographic Asian languages is another matter, however. When there are more characters in a language than there are keys on a keyboard, some sort of "input method" is required for converting multiple keystrokes into a single character. Ideographic languages require complex input methods, and often there is more than one standard method for a language. An internationalized application must support any input method chosen by the user. X11R5 provides this capability; it is described in Chapter 5, *Internationalized Text Input*.

- An internationalized program must operate regardless of the encoding of characters in the user's language. A program (or operating system) that ignores or truncates the 8th bit of every character won't work in Europe, because the accented characters used in many European languages are represented with numbers greater than 127. An application that assumes that every character is 8 bits long won't work in Japan where there are many thousands of ideographic characters. Furthermore, common Japanese usage intermixes 16-bit Japanese characters with 8-bit Latin characters, so it is not even safe to assume that characters are of a uniform width. When internationalizing an application, two areas of particular difficulty are string manipulation (how, for example, can you iterate through the characters of a string when those characters have differing widths) and text input and output. (How, for example, do you display a Japanese string that contains characters from different fonts?)

One approach to the encoding problem is to side-step it by defining a universal encoding used everywhere. The Latin-1 encoding is suitable for English and most western European languages, and this shared encoding dramatically simplifies the problem of porting applications to work in many European countries. But this approach does not work outside of Europe, and while ANSI-C provides some rudimentary internationalized string manipulation functions, it leaves issues of text input and output to the terminal hardware or terminal driver software. It is here that X11R5 makes its real contribution to internationalization—in an extension to the `setlocale` model, an internationalized X application reads a localization file at startup that contains information about the text encoding used in the locale. This information allows X to correctly parse strings into characters and figure out how to display them. There are a number of issues surrounding character encoding in internationalized applications, and it is possible to explore them in full and confusing detail. In practice, though, most of the string encoding details are hidden by the operating system, or with X internationalization, by Xlib. Section 4.1.2 explains some of the basics of text encoding in more detail.

When thinking about applications that run in other languages, it is important to recognize the distinction between an internationalized application and a multilingual application. A text editor that works in any given locale is internationalized; a mail reading program that labels its push buttons with text in the language of the locale is internationalized, but if it also allows a user to compose mail in a second language and include excerpts from a message in a third language, then it is multilingual. The requirements and problems of multilingual applications are not yet well understood, and the X Consortium made a considered decision that X11R5 would support internationalized applications but not explicitly support multilingual ones.

The following sections continue this introduction to internationalization with a description of the ANSI-C `setlocale` mechanism and a further discussion of character encoding and text representation issues.

4.1.1 Internationalization with ANSI-C

Clearly it is not feasible to write an application that has special case code for the formatting customs of every country in the world. A simpler approach is to use a library that reads a customizing database at startup time. This database would contain the currency symbol, the decimal separator symbol, abbreviations for the days of the weeks and names of the months in the local language, the collation sequence of the alphabet, etc. This is the approach taken by the ANSI-C library. The process of writing an application that is flexible enough to use the values from this database is called internationalization, and the process of creating the run-time database for a locale is called *localization*.

The first step in any internationalized application is to establish the locale—to cause the localization database to be read in. This is done with the C library function `setlocale`. It takes two arguments: a locale category and the locale name. The locale name specifies the database that should be used to localize the program, and the locale category specifies which behaviors (for example, the collation sequence of the alphabet or the formatting of times and dates) of the program should be changed. `setlocale` will most often be used as shown below:

```
setlocale(LC_ALL, "");
```

Passing the empty string as the locale name will cause `setlocale` to get the name of the locale from the operating system environment variable named **LANG**. This allows the application writer to leave the choice of locale to the end user of the application. There is no standard format for locale names, but they often have the form:

> *language*[*_territory*[*.codeset*]]

So the locale "Fr" might be used in France, while "En_GB" might specify English as used in Great Britain, and "En_US" English as used in the U.S. The *codeset* field can be used to specify the encoding (i.e., the mapping between numbers and characters) to be used for all strings in the application when there is not a single default encoding used for the language in the territory. The locale "ja_JP.ujis" is an example—"ujis" is the name of one of the encodings in common use for Japanese. The name of the default locale is simply "C." This locale is familiar to American computer users and all C programmers. Finally, note that the return value of `setlocale` is a `char *`. It returns the name of the locale that was just set, or if it is passed a locale name of **NULL** (not the same as `""`), it will return the name of the current locale.

The category `LC_ALL` instructs `setlocale` to set all internationalization behavior defined by ANSI-C to operate in the given locale. The locale may also be specified for each category individually. The standard categories (other, non-standard, categories may also be defined) and the aspects of program behavior that they control are listed below:

LC_COLLATE

This category defines the collation sequence used by the ANSI-C library functions **strcoll** and **strxfrm** which are used to order strings alphabetically.

LC_CTYPE

This category defines the behavior of the character classification and case conversion macros (such as **isspace** and **tolower**) defined in the header file *<ctype.h>*. Different languages will have different classifications for characters. Not all characters have uppercase equivalents, for example, and characters with codes between 128 and 255 which are non-printing in ASCII are important alphabetic characters in many European languages.

LC_MONETARY

This category does not affect the behavior of any C library functions. The problem of formatting monetary quantities was deemed too intricate for any standard library function, so the library simply provides a way for an application to look up any of the localized parameters it needs to do its own formatting of monetary quantities. The ANSI-C function **localeconv** returns a pointer to a structure of type **lconv** that contains the parameters (such as decimal separator, currency symbol, and flags that indicate whether the currency symbol should appear before or after positive and negative quantities, etc.) needed for numeric and monetary formatting in the current locale.

LC_NUMERIC

This category affects the decimal separator used by **printf** (and its variants), **scanf** (and its variants), **gcvt** (and related functions), **strtod**, and **atof**. It also affects the values in the **lconv** structure returned by **localeconv**.

LC_TIME

This category affects the behavior of the time and date formatting functions **strftime** and **strptime**. It defines such things as the names of the days of the week and their standard abbreviations in the language of the locale.

If you use **setlocale** and the new C library functions mentioned above (and carefully avoid the use of the old C functions that they replace), you will be well on your way to an internationalized application. For more information on **setlocale** and the functions it affects, see the documentation supplied by your vendor (a UNIX system should have reference pages for these functions). The *POSIX Programmer's Guide* by Donald Lewine, published by O'Reilly & Associates, may also be useful—it has a chapter on ANSI-C internationalization and a complete reference section of ANSI-C and POSIX (IEEE standard UNIX) functions.

4.1.2 Text Representation in an Internationalized Application

Think for a minute about the fundamentals of text representation by computer. Remember that characters displayed by your computer are represented by numbers. The correspondence between numbers and characters (on most American computers) is defined by the ASCII (American Standard Code for Information Interchange) encoding. There is nothing special about ASCII except that it is one of the most firmly established standards of the computer world. Text composed in one encoding (ASCII, for example) and displayed in another (perhaps EBCDIC, still used by IBM mainframes) will be nonsense because the number-to-character mappings of the encodings are not the same.

We've been using the term encoding rather loosely. Before we consider text representation any further, some definitions are appropriate. A *character* is an abstract element of text, distinct from a *font glyph*, which is the actual image that gets displayed. A *character set* is simply a set of characters; there are no numbers associated with those characters. We are all familiar with the character set used by ASCII. The Latin-1 character set used by many Western European Latin-based languages is an extension of ASCII that contains the accented characters required by many of those languages. An encoding is any numeric representation of the characters in a charcter set. The term *codeset* is sometimes used as a synonym for encoding. A *charset* (not the same as a character set) is an encoding in which all characters have the same number of bits. ASCII is a 7-bit encoding, for example, and is therefore a charset. Figure 4-1 diagrams the relationship between character sets, charsets, fonts, and font glyphs.

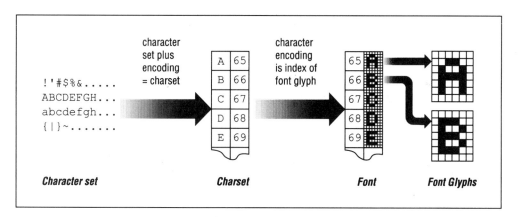

Figure 4-1. Character sets, encodings, charsets, fonts, and glyphs

The last two fields of an X font name specify a charset. By definition, the index of a font glyph in the font is the same as the encoding of the corresponding character in that charset. When the encoding of a locale is a charset, this obviously simplifies matters a great deal: text in the locale can be displayed using glyphs from a single font, and the character encoding can be used directly as the index of the corresponding font glyph.

Not all languages can be represented with a single charset, however. Japanese text, for example, commonly requires Japanese ideographic characters, Japanese phonetic characters, and Latin characters. Each of these character sets has its own standard fixed-width encoding, and is therefore a charset. Note, however, that the ideographic charset is 16-bits wide while the phonetic and Latin charsets are 8-bits wide. Full Japanese text display requires a font for each charset, and Japanese text representation requires a "super-encoding" that combines each of the component encodings. There are, in fact, several encodings commonly used for Japanese text. What they have in common is the use of "shift sequences" to indicate which charset the following character belongs to.

It is crucial to the concept of a locale that each locale has a single well-defined encoding. Many languages have only a single standardized encoding. If a language can be encoded in more than one standard way, each encoding defines a locale of its own, and the name of the encoding is part of the name of the locale.

ISO8859-1 and Other Encodings

If you examine the names of the X fonts on your system (using **xlsfonts**) you will probably find that most of them have the charset "iso8859-1." This charset is sometimes called "Latin-1" and was designed to be suitable for use by most Western European languages (Greek being a notable exception). The character set of ISO8859-1 comprises all the ASCII characters plus a wide variety of accented and special characters. (You can take a look at the characters using the **xfd** program.) Because there are fewer than 256 characters in the set, ISO8859-1 can use a state-independent 8-bit encoding. This means that all characters are 8 bits long, and there are no special shift sequences that modify the interpretation of characters. Because there are not any shift sequences, it is possible to use the encoding of all Latin-1 characters directly as font indices.

ISO8859-1 contains a superset of the ASCII characters. Every character in the ASCII character set has the same encoding in Latin-1 as it does in ASCII. (But Latin-1 does not define any control characters such as linefeed, backspace or the bell character.) Because it is an 8-bit encoding, Latin-1 strings can be represented using the usual C null-terminated array of **char**. Because the characters are a uniform 8 bits and because strings do not contain embedded shift states, it is possible to use Latin-1 strings with the standard C string manipulation routines (**strlen**, **strcat**, etc.) In conjunction with the ANSI-C internationalization facilities, the careful design of ISO8859-1 means that most programs originally written for ASCII use can easily be ported for use in most Western European countries.

But it is not so simple once we try to go beyond Western Europe and Latin-based alphabets. Japanese text, for example, commonly uses (at least within the computer industry) words written in the Latin alphabet along with phonetic characters from the *katakana* and *hiragana* alphabets and ideographic *kanji* characters. Each of these types of text has its own charset (8- or 16-bit), but they must be combined into a single encoding for Japanese text. This is done with shift sequences, bytes embedded in the running text which control the character set in which the following character will be interpreted. It is possible to use "locking shifts" which modify the interpretation of the next and subsequent characters, but this scheme is infrequently used because it makes strings of text very difficult to manipulate.

Compound Text is another text representation that is used in X applications. Compound Text strings identify their encoding using embedded escape sequences (they can also have multiple sub-strings with multiple encodings) and are therefore locale-independent. The Compound Text representation was standardized as part of X11R4 for use as a text interchange format for interclient communication. It is often used to encode text properties and for the transfer of text via selections, and is not intended for text representation internal to an application. There are new X11R5 routines that convert X Property values to and from the Compound Text representation. Note that Compound Text is not the same thing as the Compound Strings used by the Motif widget set.

Multi-byte Strings and Wide-character Strings

Strings in encodings that contain shift sequences and characters with non-uniform width can be stored in standard NULL-terminated arrays of characters, but can be difficult to work with in this form: the number of characters in a string cannot be assumed to be equal to the number of bytes, and it is not possible to iterate through the characters in a string by simply incrementing a pointer. On the other hand, strings of **char** are usefully passed to standard functions like **strcat** and **strcpy**, and assuming a terminal that understands the encoding, functions like **printf** work correctly with these strings.

As an alternative to these multi-byte strings, ANSI-C defines a wide-character type, **wchar_t**, in which each character has a fixed size and occupies one array element in the string. (The **wchar_t** is 2 bytes on some systems, 4 bytes on others, and may be 1 byte on systems that support nothing but the default C locale.) ANSI-C defines functions to convert between multi-byte and wide-character strings: **mblen**, **mbstowcs**, **mbtowc**, **wcstombs**, and **wctomb**.* As you can see here, and as you will see with the X11R5 internationalized text input and output functions, "multi-byte" is commonly abbreviated "mb" in function names, and "wide character" is abbreviated "wc." Multi-byte strings are usually more compact than wide-character strings, but wide-character strings are easier to work with. Note that ANSI-C does not provide wide-character string manipulation functions. There is, however, a contributed library of wide character functions that is shipped with the MIT X11R5 release; see the directory *contrib/lib/Xwchar*.

In an internationalized application, you must take care to handle all strings properly. Unfortunately the ANSI-C library does not provide adequate functions or conventions for sophisticated internationalized text manipulation. Note, though, that many applications can do internationalized text input and output without performing any manipulations on that text. The following list gives a few guidelines for handing internationalized strings:

- Multi-byte strings are null-terminated. There is no single convention for the termination of wide character strings, but strings passed to **wcstombs** are null-terminated. As was the case before X11R5, X text output and input functions take and return strings with a count of the characters they contain.

- If an encoding is state-dependent (i.e., if it uses locking shifts) multi-byte strings are assumed to begin in the default shift state of the encoding. There is no convention for the

---

*If your C library does not define these functions, you can try the library contributed with X11R5 in *contrib/lib/Xwchar*.

shift state at the end of a string, so when concatenating two strings, the first may need to be reset to the default shift state in order to guarantee correct interpretation of the second. In practice, state-dependent encodings are rarely used.

- None of the C library string-handling functions work with wide-character strings.

- The following C string-handling functions may be safely used with multi-byte strings (in a state-independent encoding): **strcat, strcmp, strcpy, strlen, strncmp**. Note that the string comparison routines are only useful to check for byte-for-byte equality. To compare strings for sorting, use **strcoll**.

- Multi-byte strings can be written to file or output streams. Assuming a terminal that operates in the current locale, printing a multi-byte string to **stdout** or **stderr** will cause the correct text to be displayed.

- Multi-byte strings can be read from files or from the **stdin** input stream. If the file is encoded in the current locale, or the terminal operates in the locale, then the strings that are read will be meaningful.

4.1.3 Internationalization Using X11R5

The techniques of internationalization described so far have had little to do with X, and they have been sufficient only to internationalize a terminal-based application. X applications draw text directly into their windows and get input directly from keyboard events. When an application must use multi-byte strings in an encoding that contains shift sequences and non-uniform width characters, deciding which characters to draw can be tricky, and when a language contains far more characters than fit on a keyboard, interpreting KeyPress events becomes difficult. Additionally, X clients often communicate with other clients. Because internationalized clients can run in different locales an internationalized interclient communication method is required. Also, X clients make heavy use of resource files and databases, and will need a mechanism for the correct localization of resources. The internationalization of X11R5 is based on the ANSI-C locale model, but the function **setlocale** is not sufficient for locale management in an X application. Two new functions are defined which are used along with **setlocale** when an X application starts up. Finally, all these new internationalization features of Xlib will require some changes to the Xt architecture as well.

The sections below cover these topics as follows:

- Section 4.2 describes the X locale management functions.

- Section 4.3 describes internationalized text output with X11R5.

- Section 4.4 describes string encoding changes in various Xlib functions.

- Section 4.5 describes interclient communication using internationalized properties and interlocale string conversions.

- Section 4.6 describes the localization of resource databases.

- Section 4.7 describes changes to the X Toolkit to support internationalization.

Chapter 5, *Internationalized Text Input*, covers the lengthy topic of internationalized text input with X11R5.

4.2 Locale Management in X11R5

An internationalized X application begins in the same way as a ANSI-C terminal-based internationalized program: with a call to `setlocale`. An X program, however, generally goes two steps further.

Immediately after calling `setlocale`, an application should call `XSupportsLocale` to determine if the Xlib implementation supports the current locale. This function takes no arguments and return a `Bool`. If this function returns `False`, an application will typically print a "Locale not supported" message and exit.

After verifying that the locale is supported, an application should call `XSetLocale-Modifiers`. A "locale modifier" can be thought of as an extension to the name of a locale; it specifies more information about the desired localized behavior of an application. X11R5 as shipped by MIT recognizes one locale modifier, used to specify the input method (see Chapter 5, *Internationalized Text Input*) to be used for internationalized text input for the locale.

`XSetLocaleModifiers` allows the programmer to specify a list of modifiers (usually none) which will be concatenated with a list of user-specified modifiers from an operating system environment variable (`XMODIFIERS` in POSIX). The strings passed to `XSet-LocaleModifiers` and set in the `XMODIFIERS` environment variable are a series of concatenated "@*category=value*" strings. Thus to specify that the "Xwnmo" input method should be used by an application, a user might set the XMODIFIERS as follows:

```
setenv XMODIFIERS @im=_XWNMO
```

Example 4-1 shows code that uses `setlocale` and the two functions described here to correctly establish its locale.

Example 4-1. Establishing the locale of an X application

```
#include <stdio.h>
#include <X11/Xlib.h>
/*
 * include <locale.h> or the non-standard X substitutes
 * depending on the X_LOCALE compilation flag
 */
#include <X11/Xlocale.h>

main(argc, argv)
int argc;
char *argv[ ];
{
    char *program_name = argv[0];

    /*
     * The error messages in this program are all in English.
     * In a truely internationalized program, they would not be
     * hardcoded; they would be looked up in a database of some sort.
     */

    if (setlocale(LC_ALL, "") == NULL) {
        (void) fprintf(stderr, "%s: cannot set locale.\n", program_name);
```

Example 4-1. Establishing the locale of an X application (continued)

```
        exit(1);
    }

    if (!XSupportsLocale()) {
        (void) fprintf(stderr, "%s: X does not support locale
                    program_name, setlocale(LC_ALL, NULL));
        exit(1);
    }

    if (XSetLocaleModifiers("") == NULL) {
        (void) fprintf(stderr, "%s: Warning: cannot set locale modifiers.\n",
                    program_name);
    }
        .
        .
        .

}
```

Not all systems support the `setlocale` function, but X can be built for these systems by defining the `X_LOCALE` compilation flag. When writing programs in an environment that does not have `setlocale`, include the header file *<X11/Xlocale.h>*. If this file is compiled with `X_LOCALE` defined, it defines `setlocale` as a macro for an Xlib-internal function. Otherwise, it simply includes the standard header *<locale.h>* to get the correct declaration of the real *setlocale*.

4.3 Internationalized Text Output in X11R5

Before X11R5, the Xlib drawing routines made the fundamental assumption that the encoding of a character was equal to the index of the character's glyph in the font. As explained in Section 4.1.2, this is a useful and valid assumption when text in a language can be most naturally encoded as an 8- or 16-bit wide charset. Unfortunately, it is not valid in many important cases.

X11R5 bases its new text output routines on a new Xlib abstraction, the **XFontSet**. An **XFontSet** is bound to the locale in which it is created, and contains all the fonts needed to display text in that locale, or all the independent charsets used in the encoding of that locale. Technical Japanese text, for example, often mixes Latin with Japanese characters, so for a Japanese locale, fonts might be required with the charsets jisx0208.1983-0 for Kanji ideographic characters, jisx0201.1976-0 for Kana phonetic characters, and iso8859-1 for Latin characters.

Drawing internationalized text in X11R5 is conceptually very similar to drawing text in X11R4—there are routines that allow you to query font metrics, measure strings, and draw strings. The new X11R5 functions use an **XFontSet** rather than an **XFontStruct** or a font specified in a graphics context. The drawing and measuring routines interpret text in the encoding of the locale of the fontset, and correctly map wide or multi-byte characters to the corresponding font glyph (or glyphs).

4.3.1 Creating and Manipulating Fontsets

A fontset is created with a call to **XCreateFontSet**. This function checks the current setting of the locale to determine which charsets are required for the locale, and uses a supplied *base font name list* to load a set of fonts that supply those charsets. A base font name list can be a single wildcarded font name that specifies little more than the desired size of the fonts, or it can be a (comma separated) list of partially wildcarded font names, or it can even be a list of fully-specified names. Note of course that if a fully-specified base font name list is used, it will only work for one particular locale. Generally you will want to use a very generic base font name, and allow the end user to override it (to choose individual typefaces that look good together, for example) with application resources.

XCreateFontSet returns a list of the charsets for which no font could be found, and a default string that will be drawn in place of characters from the missing charset or charsets. The list of missing charsets should be freed with a call to **XFreeStringList**. The returned default string should not be freed by the programmer. Example 4-2 shows how to create an **XFontSet**.

Example 4-2. Creating an XFontSet

```
XFontSet fontset;
char **missing_charsets;
int num_missing_charsets = 0;
char *default_string;
int i;
        .
        .
        .
fontset = XCreateFontSet(dpy,
                    "-misc-fixed-*-*-*-*-*-130-75-75-*-*-*-*",
                    &missing_charsets, &num_missing_charsets,
                    &default_string);
/*
 * if there are charsets for which no fonts can
 * be found, print a warning message.
 */
if (num_missing_charsets > 0) {
    (void)fprintf(stderr, "%s: The following charsets are missing:\n",
                program_name);
    for(i=0; i < num_missing_charsets; i++)
        (void)fprintf(stderr, "%s:    %s\n", program_name,
                    missing_charsets[i]);
    (void)fprintf(stderr, "%s: The string
                program_name, default_string);
    (void)fprintf(stderr, "%s: of any characters from those sets.\n",
                program_name);
    XFreeStringList(missing_charsets);
}
        .
        .
        .
```

If you use a very generic base font name list, be aware that **XCreateFontSet** may have to search through a large number of font names in order to find fonts of the appropriate charset. Also, when using an R5 X server, try to specify a base font name that will not require scaling. For example, many of the Japanese fonts shipped with the MIT distribution are defined at odd point sizes (11, 13, 15, etc.) instead of the even sizes more commonly used for Latin-1 fonts. If your base font name list specifies a 14-point font, the X server or font server may have to scale thousands of ideographic characters, causing a significant delay in your application; the server may even freeze up while the scaling is performed. See Chapter 2, *Font Service and Scalable Fonts*, for more information about font scaling.

The following routines also use or operate on font sets:

XFreeFontSet
> Frees an **XFontSet** and all information associated with it.

XFontsOfFontSet
> Returns the list of **XFontStruct**s and font names associated with an **XFontSet**.

XBaseFontNameListOfFontSet
> Returns a string containing the comma-separated base font name list for the given **FontSet**.

XLocaleOfFontSet
> Returns the name of the locale of the specifed **XFontSet**.

Complete documentation for these (and all functions described in this chapter) can be found in the reference section of this book.

4.3.2 Querying Fontset Metrics

Because the **XFontSet** is an opaque structure, it is not possible to read font metrics directly from an **XFontSet** as is done with an **XFontStruct**. Instead, X11R5 defines the function **XExtentsOfFontSet** which takes an **XFontSet** as its sole argument and returns a pointer to a structure of type **XFontSetExtents**. This structure is shown in Example 4-3.

Example 4-3. The XFontSetExtents structure

```
typedef struct {
    XRectangle max_ink_extent;          /* over all drawable characters */
    XRectangle max_logical_extent;      /* over all drawable characters */
} XFontSetExtents;
```

Each **XRectangle** specifies, as usual, the upper left-hand corner of a rectangle, and a positive width and height. The **max_ink_extents** rectangle specifies the bounding box around the actual glyph image of all characters in all fonts of the font set. The **max_logical_extents** rectangle describes the bounding box for all characters in all fonts of the font set that encloses the character ink plus intercharacter and interline spacing. For the layout of running text, the logical extents will be more useful. Note that these rectangles do not simply describe the biggest character in the font set, but describe a bounding box that will enclose all characters in the font set; a box big enough to accommodate the largest descent, the largest ascent, and so on. The **XFontSetExtents** structure returned by

`XExtentsOfFontSet` is private to Xlib and should not be modified or freed by the application.

4.3.3 Context Dependencies in Displayed Text

In some text, such as Arabic script, there is not a one-to-one mapping between characters and font glyphs—the glyph used to display a character depends on the position of the character in the string. In other languages, a sequence of characters may map to a single glyph or a single character may map to multiple glyphs. In cases like this, it is not possible to assume that the width of a string is the sum of the widths of its component characters, and it may not be possible to insert or delete a character from a displayed string without redrawing the surrounding characters. The only safe assumption is that context dependencies do not extend beyond whitespace in a string. An example of context dependencies in the English language is the use of ligatures in typeset text—the substitution of the special glyphs "fl" and "fi" for the character sequences "fl" and "fi." This is an artificial example though, and for practical purposes, no Latin-based language has context dependencies.

The function `XContextDependentDrawing` returns `True` if the locale associated with a font set includes context dependencies in text drawing. An internationalized application could use this function to check if it can take the various shortcuts allowed in non-context dependent locales. If `XSupportsLocale` returns `True`, then any context dependencies in the text of a locale are correctly handled by the text-measuring and text-displaying routines described below.

There is another, more difficult, kind of context dependency in languages such as Hebrew and Arabic which are drawn right-to-left except for numbers which are drawn left-to-right. In this case it is not valid to assume that characters that are adjacent in a string will be adjacent when displayed. X11R5 does not make any provisions for handling this sort of text with mixed drawing directions.

4.3.4 Measuring Strings

X11R5 provides internationalized versions of **XTextWidth** and **XTextExtents**. They require an **XFontSet** and either a multi-byte or wide-character string. They are described below:

Xmb/XwcTextEscapement*
Return the number of pixels the given string would require in the x dimension if drawn.

---

*In this and following sections, functions that operate on multi-byte (mb) strings and the equivalent functions that operate on wide characters (wc) will often be grouped together and named with this **Xmb/Xwc** syntax. For **Xmb** functions, the *text* argument is of type **char** *, and the *length* argument gives the number of bytes in the string, which may not be the number of characters. In **Xwc** functions, the *text* argument is of type **wchar_t** *, and the *length* argument specifies the number of wide characters in the string, which is not the same as the number of bytes.

`Xmb/XwcTextExtents`

    Return the text escapement as the value of the function, and also return a bounding box for all the ink in the string, and a bounding box for all the ink plus intercharacter and interline spacing.*

The term "escapement" is used instead of "width" to emphasize that **Xmb/XwcText-Escapement** returns a positive value whether text is drawn left-to-right or right-to-left. This differs from **XTextWidth** which returns a negative width for strings drawn right-to-left.

There is another pair of text extent functions that are useful when there are context dependencies in the displayed text. **Xmb/XwcTextPerCharExtents** return the escapement and extents of a string as the above functions do, but also return the ink extents and the logical extents of each character in the string. These extents are measured relative to the drawing origin of the string, not the origin of the particular glyph. Note that these extents are returned for each character of the string, not for each font glyph displayed. If a sequence of characters map to a single glyph, each of those characters will have identical extent rectangles. Similarly if a single character requires several font glyphs to display, its extents will be the combined extents of those glyphs. The dimensions of the rectangle are independent of the drawing direction of the character.†

Example 4-4 in the next section shows a use of **XmbTextExtents** and **XmbTextPerCharExtents**.

4.3.5 Drawing Internationalized Text

X11R5 provides internationalized wide-character and multi-byte versions of **XDrawString**, **XDrawImageString**, and **XDrawText**. They are listed below:

`Xmb/XwcDrawString`

    Draw the specified string. The foreground pixels of each font glyph are drawn, but the background pixels of each glyph are not.

`Xmb/XwcDrawImageString`

    Draw the specified string. Both the foreground and background pixels of each glyph are drawn.

`Xmb/XwcDrawText`

    Draw text with complex spacing or font set changes. These routines draw text described in an array of **XmbTextItem** or **XwcTextItem** structures. These structures are shown in Example 4-4.

---

*As this book goes to press, there are two major bugs in the Xsi implementation of **Xmb/XwcTextExtents**: they do not return the escapement of the string, and they do not allow the programmer to pass NULL pointers for bounding boxes that are not of interest.

†As this book goes to press, there are two major bugs in the Xsi implementation of **Xmb/XwcTextPerCharExtents**. First, the returned per-character metrics are not relative to the drawing origin—the logical extents rectangles all have an x-coordinate of 0. Second, these functions do not allow a programmer to pass NULL for bounding boxes or arrays of bounding boxes that are not of interest—a dummy pointer to valid memory must always be passed.

These functions are passed a graphics context and a font set, and draw with fonts from the font set rather than the font of the GC. For this reason, they may modify the font value of the GC. Other than the font, they use the same GC elements as their pre-X11R5 text-drawing analogs. When using these functions, remember that context dependencies may mean that it is not valid to draw or modify displayed strings a single character at a time.

Example 4-4. The XmbTextItem and XwcTextItem structures

```
typedef struct {
    char        *chars;             /* pointer to string */
    int         nchars;             /* number of bytes in string */
    int         delta;              /* pixel delta between strings */
    XFontSet    font_set;           /* fonts, None means don't change */
} XmbTextItem;

typedef struct {
    wchar_t     *chars;             /* pointer to wide char string */
    int         nchars;             /* number of wide characters */
    int         delta;              /* pixel delta between strings */
    XFontSet    font_set;           /* fonts, None means don't change */
} XwcTextItem;
```

Example 4-5 shows the use of **XwcDrawImageString**.

Example 4-5. Centering and drawing a multi-byte string

```
#include <X11/Xlib.h>

/*
 * This function draws a specified multi-byte string centered in
 * a specified region of a window.
 */
void DrawCenteredMbString(dpy, w, fontset, gc,
                          str, num_bytes, x, y, width, height)
Display *dpy;
Window w;
XFontSet fontset;
GC gc;
char *str;
int num_bytes;
int x, y, width, height;
{
    XRectangle boundingbox;
    XRectangle dummy;
    int originx, originy;

    /*
     * Figure out how big the string will be.
     * We should be able to pass NULL instead of &dummy, but
     * XmbTextExtents is buggy in the Xsi implementation.
     * Also, it should return the escapement of the string, but doesn't.
     */
    (void) XmbTextExtents(fontset, str, num_bytes,
                          &dummy, &boundingbox);
    /*
     * The string we want to center may be drawn left-to-right,
     * right-to-left, or some of both, so computing the
     * drawing origin is a little tricky.  The bounding box's x
```

Example 4-5. Centering and drawing a multi-byte string (continued)

```
   * and y coordinates are the upper left hand corner and are
   * relative to the drawing origin.
   * if boundingbox.x is 0, the the string is pure left-to-right.
   * If it is equal to -boundingbox.width then the string is pure
   * right-to-left, but it may not be either of these, so what
   * we've got to do is choose the origin so that the bounding box
   * is centered in the window without assuming that the orgin is
   * at one end or another of the string.
   */
   originx = x + (width - boundingbox.width)/2 - boundingbox.x;
   originy = y + (height - boundingbox.height)/2 - boundingbox.y;

/*
 * now draw the string
 */
 XmbDrawImageString(dpy, w, fontset, gc,
                    originx, originy,
                    str, num_bytes);
}
```

4.4 String Encoding Changes for Internationalization

Perhaps the most fundamental concern of internationalization is the encoding of strings. So far we've considered text drawing and string input, and have used multi-byte or wide-character strings in the encoding of the locale. Because X is a networked window system, however, an X client must communicate with the X server, usually with a window manager, sometimes with a session manager, and often with other clients through the X selection mechanism (which is used to implement copy-and-paste). When we allow the internationalization of X programs, we must confront the issues of communication between clients that use different locales, and of communication between an internationalized client and a "locale-neutral" X server. Furthermore we must make decisions about the encodings of any other strings used in the X and Xt specifications.

Some of the issues that must be considered are the appropriate encoding for color and font names passed to the X server, the encoding of bitmap files, the encoding of strings selected in one client and copied to another, and the encoding of resource values and names. When making decisions on questions like these, the designers of X internationalization had several choices. They could specify that particular strings were:

- In the encoding of the locale.

- In the COMPOUND_TEXT encoding, in which each string is encoded along with the name of its encoding.

- In the STRING encoding, which is Latin-1 plus the newline and tab control characters.

- In ASCII, which as the encoding of the C language, is actually fairly portable.

- In an implementation-dependent encoding.

- Not in any encoding, and are simply interpreted as a sequence of bytes.

Compound text is an encoding designed to represent text from any locale. As such it is well suited to be a standard string format for clients that communicate using string properties. It does not, however, address the problem of converting strings from one locale to another, and often this is simply not possible. In most cases it is not meaningful to select text from an application running in one locale and paste it into an application running in a different one. This is the realm of multilingual applications which are not addressed by X11R5.

Note that the above list refers to the COMPOUND_TEXT and STRING encodings. These capitalized names refer to the Atom names used in the ICCCM to specify the type of a "Property." The ICCCM also specifies a selection conversion target Atom, TEXT, which simply means a string in whatever encoding is convenient for the selection owner.

Sometimes the best choice of encodings is ASCII. It may seem unfair to non-English locales that the ASCII encoding should be singled out for special treatment, but for strings that are to be shared between X client and X server (such as Display, Property, and font and color names) some standard encoding must be specified. Because ASCII is widespread and is the usual encoding for C programming, it is a natural choice. In many cases, though, it is not the specific ASCII encoding that is important, but the fact that there is some common encoding for all the characters used by ASCII. X11R5 never actually refers to ASCII. Instead, it defines the *X Portable Character Set* as a set of basic characters that must exist in all locales supported by Xlib. Those characters are:

> a..z A..Z 0..9
> !"#$%&'()*+,-./:;<=>?@[]^_`{|}~
> <space>, <tab>, and <newline>

X11R5 also defines the *Host Portable Character Encoding* as the encoding for that character set. The encoding itself is not defined; the only requirement is that the same encoding is used for all locales on a given host machine. A string in the Host Portable Character Encoding is understood to contain only characters from the X Portable Character Set. Finally, the *Latin Portable Character Encoding* is the characters of the X Portable Character Set encoded as a subset of the Latin-1 encoding. (Latin-1 is itself a superset of ASCII.) Note that if an X client running on one host has a different portable encoding than an X server running on a different host, then translation from one encoding to the other will be required (for color names, font names, etc.) and would be done by the Xlib communication layer. In practice, however, it is likely that all systems will simply use an encoding which is a superset of ASCII, (with the possible exception of mainframes that use EBCDIC) and therefore all characters in the X Portable Character Set will share a single, standard (ASCII) encoding.

String-encoding issues arise throughout Xlib, and particularly so for functions that involve X properties and resource databases. The internationalization of client-to-window-manager and client-to-client communication via Properties is described in Section 4.5 below and the internationalization of X resource databases is discussed in Section 4.6. Here we itemize the remaining changes to the Xlib specification that involve string encodings. Table 4-1 lists Xlib functions and the encodings of the strings that are passed in and out of them. These are not so much changes to the Xlib specification as clarifications of it to make the encodings explicit.

Internationalization   57

Table 4-1. String Encodings Used by Various Xlib Functions

Function	String Encoding
XDrawImageString XDrawString XQueryTextExtents XTextExtents XTextWidth XTextItem structure XChar2b structure	No encoding; "characters" are treated as glyph indexes into the font, independent of locale.
XServerVendor ServerVendor macro	If the X server uses the Latin Portable Character Encoding, this function will return a string in the Host Portable Character Encoding; otherwise the encoding is implementation-dependent.
XOpenDisplay XDisplayName DisplayName macro XDisplayString DisplayString macro	Display names in the Host Portable Character Encoding are supported; additional encodings are implementation dependent.
XAllocNamedColor XLookupColor XStoreNamedColor XParseColor	Color names in the Host Portable Character Encoding are supported; Xlib implementations may support additional encodings, and may look up color names in locale-specific databases before passing them to the server.
XLoadFont XLoadQueryFont	Font names in the Host Portable Character Encoding are supported; implementations may support additional encodings.
XListFonts XListFontsWithInfo	Font patterns in the Host Portable Character Encoding are supported; implementations may support additional encodings. Returned strings are in the Host Portable Character Encoding if the server returns strings in the Latin Portable Character Encoding; otherwise the encoding is implementation-dependent.
XSetFontPath XGetFontPath	The encoding and interpretation of the font path is implementation-dependent.
XParseGeometry XGeometry XWMGeometry	Geometry strings in the Host Portable Character Encoding are supported; implementations may support additional encodings.
XInternAtom	Atom names in the Host Portable Character Encoding are supported; implementations may support additional encodings.

Table 4-1. String Encodings Used by Various Xlib Functions (continued)

Function	String Encoding
XGetAtomName	The returned atom name is in the Host Portable Character Encoding if the server returns a value in the Latin Portable Character Encoding.
XStringToKeysym	Keysym names in the Host Portable Character Encoding are supported; implementations may support additional encodings.
XKeysymToString	The returned string is in the Host Portable Character Encoding.
XInitExtension XQueryExtension	Extension names in the Host Portable Character Encoding are supported; implementations may support additional encodings.
XListExtensions	The returned strings are in the Host Portable Character Encoding if the server returns strings in the Latin Portable Character Encoding.
XReadBitmapFile	The bitmap file is parsed in the encoding of the current locale.
XWriteBitmapFile	The file is written in the encoding of the current locale.
XFetchBytes XFetchBuffer XStoreBytes XStoreBuffer	No encoding; data in cut buffers is treated as uninterpreted bytes.
XGetErrorDatabaseText	Name and message arguments in the Host Portable Character Encoding are supported; implementations may support additional encodings. The *default_string* argument is encoded in the current locale, and the returned text is also in encoded in the current locale.
XGetErrorText	The returned text is in the current locale.
XSetWMProperties XSetStandardProperties XStoreName XSetIconName XSetCommandP XSetClassHint	Strings in the Host Portable Character Encoding are supported; implementations may support additional encodings. The strings are set as the values of a property of type STRING.

Internationalization

Table 4-1. String Encodings Used by Various Xlib Functions (continued)

Function	String Encoding
XFetchName XGetIconName XGetCommand XGetClassHint	Returned strings are in the Host Portable Character Encoding if the data returned by the server is in the Latin Portable Character Encoding.

4.5 Internationalized Interclient Communication

When writing an internationalized application it is not safe to assume that all interclient communication with text properties will be done with Latin-1 or ASCII strings. X11R5 provides some new functions that do not make this assumption. The first is a convenience routine for communication with window managers. **XmbSetWMProperties** is a function very similar to **XSetWMProperties**, except that the *window_name* and *icon_name* arguments are multi-byte strings (rather than **XTextProperty** pointers) in the encoding of the locale. If these strings can be converted to the **STRING** encoding (Latin-1 plus newline and tab), then their corresponding **WM_NAME** and **WM_ICON_NAME** properties are created with type **STRING**. If this conversion cannot be performed, the strings are converted to Compound Text (this conversion can always be done, by the definition of Compound Text), and the properties are created with type **COMPOUND_TEXT**. Note that there is no wide-character version of this function.

Since X properties have a single contiguous block of data as their value, they cannot directly represent types such as **char ****. But sometimes such a complex type must be represented (imagine a text editor setting a property to a set of disjoint selected strings). To allow this, X11R4 defined the **XTextProperty** structure (shown in Example 4-6) and the functions **XStringListToTextProperty** and **XTextPropertyToStringList**.

Example 4-6. The XTextProperty structure

```
typedef struct {
        unsigned char *value;    /* property data */
        Atom encoding;           /* type of property */
        int format;              /* 8, 16, or 32 */
        unsigned long nitems;    /* number of items in value */
} XTextProperty;
```

These functions assume input strings are in Latin-1 and always create properties of type STRING, which is not correct behavior in internationalized applications. So X11R5 provides the new functions **Xmb/XwcTextListToTextProperty** and **Xmb/XwcTextPropertyToTextList** which operate correctly with localized strings, converting between text encoded in the locale and **STRING** or **COMPOUND_TEXT** types. The **Xmb/wcTextListToTextProperty** functions take a new argument of type **XICCEncodingStyle**, which is shown in Example 4-7.

Example 4-7. The XICCEncodingStyle type

```
typedef enum {
          XStringStyle,             /* STRING */
          XCompoundTextStyle,       /* COMPOUND_TEXT */
          XTextStyle,               /* text in owner's encoding (current locale) */
          XStdICCTextStyle          /* STRING, else COMPOUND_TEXT */
} XICCEncodingStyle;
```

The *style* argument to these functions specifies how the text is to be converted. The possible values have the following meanings:

- **XStringStyle** specifies that the text should be converted to the **STRING** encoding, and the encoding field of the returned **XTextProperty** should be set to the Atom **STRING**. Note that text cannot always be converted to this type without loss of data—only characters that are in the Latin-1 character set will be convertible.

- **XCompoundTextStyle** specifies that the text should be converted to the Compound Text encoding and the encoding field of the returned **XTextProperty** should be set to the Atom **COMPOUND_TEXT**.

- **XTextStyle** specifies that the text should be left unconverted in the encoding of the current locale. The encoding field of the returned **XTextProperty** structure is set to an Atom which names that encoding.

- **XStdICCTextStyle** specifies that the text should be converted to STRING if that conversion is possible and otherwise it should be converted to Compound Text. The encoding field of the returned **XTextProperty** will be set to the Atom **STRING** or **COMPOUND_TEXT** depending on which conversion was performed.

The returned **XTextProperty** is suitable to pass to **XSetTextProperty**.

The other two routines, **Xmb/XwcTextPropertyToTextList**, perform the conversion in the opposite direction. They are passed an **XTextProperty** (obtained with a call to **XGetTextProperty**, perhaps) and return an array of pointers to **char *** or an array of pointers to **wchar_t ***. These routines do not require an argument of type **XICCEncodingStyle**; they always convert from the encoding of the property to the encoding of the current locale if such a conversion is possible. The application is responsible for freeing the memory allocated by these functions. To free the array of multi-byte strings (and the strings themselves) returned by **XmbTextPropertyToTextList** use **XFreeStringList**, which is a pre-X11R5 function. To free the array of wide-character strings (and the strings themselves) allocated by **XwcTextPropertyToTextList** use the new function **XwcFreeStringList**.

These four functions return an integer. The possible values and their meanings are as follows:

Success
> The conversion is completely successful; all characters were converted.

XNoMemory

There was not enough memory available to perform the conversion.

XLocaleNotSupported

The current locale is not supported. By definition, no conversions are possible to or from the encoding of an unsupported locale. This error code will never be returned if **XSupportsLocale** has returned **True** for the current locale.

XConverterNotFound

No converter could be found between the encoding of the text property and the current locale. There is always a converter for converting between **STRING** and **COMPOUND_TEXT** and encoding of the current locale (if that locale is supported, of course), so **Xmb/wcTextListToTextProperty** never returns this error code, and **Xmb/XwcTextPropertyToTextList** will never return it if the text property is in the **STRING** or **COMPOUND_TEXT** encodings.

any value > 0

There were unconvertible characters in the string, and the return value indicates how many. Even when the current locale is supported, and an appropriate converter is found, it is by no means guaranteed that all the characters of the string can be converted. If two locales use the same character set but simply encode those characters differently, then strings will be fully convertible between the locales. But imagine trying to convert from French text to ASCII—any accented characters would be unconvertible because they simply do not exist in the ASCII character set. When converting between languages as dissimilar as Arabic and Korean, for example, there will be no convertible characters.* Note that the return value **Success** has a value of 0, and the other return values, **XNoMemory**, **XLocaleNotSupported**, and **XConverterNotFound** all have negative values. Therefore any positive return value indicates unconvertible characters.

Table 4-2 shows the possible results of the conversions performed by **Xmb/XwcTextListToTextProperty** and **Xmb/XwcTextPropertyToTextList**.

---

*If Korean is the current (supported) locale, and the Arabic text has been "wrapped" into a Compound Text encoding, a converter will exist between Compound Text and the current locale, but no meaningful conversion will be performed. Until the advent of multilingual applications (or specialized applications using a special Korean/Arabic locale) such a conversion attempt (triggered by a user's copy-and-paste actions, for example) will not be meaningful, and should be ignored or produce an error message.

Xmb/XwcTextListToTextProperty		
XICCEncodingStyle	Converter found?	Characters convertible?
XStringStyle	yes	maybe
XCompoundTextStyle	yes	yes
XTextStyle	yes	yes
XStdICCStyle	yes	yes

Xmb/XwcTextPropertyToTextList		
Encoding of property	Converter found?	Characters convertible?
same as current locale	yes	yes
STRING	yes	maybe
COMPOUND_TEXT	yes	maybe
other locale	maybe	maybe

When there are unconvertible characters in a string, the conversion functions substitute a locale-dependent default string (encoded in the current locale). The value of the default string may be queried with **XDefaultString**, and may be the empty string (" "). There is no way to set the value of the default string. The default string is independent of the default string used by the X11R5 text-drawing routines when an **XFontSet** does not contain all the characters needed to represent text in a locale.

4.6 Localization of Resource Databases

We've seen that X resources are a useful way to allow the localization of strings—rather than hardcoding its strings, an X client can look them all up by name from a locale-dependent resource file. The twist here is that although resource values can be localized, and may contain text in the encoding of the locale, resource *names* must still be hardcoded into the application. As you might expect, X11R5 specifies that resource names in the Host Portable Character Encoding are always supported, and that any other encodings are implementation-dependent. What this means is that a Chinese user who wishes to customize the behavior of an application written by a Japanese programmer will have to specify values for resources that are named using Latin characters in the X Portable Character Set. Those resource names may be English phonetic representations of Japanese words which are mnemonic to the Japanese programmer, but which are meaningless to the Chinese (or American) user. This situation is unfortunate but there is no way around it within the scope of the X Resource Manager mechanisms. If resource names are to be localized, they would have to be looked up in a database as well, and then we would need hardcoded names for the names. Another approach would be to use resource numbers in place of resource names. These remain constant across all locales, but where a resource name is mnemonic to the original programmer, at least, a resource number would be mnemonic to no one.

When a resource file or string are parsed into an **XrmDatabase,** that parsing is done in the current locale, and the database is bound to that locale even if the current locale changes. We can speak of the "locale of the database" in the same way that we speak of the "locale of the **XFontSet.**" To determine the locale of a database, call **XrmLocaleOfDatabase.**

The internationalization of resources requires additions to the Xlib specification to make explicit the encoding and interpretation of the strings that are passed in and out of the **Xrm** functions. Table 4-3 lists the resource manager functions that have been respecified. X11R5 also introduces a number new **Xrm** functions, but most of these changes are not related to internationalization, and are described in Chapter 6, *Resource Management.*

Table 4-3. String Encoding and Locale Changes to Xrm Functions

Function	String Encoding and Locale Changes
XrmStringToQuark XrmStringToQuarkList XrmStringToBindingQuarkList	Quark names in the Host Portable Character Encoding are supported; implementations may support additional encodings.
XrmQuarkToString	No specified encoding; the returned string is equal byte-for-byte to the string originally passed to one of the string-to-quark routines.
XrmGetFileDatabase	The file is parsed in the current locale.
XrmGetStringDatabase	The string is parsed in the current locale.
XrmPutLineResource	The line is parsed in the locale of the database. The resource name part of the line and the colon are in the Host Portable Character Encoding or some implementation-dependent encoding.
XrmPutFileDatabase	The resource file is written in the locale of the database. Resource names in the Host Portable Character Encoding, and resource values in the encoding of the locale of the database are supported; implementations may support additional encodings.
XrmPutResource	Resource specifiers and types in the Host Portable Character Encoding are supported; implementations may support additional encodings. The resource value is stored as uninterpreted bytes.
XrmQPutResource	The resource value is stored as uninterpreted bytes.
XrmPutStringResource	Resource specifiers in the Host Portable Character Encoding are supported; implementations may support additional encodings. The resource value is stored as uninterpreted bytes. The resource type is set to the quark for the string "String" encoded in the Host Portable Character Encoding.

Table 4-4. String Encoding and Locale Changes to Xrm Functions

Function	String Encoding and Locale Changes
XrmQPutStringResource	The resource value is stored as uninterpreted bytes. The resource type is set to the quark for the string "String" encoded in the Host Portable Character Encoding.
XrmGetResource	Resource names and classes in the Host Portable Character Encoding are supported; implementations may support additional encodings.
XrmMergeDatabases	The database values and types are merged as uninterpreted bytes regardless of the locales of the databases. The locale of the target database is not changed.
XResourceManagerString	The **RESOURCE_MANAGER** property is converted from **STRING** encoding to the encoding of the current locale in the same way that XmbTextPropertyToTextString performs conversions.
XrmParseCommand	The option strings in the **XrmOptionDescList** are compared byte-for-byte with the characters in **argv**, independent of locale. The name argument and the resource specifier strings in the **XrmOptionDescList** are in the Host Portable Character Encoding or in an additional implementation-dependent encoding. The resource values are stored in the database as uninterpreted bytes, and all database entries are created with their type set to the quark for the string "String" in the Host Portable Character Encoding.
XGetDefault	The use of this function is discouraged.

4.7 Internationalization Changes to the X Toolkit

The changes to the X Toolkit for X11R5 mostly have to do with internationalization and the additions to the X Resource Manager. Xt changes for internationalization are described below. Changes involving resource management are described in Chapter 6, *Resource Management*, and the remaining changes are documented in Chapter 7, *Other Changes in X11R5*.

4.7.1 String Encoding and Locale Dependencies in Xt

The X Toolkit specification has not been so thoroughly revised as the Xlib spec to make explicit the expected encodings of all strings. Generally, it will be true that Xt variables or arguments of type `String` should be in the encoding of the locale, but caution is necessary: the widget name passed to `XtCreateWidget` is of type `String`, for example, but since it may be used in resource specifications it should be in the Host Portable Character Encoding if the application is to operate in more than a single locale. Neither is the spec explicit about such things as the encoding of translation tables or the localized behavior of resource converters like `XtCvtStringToBoolean`. None of these are critical problems; the Xt programmer who wishes to write internationalized applications should be aware, however, that there are internationalization issues in Xt that remain to be worked out.

4.7.2 Establishing Locale in an Xt Application

Resource specifications in X11R5 are parsed in the current locale, which means that an application should have established its locale before reading its app-defaults file and creating its resource database. However, it should be possible to specify the locale for an application using a resource, which means that the resources should be read before the locale is set. The X Toolkit in X11R5 resolves this catch-22 by parsing resources in two steps: first it scans the command line and per-display resource string for the setting of the locale, then, once the locale is set, it fully parses all the resource specifications.

The locale and resource initialization sequence is as follows:

1. The application starts up in the default locale. The programmer does not call `setlocale`, but registers a *language procedure* by calling `XtSetLanguageProc`. This language procedure will later be called to set the locale.

2. The application then typically calls `XtInitialize` or `XtAppInitialize` or `XtOpenDisplay`. These initialization routines call `XtDisplayInitialize` which scans (but doesn't actually parse—this scan is done in a way that is independent of the initial locale of the process) the command line and the `RESOURCE_MANAGER` property on the root window of the default screen for the value of the `xnlLanguage` resource. (The class of this resource is `XnlLanguage`, and it can be set from the command line using the -xnlLanguage option. The "nl" stands for "native language.") The *language string* obtained from this resource (or the empty string if the resource doesn't exist) is passed to the language procedure registered with `XtSetLanguageProc`. If no lan-

guage procedure was registered, **XtDisplayInitialize** continues exactly as it did in X11R4.

3. The language procedure uses the passed string to set the locale. Note that the language procedure can pass the empty string directly to **setlocale** which will take it as a signal to set the locale based on the value of the appropriate operating system environment variable. The language procedure should also call **XSupportsLocale** to verify that the locale is supported and **XSetLocaleModifiers** to set any locale modifiers. Finally, the language procedure must return the name of the locale it set (which is the return value of **setlocale**).

4. Now **XtDisplayInitialize** saves the return value of the language procedure for use by **XtResolvePathname** as a pathname substitution when searching for the appropriate application defaults file for the locale.

Note that **XtDisplayInitialize** could make the call to **setlocale** itself, but that this was deemed inappropriate by the designers. If no language procedure is registered, **XtDisplayInitialize** behaves as it did in X11R4, and the locale is never set. For most applications the default language procedure will be sufficient: it calls **setlocale**, **XSupportsLocale**, and **XSetLocaleModifiers** and it returns the name of the locale it set. Note that the default procedure is not actually registered by default; you must explicitly register it or you will get X11R4 behavior. To register it, call **XtSetLanguageProc** with a procedure argument of **NULL**. Example 4-8 shows how to initialize Xt using the default language procedure to correctly set the locale.

Example 4-8. Establishing the locale in an Xt application

```
main(argc, argv)
int argc;
char **argv;
{
    Widget toplevel;

    /* register the default language proc */
    /* no app-context, no function, no tag */
    XtSetLanguageProc(NULL, (XtLanguageProc)NULL, NULL);

    /* this function invokes XtDisplayInitialize which
     * will call the language procedure. */
    toplevel = XtAppInitialize(...);
        .
        .
        .
```

4.7.3 XFontSet Resources

The **XFontSet** abstraction defined by X11R5 Xlib for internationalized text output will be an important resource for any internationalized widget that draws text. The X11R5 Xt Intrinsics give **XFontSet** almost the same support they give the **XFontStruct**. They define:

• **XtNfontSet**, a name for an **XFontSet** resource.

- **XtCFontSet**, a class for an **XFontSet** resource.

- **XtRFontSet**, the representation type for an **XFontSet** resource.

- A pre-registered String-to-XFontSet converter.

- **XtDefaultFontSet,** a string constant guaranteed to work with the pre-registered String-to-XFontSet converter.

When the constant **XtDefaultFontSet** is passed to the pre-registered String-to-XFont-Set converter, it queries the resource database for the value of a resource with name **xt-DefaultFontSet** and class **XtDefaultFontSet**. If this resource exists and has a valid value, the **XFontSet** is created using the resource value as the base font name list. If the resource doesn't exist or no font set can be created from it, the converter falls back onto an implementation-defined default font set list.

Unfortunately there is no standard command-line option analogous to **−font** defined by the Xt Intrinsics which will set this **xtDefaultFontSet** resource. Applications can provide this command-line option themselves, or a user can specify a font set with the **−xrm** option:

```
imail −xrm "*xtDefaultFontSet: −*−*−*−R−*−*−*−140−100−100−*−*−*−*"
```

4.7.4 Other Xt Changes for Internationalization

The three other changes to Xt for internationalization are as follows:

- To allow the localization of error messages, the high-level Xt error and warning handling routines are no longer required to use the single file */usr/lib/X11/XtErrorDB* (on POSIX systems) as the error message database. Unfortunately, the app-context based design of the error and warning handlers means that these handers are not passed a handle to the Display that the error occurred on. This implies that they cannot use **XtResolve-Pathname** (which requires the display to look up the language string to use in path substitutions) to find an appropriate error database for the locale. For this reason X11R5 does not specify a standard error database search path, but simply states that the source of the error and warning message text is implementation-dependent. What this means to the programmer of internationalized applications is that you cannot portably rely on the default high-level Xt warning and error handlers to find the localized text of your error messages. You should register an error handler of your own or display your error messages through some entirely different mechanism.

- X11R4 specified that the language string obtained from the **xnlLanguage** resource should be in the form:

    language[_*territory*][.*codeset*]

This was deemed an unnecessary restriction, and for X11R5 the specification has been changed to state that the language string (obtained from the **xnlLanguage** resource or returned by the new language procedure) has a "language part," a "territory part," and a "codeset part," but that the format of the string is implementation-dependent.

- The internationalization of X text input with input methods (see Chapter 5, *Internationalized Text Input*) requires that an input method have a way to intercept X events before they are processed by the application. An input method does this by registering an event filter, and all applications that perform internationalized text input are required to call the function **XFilterEvent** each time they receive an event. To support internationalized input, **XtDispatchEvent** has been modified to make this required call to **XFilterEvent**. Furthermore, if an event arrives that triggers a grab registered by **XtGrabButton** or **XtGrabKey**, and that event is filtered by **XFilterEvent**, then **XtDispatchEvent** breaks the grab by calling **XtUngrabPointer** or **XtUngrabKeyboard** with the timestamp of the event. This is done because when an input method filters an event, the application should behave as if that event never arrived.

4.8 Summary: Writing an Internationalized Application

This chapter has covered a lot of tricky material. The following guidelines summarize the requirements for ANSI-C and X11R5-based internationalization:

- Set the locale desired by the user by calling **setlocale** with the empty string (" ") as the locale name argument. Verify that the locale is supported by Xlib with **XSupportsLocale**. Set the X locale modifiers as desired by the user by passing the empty string to **XSetLocaleModifiers**. In an X Toolkit application, use **XtSetLanguageProc** to register a procedure to set the locale. The default language procedure (which is not actually registered by default) performs all of the above functions.

- Use ANSI-C functions such as **strcoll** and **strftime** which make use of the current setting of the locale. Avoid the superseded functions that do not.

- Place all strings which will be displayed by the application in an X resource file. Use X Resource Manager functions in the application to look those strings up.

- Do not assume that the strings your application handles have a uniform state-independent encoding. Treat them as multi-byte strings or convert them to wide-character strings.

- Create an **XFontSet** for the locale and use it with the new X11R5 text output functions to measure and display multi-byte and wide-character strings.

- Use **XmbSetWMProperties** to set the essential properties for communication with the window manager.

- Use the new X11R5 Property routines to convert from or to the encoding of the current locale when setting or reading text properties.

- Pay attention to the encoding of strings such as Atom and Display names, font and color names, resource names, and resource values specifications.

- Use the new X input method mechanisms to get correctly encoded multi-byte and wide-character input. Chapter 5, *Internationalized Text Input*, explains how to do this.

5

Internationalized Text Input

Converting user keystrokes into text in the encoding of the locale is perhaps the most difficult task of internationalization. This chapter is a continuation of the last, and assumes knowledge of the basics of internationalization covered in that chapter. The first two sections provide an overview of the internationalized text input model used by X11R5, and are valuable to any programmer writing internationalized applications. The remaining sections describe the new Xlib functions and datatypes for internationalized text input, and are quite detailed. Programmers who will be writing output-only applications or who will be using toolkits or widgets with internationalized text input capabilities built in can skip these sections.

In This Chapter:

5
Internationalized Text Input

In an internationalized program, you can't assume any particular mapping between keystrokes and input characters. An internationalized program must run in any locale on a single workstation, using a single keyboard. The mapping between keystrokes and Japanese characters is very different (and more complex) than the mapping between keystrokes and Latin characters, for example. When there are more characters in the codeset of a locale than there are keys on a keyboard, some sort of *input method* is required for mapping between multiple keystrokes and input characters. X11R5 supports the internationalization of keyboard input with the new abstractions *X Input Method* (**XIM**) and *X Input Context* (**XIC**) and the new functions, **XmbLookupString** and **XwcLookupString**, which return a string in the encoding of the locale. Because internationalized text input is a complex topic, we begin with a discussion of the important issues of internationalized text input in Section 5.1 and an overview of the X input method architecture in Section 5.2. The remaining sections explain the individual topics required in order to implement internationalized text input.

Before beginning with internationalized text input, bear in mind that input methods are a technology that has previously been used only in *ad hoc* ways for specific languages. Driven by industry demand, it has very quickly advanced from research topic to X Consortium standard, and now must operate correctly in any locale. It is a difficult problem and X11R5 does not provide a complete solution. One frustration is the ambiguity, in places, of the XIM specification. This book attempts to resolve those ambiguities in reasonable ways, but in practice, much remains "implementation defined," and XIM programs may have to be tailored to operate correctly with a few particular target input methods. None of the input methods that are shipped with X11R5 are part of the core distribution, and none are fully robust or well documented (not in English, at least). The XIM designers envision that their internationalized text input mechanism will be incorporated within toolkits and Xt widgets, and thus will be hidden from most programmers. Until these widgets are available, however, performing truly internationalized text input may be a difficult task.

The following items support internationalized text input in X11R5:

- A variety of new functions and datatypes in the Xlib specification.

- Two implementations of the new specification, shipped as part of the core MIT distribution. The default implementation contains support for simple (generally European) input methods directly within Xlib.

- Contributed input methods that work with each of the Xlib implementations. The input method that works with the default implementation supports Japanese, Korean, and Chinese input.

As mentioned in the previous chapter, X11R5 as shipped from MIT contains two separate implementations of the new internationalization facilities. The "Xsi" implementation is the default on all but Sony machines which use the "Ximp" implementation. Each implementation defines its own protocol for communication with input methods which are implemented as separate processes. Therefore, the contributed Ximp input method will not work if Xlib has been built with the Xsi implementation, and vice versa.

5.1 Issues of Internationalized Text Input

Think for a moment about how we use a keyboard to enter text into a computer. There are not enough keys on a standard keyboard for all the lowercase and uppercase letters used in English as well as the number and punctuation characters, so we use a shift key to effectively double the number of characters we can enter.

But for many European languages, this technique is not sufficient. The most common accented characters may appear directly on a keyboard (the é, è, and ç in French, for example) but this still leaves a variety of other characters that cannot be entered with any single shifted or unshifted keystroke. French typewriters have a key that will produce an umlaut or a caret, without advancing the carriage, so to produce a û, for example, you would strike the caret key followed by the "u" key. In computer systems, a variety of methods have been developed for entering these accented characters. Often they involve a Compose key (found on many DEC keyboards) or any "dead key" which, does not send a code when struck but places the keyboard into a special compose mode (sometimes indicated by a light on the keyboard) in which one or more of the following keystrokes are combined into a single character. If this sort of input method is implemented in the keyboard hardware or in the operating system software, then it behaves transparently to the programmer who can simply read characters, assured that the user will have some way of entering any text desired.

As with internationalized text output, it is with the Asian ideographic languages that things become complicated. Japanese and Korean both have phonetic alphabets that are small enough to physically map onto a keyboard. It is sometimes adequate to leave text in this phonetic alphabet, but usually the user will want the final text to be in the full ideographic language. Input methods for these languages commonly have the user type the phonetic symbols for a particular word or words and signal somehow when this composition or pre-editing is finished. The input method then looks up that string of phonetic characters in a dictionary and converts it to the equivalent character or characters in the ideographic system. Sometimes there will be more than one character with a given phonetic representation, in which case the user will have to select between them.

These methods are obviously more complex than European compose methods. They are modal, and must display a lot of state information. It is not enough to have a keyboard light that tells users that they are composing an ideographic character; the computer must display the phonetic characters as the user types them, allow the user to edit them, and then when the user is done, compose them into an ideographic character or characters. The conversion from phonetic to ideographic characters requires a large dictionary, and finally, as noted above, the input method may have to display a menu or popup dialog box so the user can choose among ideograms with the same phonetic representation.

Because input methods can be so large and complex, and because they vary so much from locale to locale, it does not make sense to link every application with a generic input method which is somehow localized at application startup. Instead, an *input manager* is usually run as a separate process that communicates with the X server and with the application. At application startup, the setting of the locale or the "im" locale modifier determines to which input manager the application establishes a connection. X11R5 provides new routines and datatypes in Xlib which support this sort of internationalized text input. The next section provides an overview of the Xlib architecture for internationalized text input.

5.2 Overview of the X Input Method Architecture

The sections below present an overview of the concepts, datatypes, and functions used in X11R5 to support input methods. An understanding of material presented here will make the implementation details presented in later sections easier to follow.

5.2.1 Input Methods and Input Servers

An internationalized X application gets user text input by communicating with an input method. At application startup, the application is localized by opening the particular input method appropriate for the locale. Often, opening an input method causes Xlib to establish a connection to another process known as the "input manager" or "input server." The input manager can provide input method service to multiple X clients that use the same locale. Sometimes an input manager will connect to a third process, the translation server, which performs dictionary lookup and translation from pre-edit text (often phonetic) to composed text (often ideographic). The details of input method architecture are of course implementation dependent. Simple input methods, for example, can be implemented directly in Xlib, without need of other processes. The default Xsi implementation shipped with the MIT distribution does just this for European compose methods that do not require any dictionary lookup or graphical feedback. Figure 5-1 diagrams several possible connections between a client and its input method.

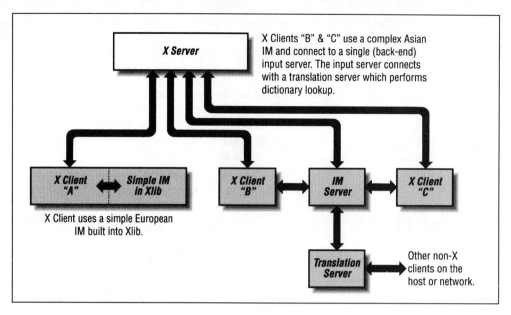

Figure 5-1. Possible input method architectures

The XIM architecture was designed to support two models of input method, known as front-end and back-end methods. A *front-end input method* intercepts events from the X server before they reach the application. A *back-end method* filters events from the application, before the application has processed them. Because internationalized programs must support either model of input method, the distinction is of little importance to the programmer. It is discussed in the XIM specification, however, and you may run across it in other discussions of input methods.

Recall the distinction between internationalized and multilingual applications. There is nothing to prevent an application from opening multiple input methods for multiple locales, but internationalized applications will generally operate only in a single locale and will therefore only need a single input method.

5.2.2 User Interaction with an Input Method

In order for a complex input method to provide feedback or otherwise interact with the user, it must have regions of the screen that it can draw text or bitmaps into. The X Input Method specification defines three of these areas:

* The *Status* area is an output-only window in which the input method can display information about its internal state. It can be thought of as a logical extension of the keyboard mode indicators, such as the Caps Lock indicator. The client generally provides this area to the input method, but the input method is solely responsible for its contents.

- The *Preedit* area is the region for the display of the intermediate text typed while composing a character. The client generally provides this area to the input method, which is responsible for its contents.

- The *Auxiliary* area is a transient window used for any popup menus or dialog boxes that are needed by the input method. This area is managed entirely by the input method.

The location and use of the Preedit and Status areas depend on the interaction style used between the application and the input method. Four interaction styles are defined by the X Input Method specification.

- In the *root-window* pre-editing style, the input method displays data outside of the application in a window that is a child of the root window.

- In the *off-the-spot* pre-editing style, the input method displays pre-edit data in a fixed location of the application window, often in a "message line" near the bottom.

- In the *over-the-spot* pre-editing style, the input method displays pre-edit data a window of its own which is placed over the current insertion point.

- In the *on-the-spot* pre-editing style, the input method directs the application to display the pre-edit data. When using this style, the application can display the pre-edit text in a way that matches the display of the already composed text.

The client must choose an interaction style from a list of styles supported by the input method, and must provide the Preedit and Status areas as required by that style. Additionally, in the case of on-the-spot pre-editing, the client must supply callbacks that the input method can call to control the pre-edit process.

5.2.3 The X Input Method

An application that wishes to use an input method must first call **XOpenIM**. This function establishes a connection to the input method appropriate for the current locale, and returns an opaque handle of type **XIM**. Opening an input method is conceptually similar to opening a display, and the **XIM** returned is analogous to the **Display *** returned by **XOpenDisplay**. An input method is bound to the particular locale that was in effect when it was created, even if this locale is subsequently changed. **XOpenIM** and related functions are documented in Section 5.4.1.

5.2.4 The X Input Context

Just as the X server can display multiple windows for a single client, an input method can maintain multiple *input contexts* for an application. The function **XCreateIC** creates a new input context in an input method. The function returns an opaque handle of type **XIC**. Like the **Window** or **GC** types, **XIC** has a number of attributes which can be set. These attributes control the interaction style for input done under that context, the regions to be used for the Preedit and Status areas, the **XFontSet** with which the text should be drawn, and so on. `XCreateIC` and related routines to set and get the values of input context attributes are documented in Section 5.5.

A text editor that supported multiple editing windows within a single top-level window could choose to create one IC for each editing window, or to share only one IC among all such windows. In the first case, each window would have different Preedit and Status areas, and each could be in a different intermediate state of pre-editing. In the second case, there would be a single Preedit and a single Status area shared by all editing windows, and the application would probably reset the state of the IC each time the input focus moved from one window to another.

5.2.5 Input Context Focus Management

Because there is only one keyboard associated with an X display, X allows only one window to have the input focus at a time. For the same reason, only one input context (per application) can have the focus at a time. The function `XSetICFocus` causes key events to be directed to a particular IC. It should be called at least once by every application that uses input contexts. In addition, the application should set the `FocusWindow` attribute of the IC to the window in which the key events will occur.

If an application has multiple text entry windows using multiple input contexts, that application will have to call `XSetICFocus` every time the input focus changes. An application that shares a single IC among multiple text entry windows will have to set the `Focus-Window` attribute of that IC each time the focus changes. Note that focus changes can be changes of the focus window known to the X server, or they can be application-internal focus changes, controlled by event redirection as is done in Xt and other toolkits.

5.2.6 Pre-edit and Status Area Geometry Management

Depending on interaction style, an input method may require screen space to display pre-edit and status information. The application is responsible for providing these areas, but except for the on-the-spot interaction style, the input method will handle all output to them. When an input method requires screen space, the application should query its desired size and attempt to honor it. Note however that the input method must make do with whatever area it is given. This geometry management and geometry negotiation is handled through attributes of each input context and with a "geometry callback" function. These are described in Section 5.7 and Section 5.8.1.

5.2.7 Pre-edit and Status Callbacks

When using the on-the-spot interaction style, the IM will request the application to display pre-edit and status information for it. This is more complicated for the application, but because the application has finer control over the positioning of the information, it allows the appearance of a seamless interface with the IM. The IM makes requests of the application through a series of callback functions specified as attributes of the IC. The prototypes and responsibilities of these functions will be described in Section 5.8.

5.2.8 Getting Composed Input

When the application gets a **KeyPress** event, it should use that event in a call to **XmbLookupString** or **XwcLookupString**. These functions are analogs of **XLookupString**, but return multi-byte or wide-character strings in the codeset of the locale, where **XLookupString** can only return Latin-1 strings. Because it may take multiple keystrokes to enter a single character of text, these functions may return a status code that indicates that no composed input is ready.

Some input methods intercept keyboard events before the application has a chance to see them. If this is the case, they will send a synthetic **KeyPress** event with a keycode of 0 when there is composed input that should be looked up by the application.

5.2.9 Filtering Events

In order for an input method to perform pre-editing of input, it must have access to all **KeyPress** events. These events are passed to it through one of the internationalized **LookupString** functions. All but the most simple input methods, however, need access to other events as well. An IM that displays graphical feedback to the user will have to receive expose events, and an IM that displays a menu of homonyms, for example, will need to receive mouse motion and button events. **XFilterEvent** provides the hook that makes this possible. This function must be called from within an application's event loop before each new event is processed. If the IM has registered a (Xlib-internal) filter for that event, **XFilterEvent** invokes the filter and the IM has a chance to examine the event. If the IM is interested in the event, **XFilterEvent** will return **True**, and the application should not dispatch the event any further. Notice that an IM can use **XFilterEvent** to filter KeyPress events before the application can call one of the **LookupString** functions, but this is not the primary purpose of the function.

It is not safe to assume that the IM will only need events that the application currently receives, so the IM places an event mask for events in which it is interested in an attribute of each IC. The application is responsible for requesting to receive those events in the window of the IC.

5.2.10 The Big Picture

With the above explanations in mind, we can now consider the saga of a keystroke as it is processed through an internationalized application. Figure 5-2 diagrams the path a character follows between being typed on the keyboard and being displayed on the screen in an internationalized application.

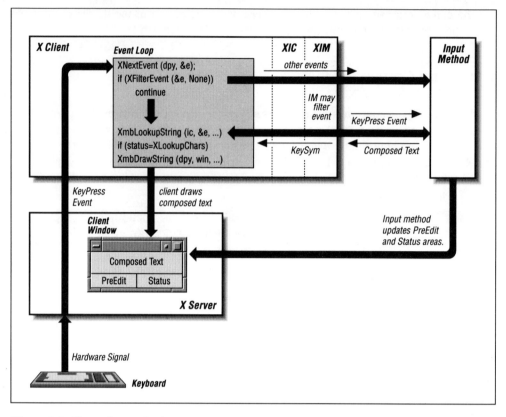

Figure 5-2. How a keystroke becomes a displayed character in an internationalized application

1. When the user strikes a key on the keyboard, the keyboard sends a hardware-specific key-code to the X server.

2. The X server sends an event to the client or clients that have expressed interest in key-stroke events for the window that had focus when the keystroke occurred.

3. The keystroke event will be received in the client's event loop by a call to **XNext-Event**.

4. The event is immediately passed to **XFilterEvent** to give the input method the opportunity to use it. Generally, the input method will not filter a **KeyPress** event.

5. Back in the application, if **XFilterEvent** returns **True**, then the application will dis-card the event and wait for the next one.

6. Otherwise, the application will go ahead and process the event. For every **KeyPress** event, the application will call **XmbLookupString** or **XwcLookupString**.

7. The input method now processes the keystroke: it adds a new character to its pre-edit text and updates the display in the Preedit and Status areas of the application. If the key-stroke is a control character such as Delete, the input method may modify the pre-edit text.

8. If the keystroke indicates that the user is done pre-editing and wishes to compose the pre-edited text, the input method does any necessary translation and the result becomes the return value of **Xmb/XwcLookupString**. In most applications, this returned string will be immediately echoed in the window with a call to one of the internationalized text drawing functions. If the keystroke merely adds to the pre-edit text, then the status value returned by **Xmb/wcLookupString** indicates that there is no composed text ready.

The above sections have presented an overview of the XIM architecture. The sections below describe how to write programs with input methods and input contexts. They explain how to implement each of the steps in the "big picture" above.

5.3 XIM Programming Interface

The input method programming interface departs in some ways from the style established by the rest of Xlib. Functions that set, modify, or query the attributes of an **XIM** or **XIC** have a variable-length argument list interface, similar to the interface of the X Toolkit **XtVaSet-Values** function, for example. Attributes are specified by a null-terminated list of name/value pairs. Names are null-terminated character strings (of type **char ***), and values are of type **XPointer**, which is a new Xlib generic pointer type, like **XtPointer**, which replaces the non-standard **caddr_t**. There are predefined symbols for all of the **XIM** and **XIC** attribute names. These are named similarly to X Toolkit resource names: they are prefixed with **XN** (not **XtN**) and words in the name are separated by capitalization rather than underscores. They differ from the Xt convention in that the first letter after the **XN** prefix *is* capitalized. Example 5-1 shows this naming convention and the varargs interface used in C code. There is only a single defined **XIM** attribute, which is explained in Section 5.4.2. There are a number of **XIC** attributes, which are explained in Section 5.6.

Example 5-1. The XIM varargs interface and attribute naming conventions

```
status = XSetICValues(ic, XNFocusWindow, w,
                      XNGeometryCallback, HandleIMGeometry,
                      NULL);
```

The **XNPreeditAttributes** and **XNStatusAttributes** attributes of an input context have a number of sub-attributes. In order to set or query these values, the programmer must specify a nested argument list of type **XVaNestedList ***. A value of this type is created with a call to the function **XVaCreateNestedList**. This function takes a dummy integer argument (as required by ANSI-C) followed by a null-terminated variable length list of name/value pairs. **XVaCreateNestedList** can be conveniently called from within an argument list to another function, as is shown in Example 5-2.

Example 5-2. A nested call to XVaCreateNestedList

```
XVaNestedList nlist;
ic = XCreateIC(im, XNInputStyle, XIMPreeditPosition | XIMStatusNothing,
               XNPreeditAttributes, nlist = XCreateVaNestedList(
                      0,  /* dummy argument */
                      XNSpotLocation, cursor_location,
                      XNFontSet, font_set,
```

Example 5-2. A nested call to XVaCreateNestedList (continued)

```
                            NULL),
                XNFocusWindow, focus_window,
                NULL);
XFree(nlist);
```

Nested argument lists can also be used to specify top-level attributes. To do this, use the special name **XNVaNestedList** which will cause the contents of the following nested list to be logically inserted into the argument list at the current position.

Note that **XVaCreateNestedList** allocates memory for the list it returns, which must be freed with a call to **XFree**. Also note that if any of the values in the list are pointer types, the data pointed to must remain valid for the lifetime of the list.

The designers of the XIM specification chose this varargs-and-named-attributes interface over the more familiar structure-and-flags interface used by **XChangeWindow-Attributes** and **XChangeGC**, for example, because they felt it provided "more flexibility." The perceived flexibility to the programmer is probably a matter of personal taste, but the varargs interface certainly provides more flexibility for future extensions—new attributes and vendor- or IM-specific attributes can easily be added without destroying binary compatibility.

5.4 XIM Functions

An **XIM** is an opaque structure that serves as a handle to the input method. Because input methods are generally implemented as separate processes, we generally talk about "opening," not "creating," an input method. In this respect, an **XIM** can be thought of as analogous to a **Display ***. The sections below explain how to open and close a connection to an input method, and how to query the values of input method attributes.

5.4.1 Opening and Closing an Input Method

A connection to an input method is opened with a call to **XOpenIM**. This function takes as arguments the Display, an **XrmDatabase**, and a resource name and resource class of type **char ***. The database is used by the input method to look up resources private to it. The resource name and class are used as resource name and class prefixes by the input method when looking up resources for input contexts. In an Xt program, the database created when the display is initialized can be used. In Xlib programs, the programmer will have to explicitly build the database, or simply pass an empty one.

XOpenIM also uses the current locale and locale modifiers as implicit arguments. The locale determines the default input method that **XOpenIM** will connect to, as well as the encoding of the strings which will be returned by **Xmb/XwcLookupString**. The locale is bound to an input method when it is open—the locale that was in effect when the input method was opened will be used by all input contexts of that input method regardless of the current locale when they are created.

The locale determines a default input method to be opened by **XOpenIM**, but it cannot be assumed that only one input method will be available in each locale. Therefore X defines a locale modifier named "im" which can be used to override the default input method of the locale. The programmer should call **XSetLocaleModifiers** to set all X locale modifiers ("im" is currently the only one). The user can specify a desired input method by setting the (UNIX) environment variable **XMODIFIERS** to a string of the form "@im=*input method name.*"

When an input method will no longer be used, it may be closed with a call to **XCloseIM**.

Example 5-3 shows how to establish the locale and open a connection to the input method for that locale.

Example 5-3. Establishing the locale and opening an XIM

```
#include <stdio.h>
#include <X11/Xlib.h>
/*
 * include <locale.h> or the non-standard X substitutes
 * depending on the X_LOCALE compilation flag
 */
#include <X11/Xlocale.h>

main(argc, argv)
int argc;
char *argv[ ];
{
    Display *dpy;
    XIM im;
    char *program_name = argv[0];

    /*
     * The error messages in this program are all in English.
     * In a truely internationalized program, they would not
     * be hardcoded; they would be looked up in a database of
     * some sort.
     */

    if (setlocale(LC_ALL, "") == NULL) {
        (void) fprintf(stderr, "%s: cannot set locale.\n",program_name);
        exit(1);
    }

    if ((dpy = XOpenDisplay(NULL)) == NULL) {
        (void) fprintf(stderr, "%s: cannot open Display.\n", program_name);
        exit(1);
    }

    if (!XSupportsLocale()) {
        (void) fprintf(stderr, "%s: X does not support locale
                    program_name, setlocale(LC_ALL, NULL));
        exit(1);
    }

    if (XSetLocaleModifiers("") == NULL) {
        (void) fprintf(stderr, "%s: Warning: cannot set locale modifiers.\n",
                    program_name);
    }
```

Example 5-3. Establishing the locale and opening an XIM (continued)

```
/*
 * Connect to an input method.
 * In this example, we don't pass a resource database
 */
if ((im = XOpenIM(dpy, NULL, NULL, NULL)) == NULL) {
    (void)fprintf(stderr, "%s: Couldn't open input method\n",
                  program_name);
    exit(1);
}
         .
         .
         .
```

5.4.2 Querying Input Method Values

The function **XGetIMValues** is used to query attributes of the input method. At this point, there is only one defined attribute, named **XNQueryInputStyle**. This is a read-only attribute that specifies the interaction styles supported by the input method. When an input context is created, one of the interaction styles from this list must be specified. Because the one attribute currently defined for input methods is read-only, there is no **XSetIMValues** procedure.

To get the list of supported interaction styles, call **XGetIMValues** passing the IM, the name **XNQueryInputStyle**, and the address of a variable of type **XIMStyles** *. The XIMStyles structure is shown in Example 5-4.

Example 5-4. The XIMStyles structure

```
typedef unsigned long XIMStyle;

typedef struct {
    unsigned short count_styles;
    XIMStyle *supported_styles;
} XIMStyles;
```

The call to **XGetIMValues** will return a pointer to a **XIMStyles** structure which contains a list of supported styles and the number of styles in the list. The client is responsible for freeing the **XIMStyles** structure when done with it.

Each **XIMStyle** in the list of supported styles is an **unsigned long** in which various bit flags describing the style are set. The valid flags and their meanings are described below:

XIMPreeditCallbacks

> The client must provide pre-edit callback procedures so that the input method can cooperate with the application to perform on-the-spot pre-editing.

XIMPreeditPosition

> The client must provide the location of the insertion cursor so that the input method can do over-the-spot pre-editing.

XIMPreeditArea

> The client must provide geometry management of an area in which the input method can do off-the-spot pre-editing.

XIMPreeditNothing

> The input method can perform root window pre-editing with no geometry management provided by the client.

XIMPreeditNone

> The input method does not do any pre-editing, or does not display any pre-edit data.

XIMStatusCallbacks

> The client must provide status callback procedures so that the input method can request the application to display status data when needed.

XIMStatusArea

> The client must provide geometry management of an area in which the input method can display status values.

XIMStatusNothing

> The input method can display status information in the root window with no geometry management provided by the client.

XIMStatusNone

> The input method does not display any status information.

When examining the **supported_styles** list, you may assume that each **XIMStyle** will have only one **XIMPreedit** flag and one **XIMStatus** flag set.* Example 5-5 in Section 5.5.2 shows how to query the supported styles of an input method.

5.5 XIC Functions

An input context is to an input method almost as a Window is to a Display. Each independent internationalized text input stream requires an IC, and the attributes of an IC define the behavior and appearance of the IM for that input stream. The sections below describe how to choose an input style for an IC, how to create and destroy an IC, how to set and get the attribute values of an IC, how to reset an IC, and how to set focus to an IC. The attributes of an IC are documented in Section 5.6.

---

*The XIM spec places no restrictions on how many flags may be set in an **XIMStyle**, but it does not assign any meaning to a style which has multiple **XIMPreedit** or **XIMStatus** flags.

5.5.1 Choosing an Interaction Style

The input or interaction style to be used by an input context must be specified when the input context is created. The style chosen must be one of those supported by the input method, and must also be supported by the client. The simplest of applications may choose to provide only minimal interaction with the input method, and may support only the **XIMPreedit-Nothing** and **XIMStatusNothing** interaction styles, forcing the input method to display its information in the root window. More complicated applications will probably support at least **XIMPreeditArea** and **XIMStatusArea** styles, as well as the "do nothing" styles. Generally, the right choice of interaction style is the most complicated (and therefore most user-friendly) style supported both by the application and the input method. An application may also choose to provide a resource so that the user can specify a desired style. Note that the choice of Preedit interaction style must be made independently of the Status style.

Section 5.4.2 lists the possible interaction styles, and explains how to query an input method for supported styles. Example 5-5 shows how to select Preedit and Status interactions styles and create an IC to use those styles.

5.5.2 Creating and Destroying Input Contexts

An **XIC** is created with a call to **XCreateIC** and destroyed with a call to **XDestroyIC**. **XCreateIC** takes an **XIM** as its first argument followed by a **NULL**-terminated variable-length argument list of attribute name/attribute value pairs. The IC is created in the locale of the IM, regardless of the current locale. The names of the IC attributes and their meanings are described in Section 5.6. Note that the **XNInputStyle** and **XNFontSet** attributes must be specified when an input context is created, and depending on the input style, **XNSpotLocation** and all of the callback attributes may also have to be specified at creation time. The **XNClientWindow** attribute need not be specified when the IC is created, but must be specified before any input is done with the IC. Example 5-5 shows how to choose an interaction style and create an IC.

Example 5-5. Choosing an interaction style and creating an IC

```
#include <stdio.h>
#include <X11/Xlib.h>
#include <X11/Xlocale.h>

main(argc, argv)
int argc;
char *argv[ ];
{
    Display *dpy;
    Window win;
    XFontSet fontset;
    XIM im;
    XIC ic;
    XIMStyles *im_supported_styles;
    XIMStyle app_supported_styles;
    XIMStyle style;
```

Programmer's Supplement for Release 5

```
XIMStyle best_style;
XVaNestedList list;
char *program_name = argv[0];
int i;
    .
    .
    .

/* figure out which styles the IM can support */
XGetIMValues(im, XNQueryInputStyle, &im_supported_styles, NULL);

/* set flags for the styles our application can support */
app_supported_styles = XIMPreeditNone | XIMPreeditNothing | XIMPreeditArea;
app_supported_styles |= XIMStatusNone | XIMStatusNothing | XIMStatusArea;

/*
 * now look at each of the IM supported styles, and
 * chose the "best" one that we can support.
 */
best_style = 0;
for(i=0; i < im_supported_styles->count_styles; i++) {
    style = im_supported_styles->supported_styles[i];
    if ((style & app_supported_styles) == style) /* if we can handle it */
        best_style = ChooseBetterStyle(style, best_style);
}

/* if we couldn't support any of them, print an error and exit */
if (best_style == 0) {
    (void)fprintf(stderr, "%s: application and program do not share a\n",
                    program_name);
    (void)fprintf(stderr, "%s: commonly supported interaction style.\n",
                    program_name);
    exit(1);
}

XFree(im_supported_styles);

/*
 * Now go create an IC using the style we chose.
 * Also set the window and fontset attributes now.
 */
list = XVaCreateNestedList(0, XNFontSet, fontset, NULL);
ic = XCreateIC(im, XNInputStyle, best_style,
                    XNClientWindow, win,
                    XNPreeditAttributes, list,
                    XNStatusAttributes, list,
                    NULL);
XFree(list);
if (ic == NULL) {
    (void) fprintf(stderr, "Couldn't create input context\n");
    exit(1);
}
    .
    .
    .
}

/*
```

```
 * This function chooses the "more desirable" of two input styles.  The
 * style with the more complicated Preedit style is returned, and if the
 * styles have the same Preedit styles, then the style with the more
 * complicated Status style is returned.  There is no "official" way to
 * order interaction styles; this one seems reasonable, though.
 * This is a long procedure for a simple heuristic.
 */
XIMStyle ChooseBetterStyle(style1,style2)
XIMStyle style1, style2;
{
    XIMStyle s,t;
    XIMStyle preedit = XIMPreeditArea | XIMPreeditCallbacks |
        XIMPreeditPosition | XIMPreeditNothing | XIMPreeditNone;
    XIMStyle status = XIMStatusArea | XIMStatusCallbacks |
        XIMStatusNothing | XIMStatusNone;

    if (style1 == 0) return style2;
    if (style2 == 0) return style1;
    if ((style1 & (preedit | status)) == (style2 & (preedit | status)))
        return style1;

    s = style1 & preedit;
    t = style2 & preedit;
    if (s != t) {
        if (s | t | XIMPreeditCallbacks)
            return (s == XIMPreeditCallbacks)?style1:style2;
        else if (s | t | XIMPreeditPosition)
            return (s == XIMPreeditPosition)?style1:style2;
        else if (s | t | XIMPreeditArea)
            return (s == XIMPreeditArea)?style1:style2;
        else if (s | t | XIMPreeditNothing)
            return (s == XIMPreeditNothing)?style1:style2;
    }
    else { /* if preedit flags are the same, compare status flags */
        s = style1 & status;
        t = style2 & status;
        if (s | t | XIMStatusCallbacks)
            return (s == XIMStatusCallbacks)?style1:style2;
        else if (s | t | XIMStatusArea)
            return (s == XIMStatusArea)?style1:style2;
        else if (s | t | XIMStatusNothing)
            return (s == XIMStatusNothing)?style1:style2;
    }
}
```

5.5.3 Querying and Modifying an XIC

Attributes of an XIC can be set with a call to XSetICValues and can be queried with a
call to XGetICValues. Both functions take an XIC as their first argument, followed by a
NULL-terminated variable-length argument list of attribute name/attribute value pairs. The
names, types, and usage of the attributes are explained in Section 5.6. Note that some of the

attributes are read-only, some must be specified when the IC is created, and others must be specified once and may not be changed once specified.*

The value arguments passed to **XGetICValues** must be valid pointers to locations in which to store the requested attribute values. **XGetICValues** will allocate memory for the storage of some of these attributes, and this memory must be freed by the client with a call to **XFree**.†

To query the values of Preedit and Status sub-attributes, create a nested list of name/value pairs, where the values are pointers to storage and pass this nested list as the value of the **XNPreeditAttributes** or **XNStatusAttributes** attributes. You cannot query the value of all sub-attributes by passing a **XVaNestedList *** as the value of **XNPreedit-Attributes** or **XNStatusAttributes**—**XGetICValues** does not build and return a nested list of sub-attributes

Both **XSetICValues** and **XGetICValues** return a **char *** which is **NULL** if no errors occurred, or points to the name of the first attribute that could not be set or queried.

5.5.4 Resetting an Input Context

If text input is interrupted while pre-editing is in progress, the input context may be left in a non-initial internal state. To reset the state of an **XIC**, call **XmbResetIC** or **XwcReset-IC**. Both reset the IC to its initial state and discard any pending input. Both functions may return the current pre-edit string, but it is implementation dependent how and whether they do this. The only difference between these functions is in the type of string they return. The returned string, if any, should be freed by the client with **XFree**.

---

*Some attributes, such as **XNGeometryCallback** and **XNArea**, have values that are pointer types. The spec does not say whether the values pointed to by these attributes are copied. It appears that the Xsi implementation (the default) does make a copy of all these attribute values, with the exception of the **XNResourceName** and **XNResourceClass** attributes, which are strings and not of fixed length.

†The spec is self-contradictory about which attributes will have memory allocated for them. It says, "Each argument value (following a name) must point to a location where the value is to be stored. **XGetICValues** allocates memory to store the values, and client [sic] is responsible for freeing each value by calling **XFree**." The first sentence indicates that the program provides memory for the attribute value. The second indicates that the program provides memory for a pointer to the attribute value. The Xsi implementation (the default) takes the first approach, and the Ximp implementation takes the second. So, for example, to query the value of the **XNFocusWindow** attribute, you would pass the address of a **Window** to **XGetICValues** if using the Xsi implementation, but the address of a **Window *** if using the Ximp implementation. In the second case, the returned **Window *** value points to allocated memory which must be freed. When querying attributes like **XNResourceName** and **XNGeometry-Callback**, which have values that are pointer types, it is not clear what types should be passed in the query, nor is it clear whether the returned pointer points to a copy of the value which must be freed, or to the value itself which must not be freed. As a programmer, your best bet is to avoid the use of **XGetICValues**, except when necessary for the **XNFilterEvents** and **XNAreaNeeded** attributes.

5.5.5 Setting Input Context Focus

When the focus window of an input context receives the application input focus, the application should call **XSetICFocus** on that IC. Use **XUnsetICFocus** when the focus window of an IC loses focus, or simply call **XSetICFocus** on the IC of the new focus window. This will allow the input method to perform internal housekeeping and display special graphics (such as a highlighted border) in the Pre-Edit and Status windows of the IC that has the focus.

If you are using a single IC to handle input across several windows, and the input focus shifts from one of these windows to another, then the IC's **XNFocusWindow** attribute should be changed, you needn't call **XSetICFocus**. Depending upon your user interface, you may also want to reset the IC when focus changes like this.

5.5.6 Input Context Utility Functions

The following utility functions are sometimes useful when using input methods and input contexts:

XIMOfIC Returns the IM associated with a given IC.

XDisplayOfIM
> Returns the Display associated with a given IM.

XLocaleOfIM
> Returns the locale associated with a given IM. The returned string is owned by Xlib and should not be freed by the client. It will be freed by Xlib when the IM is closed.*

5.6 Input Context Attributes

The behavior of an input method for a particular stream of input is controlled by the attributes of the input context of that stream. There is an attribute, for example, that specifies the interaction style (which must be one of the styles supported by the IM), there are attributes that specify the pre-edit callbacks to be called by the input method when over-the-spot interaction is being used, and there are attributes that specify the foreground and background pixels and colormap for the IM to use when drawing in its Preedit area.

Some attributes are used for communication in the other direction. One is used by the input method to tell the client which types of X events it requires, and another is used by the input method to request a new size for its Preedit and Status areas. Most attributes may be freely modified, but note that some must be set when the IC is created, others must be set exactly once, and others still are read-only and must never be set.

---

*The spec does not state whether the client should free this string, nor when it will be freed by Xlib.

The attributes are listed below. Most attributes provide default values, but recall that some must be specified, either when the IC is created or at some later time before it is used.

5.6.1 XNInputStyle

The **XNInputStyle** attribute specifies the interaction style to be used by the input method for this input context. It is of type **XIMStyle**. It must be one of the supported styles queried from the input method with **XGetIMValues**. This attribute must be specified when the IC is created. It may be queried but not changed.

5.6.2 XNClientWindow

The **XNClientWindow** attribute specifies the window in which the input method will display its Preedit and Status areas. It is of type **Window**. All geometry values for those areas are specified relative to this window. This attribute must be specified (with **XCreateIC** or **XSetICValues**) before any input is done, and once set may not be changed.

5.6.3 XNFocusWindow

If a single IC is used to handle multiple input streams within a single client window (as in a multi-buffer text editor that displays several paned editing windows and provides pre-editing in a message line at the bottom of the client window), the **XNFocusWindow** attribute (of type **Window**) is used to specify which sub-window currently has the focus. The input method may select events on this window, send synthetic events to it, set or change properties on it, or grab the keyboard within it. If not specified, this attribute will default to the value of **XNClientWindow**. If this attribute is specified, it should generally be a child of the client window. The value of **XNFocusWindow** may be changed freely.

5.6.4 XNResourceName and XNResourceClass

The **XNResourceName** and **XNResourceClass** attributes are null-terminated strings which completely specify the resource name and class used to obtain resources for the client window. If the input method allows per-IC customization using X resources, those resources will be looked up using the name and class hierarchies specified by **XNResourceName** and **XNResourceClass**. If your application is named "iedit" with class name "Iedit," and the client window is a widget named "itext" of class "IText" and it is within a top-level manager widget named "main" of class "Form," then the **XNResourceName** attribute should be set to "iedit.main.itext," and the **XNResourceClass** attribute should be set to "IEdit.Form.IText." If these attributes are not set, the input method will not be able to look up resource values for the IC in its resource database. Both attributes may be set at any time, but because resource lookup is generally done only when an IC is created, they will only be useful if specified to **XCreateIC**. The specification does not say whether or not the values of these strings are copied. To be safe, the strings passed as values of **XNResourceName** and **XNResourceClass** should not be freed or modified until the IC is destroyed or new values are provided for those attributes.

5.6.5 XNGeometryCallback

The **XNGeometryCallback** attribute, of type **XIMCallback ***, specifies a procedure which an input method may call to request a different size for it's Preedit or Status areas. Because the client is never obliged to meet IM geometry requests, specifying this attribute is optional.

5.6.6 XNFilterEvents

The **XNFilterEvents** attribute is used by the input method to notify the client of the X events it needs to receive. It is an event mask, a long integer of the format passed to **XSelectInput**. The client must query this resource before any input is done and augment the event mask for the **XNClientWindow** with it. This attribute is read-only and should never be set.

5.6.7 XNPreeditAttributes and XNStatusAttributes

Each of these attributes specifies a list of sub-attributes that control the position, behavior, and appearance of the Preedit and Status areas of the IC. They have type **XVaNested-List** and should be created with a call to **XVaCreateNestedList**. Most of these attributes are used by the input method for both the Preedit and the Status areas. They are ignored, of course, for **XIMPreeditNone** and **XIMStatusNone** interaction styles. All of these attributes except the callbacks are ignored for interaction styles **XIMPreedit-Callbacks** and **XIMStatusCallbacks**. They are described individually below.

XNArea

The **XNArea** attribute is a pointer to an **XRectangle**. If the interaction style is **XIMPreeditArea** or **XIMStatusArea**, then the rectangle defines the region of the client window in which pre-editing and status display is to take place. An input method may create sub-windows of the client window that conform to this geometry. If the pre-edit interaction style is **XIMPreeditPostion** instead of **XIMPreeditArea**, then this attribute specifies a clipping region in the focus window of the IC to be used in conjunction with the **XNSpotLocation** attribute to implement over-the-spot pre-editing. This attribute must be specified if any of the above interaction styles are in use. For all other pre-edit and status interaction styles, this attribute is ignored.

XNAreaNeeded

The **XNAreaNeeded** attribute is also a pointer to an **XRectangle**. It is used for geometry negotiation between client and input method for the **XIMPreeditArea** and **XIMStatusArea** interaction styles, and is ignored for all other styles. The client may provide a hint to the input method about the area it is likely to get by setting a non-zero width or height in this attribute (the x and y values are ignored). The client may query the input method's preferred size for those areas by reading the value of this attribute. A well-behaved input method will not request a size larger than any hints it has received. Note that neither step is required—the client can always set any size it desires with the **XNArea** attribute. See Section 5.7 for more details on geometry negotiation.

XNSpotLocation

The **XNSpotLocation** attribute is a pointer to **XPoint**. It is used when the Preedit interaction style is **XIMPreeditPosition** and is ignored for all Status interaction styles and all other Preedit interaction styles. The value of this attribute should be set to the position (in the focus window) at which the next character would be drawn. The input method will use this point and the clipping region specified in **XNAreaNeeded** to implement over-the-spot pre-editing in a sub-window of the focus window. Each time a newly-composed character is drawn or the text modified in any way, the value of this attribute should be changed to reflect the new value of the "spot." When the interaction style is **XIMPreeditPosition**, this attribute must be specified when the IC is created.

XNColormap

The **XNColormap** attribute specifies the colormap which the input method should use for any windows it creates itself. It is of type **Colormap**. If the colormap is unspecified, the input method will provide a default.

XNStdColormap

The **XNStdColormap** attribute provdes an alternate method of specifying the colormap to be used by the input method. It is of type **Atom**, and should be set to a value appropriate for a call to **XGetStandardColormap**. If both this attribute and the **XNColormap** attribute are passed in a call to **XSetICValues**, it is implemenation-dependent which will take precedence.

XNForeground

The **XNForeground** attribute specifies the foreground pixel value to be used by the input method. It is of type `unsigned long`.

XNBackground

The **XNBackground** attribute specifies the background pixel value to be used by the input method. It is of type `unsigned long`.

XNBackgroundPixmap

The **XNBackgroundPixmap** attribute specifies a pixmap to be used as the background of the Preedit or Status window created by the input method. It is of type `Pixmap`.

XNFontSet

The **XNFontSet** attribute specifies a fontset to be used by the input method for text drawing in the Preedit or Status window. It is of type `XFontSet`. The locale of the specified fontset must match the locale of the input method. This attribute must be specified when the IC is created.

XNLineSpacing

The **XNLineSpacing** attribute specifies the line spacing* to be used by the input method when displaying multi-line text. It is of type `int`.

XNCursor

The **XNCursor** attribute specifies the mouse cursor to be used in the Preedit or Status windows. It is of type `Cursor`.

Pre-edit and Status Callbacks

There are seven callback attributes, four of which must be specified for **XIMPreedit-Callbacks** interaction style, and three of which must be specified for **XIMStatus-Callbacks** interaction style. Each callback attribute is of type **XIMCallback ***. This type, the callback prototypes, and requirements will be explained in Section 5.8. If the **XIMPreeditCallbacks** or **XIMStatusCallbacks** interaction styles are in use, the

---

*The spec simply says "line spacing" and does not specify whether the value should be a baseline-to-baseline spacing or just interline spacing. A baseline-to-baseline spacing was probably the intent, but it will be safest to leave this attribute unspecified and use the IM default.

appropriate callbacks must be specified when the IC is created. The callback attributes are the following:

- **XNPreeditStartCallback**, called when pre-editing starts. It gives the client the opportunity to provide feedback to the user, to rearrange characters in the window to make room for pre-editing, etc.

- **XNPreeditDoneCallback**, called when a character is composed and pre-editing stops. It gives the client the opportunity to provide feedback to the user, close up any space opened for pre-editing, etc.

- **XNPreeditDrawCallback**, called when the input method wants the client to draw characters in the window.

- **XNPreeditCaretCallback**, called when the input method wants the client to move the text-insertion cursor (which for some applications may have the shape of a caret).

- **XNStatusStartCallback**, called when the input context gets the focus. It gives the client the chance to provide user feedback.

- **XNStatusDoneCallback**, called when the input context loses focus (or is destroyed). It gives the client the chance to provide user feedback.

- **XNStatusDrawCallback**, called when the input method wants the client to draw text or a bitmap into the status area.

5.7 Negotiating Preedit and Status Area Geometries

For the **XIMPreeditArea** and **XIMStatusArea** interaction styles, the input method needs an area of the application window in which it can create a sub-window and perform its necessary pre-editing and display status information. The application is responsible for providing these areas to the input method (with the **XNArea** sub-attribute) and the input method must accept whatever area it is given.

The simplest applications may simply force the input method to use some pre-defined area, but slightly more flexible applications will want to query the input method for its desired size. To allow this, a protocol for geometry negotiation between application and input method has been defined. The protocol uses the **XNAreaNeeded** sub-attribute of an input context in two distinct ways: when the application sets this attribute with a non-zero width and/or height, the input method interprets these as hints about the size that will eventually be assigned to it by the client. When the application queries the value of the **XNAreaNeeded** attribute, it is returned the input method's preferred size which it may choose to honor when setting the size in the **XNArea** attribute.

An example best demonstrates the use of this protocol: Suppose an internationalized client wants to place the pre-edit area across the bottom of its application window. This means that the width of the area is constrained to be the width of the window, but the height of the area is not constrained. So the application specifies the width of the **XNAreaNeeded** attribute to be the width of the window and leaves the height of the attribute set to 0. Now the input method may use this information to re-compute its desired size. If it would have liked a one line pre-edit area 500 pixels wide, for example, and has just received a hint that it will not get an area wider than 350 pixels, it might choose to request a pre-edit area that is two lines high. Now when the application queries the **XNAreaNeeded** attribute it will get the input method's new desired size. If an application has no constraints for the input method, it can omit the first step and simply read from **XNAreaNeeded**.

This negotiation protocol is not reserved for application startup; it may take place at any time. Note that if the application changes the **XNFocusWindow** attribute of an IC or the **XNFontSet** or **XNLineSpacing** sub-attributes of the pre-edit or status areas, the input method will probably have a new desired size for those areas, and the application should redo the geometry negotiation process. When the application's window is resized, the application will probably want to place the pre-edit and status areas at a new location, and may also have new constraints on their size. The application should set its size constraints in **XNArea-Needed** even if those constraints have not changed since the last time geometry was negotiated.* Example 5-6 shows a procedure that handles the geometry negotiation process. It was designed to be called from an application's event loop when the main window is resized.

Example 5-6. Negotiating Preedit and Status area geometries

```
#include <X11/Xlib.h>

/*
 * This procedure sets the application's size constraints and returns
 * the IM's preferred size for either the Preedit or Status areas,
 * depending on the value of the name argument.  The area argument is
 * used to pass the constraints and to return the preferred size.
 */
void GetPreferredGeometry(ic, name, area)
XIC ic;
char *name;            /* XNPreeditAttributes or XNStatusAttributes */
XRectangle *area;      /* in: constraints;  out: IM preferred size */
{
    XVaNestedList list;

    list = XVaCreateNestedList(0, XNAreaNeeded, area, NULL);
    /* set the constraints */
    XSetICValues(ic, name, list, NULL);
    /* query the preferred size */
    XGetICValues(ic, name, list, NULL);
    XFree(list);
}

/*
 * This procedure sets the geometry of either the Preedit or Status
 * Areas, depending on the value of the name argument.
 */
void SetGeometry(ic, name, area)
XIC ic;
char *name;            /* XNPreeditAttributes or XNStatusAttributes */
XRectangle *area;      /* the actual area to set */
{
    XVaNestedList list;
```

---

*The spec makes no statement about the duration of the validity of the application's constraints.

Example 5-6. Negotiating Preedit and Status area geometries (continued)

```
        list = XVaCreateNestedList(0, XNArea, area, NULL);
        XSetICValues(ic, name, list, NULL);
        XFree(list);
}

/*
 * Called when the window is resized.  If the interaction style
 * uses the Preedit or Status areas, then their size needs to
 * be re-negotiated.  This procedure places both the Preedit and
 * Status areas at the bottom of the window, and constrains the
 * Preedit area to occupy no more than 4/5ths of the window width
 * on the right hand side of the window, and constrains the Status
 * area to occupy no more than 1/5th of the window on the left.
 * It does not constrain the height of these areas at all.
 */
void NegotiateICGeometry(ic, event, style, preedit_area, status_area)
XIC ic;
XEvent *event;
XIMStyle style;
XRectangle *preedit_area, *status_area;
{
    if ((preedit_area != NULL) && (style & XIMPreeditArea)) {
        preedit_area->width = event->xconfigure.width*4/5;
        preedit_area->height = 0;
        GetPreferredGeometry(ic, XNPreeditAttributes, preedit_area);
        preedit_area->x = event->xconfigure.width - preedit_area->width;
        preedit_area->y = event->xconfigure.height - preedit_area->height;
        SetGeometry(ic, XNPreeditAttributes, preedit_area);
    }
    if ((status_area != NULL) && (style & XIMStatusArea)) {
        status_area->width = event->xconfigure.width/5;
        status_area->height = 0;
        GetPreferredGeometry(ic, XNStatusAttributes, status_area);
        status_area->x = 0;
        status_area->y = event->xconfigure.height - status_area->height;
        SetGeometry(ic, XNStatusAttributes, status_area);
    }
}
```

Finally, an application may choose to provide a callback procedure that will be called by the input method to request a new size for its pre-edit or status areas. This callback may be triggered by changes to attributes such as **XNFontSet** as described above, or may be triggered directly by the user's interactions with the input method (an input method could provide "resize handles" on its pre-edit area, for example). If an application provides a geometry callback, it should attempt to honor any resize requests made by the input method. (An input method might choose whether or not to display "resize handles" on its pre-edit area depending on the presence or absence of such a callback.) The prototype geometry callback is described in Section 5.8.1.

5.8 Geometry, Preedit, and Status Callbacks

An application interacting with an input method using the **XIMPreeditArea** and/or **XIMStatusArea** styles may optionally provide a callback to be called when the input method would like to renegotiate the size of its pre-edit or status areas. An application using the **XIMPreeditCallbacks** style must provide a suite of pre-edit callback routines that allow the input method and application to cooperate and provide pre-editing that appears to be an integral part of the application itself. Similarly, an application using the **XIMStatusCallbacks** must provide a suite of callbacks for the display of status information.

Each callback attribute is of type **XIMCallback**, which is shown in Example 5-7.

Example 5-7. The XIMCallback structure

```
typedef void (*XIMProc)();

typedef struct {
    XPointer client_data;
    XIMProc callback;
} XIMCallback;
```

If you have used X Toolkit callbacks, you will be familiar with the use of the **client_data** field. This is untyped data registered with the callback and passed to the callback every time it is invoked. When a single callback procedure is registered on several different callback attributes, the **client_data** can serve in a **switch** statement to determine how the callback should behave. It is also often used to pass data to the callback (such as a window ID or a widget pointer), which the callback would otherwise not have access to. The type of *client_data* is **XPointer**, which is a new Xlib generic pointer type, like **XtPointer**.

Most of the callback procedures have the prototype shown in Example 5-8.

Example 5-8. A prototype XIM callback procedure

```
void CallbackPrototype(ic, client_data, call_data)
    XIC ic;
    XPointer client_data;
    XPointer call_data;
```

The **XIC** passed to the callback procedure will be the input context that caused the callback to be invoked. The *client_data* argument will be the untyped data registered with the callback as described above. It is up to the callback to know the actual type of this data and cast it as appropriate before use. The *call_data* argument is data passed by the input method to the callback; it is the data required by the callback to perform whatever action the input method needs done. Each callback passes a different type in this argument. Note that the Xlib header files do not actually define **CallbackPrototype**, only the type **XIMProc** shown in the previous example. Since the definition of the **XIMProc** type does not have a prototype, callback procedures may be written with any desired types for *client_data* and *call_data*.

5.8.1 The Geometry Callback

The geometry callback (**XNGeometryCallback**) is triggered when the input method would like to renegotiate the geometry of its pre-edit or status areas. It is not passed any data in its *call_data* argument. Note that this callback does not indicate whether the input method wants renegotiation of the pre-edit area or the status area or both. If the application and the input method are interacting through both **XIMPreeditArea** and **XIMStatus-Area** styles, then the application should renegotiate the geometry of both areas. The geometry negotiation process is described in Section 5.7.

5.8.2 The PreeditStartCallback and the PreeditEndCallback

The **XNPreeditStartCallback** and **XNPreeditEndCallback** are called when the input method begins and ends pre-editing. They give the application the opportunity to do any necessary internal setup or cleanup and provide graphical feedback to the user that the application is entering or leaving pre-edit mode. Both callbacks are passed **NULL** as their *call_data* values. **XNPreeditStartCallback** will not be called twice for the same IC without an intervening call to **XNPreeditEndCallback**.

The **XNPreeditStartCallback** has one additional requirement. It must return an int (and therefore does not satisfy the general callback prototype given above) to the input method which indicates the maximum number of bytes the application is able to handle in the pre-edit string. If this callback returns a positive value, the input method should not expect the application to be able to successfully display pre-edit strings any longer than that value. If the callback returns the value -1, it indicates that the application can handle pre-edit strings of any length.

5.8.3 The PreeditDrawCallback

This callback is called when the input method wants the application to insert, delete, or replace text in the pre-edit string. It is also used by the input method to request that some characters or substrings be highlighted (to indicate a selected region of the pre-edit string, for example). The callback is expected to display the pre-edit text to the user and will have to maintain an internal pre-edit string. The pre-edit text will likely appear within the running text of the application, but cursor and character positions referred to in this callback are all relative to the beginning of the pre-edit string. The **XNPreeditDrawCallback** is passed *call_data* of type **XIMPreeditDrawCallbackStruct**, which is shown in Example 5-9.

Example 5-9. The XIMPreeditDrawCallbackStruct

```
typedef unsigned long XIMFeedback;

#define XIMReverse      1L
#define XIMUnderline    (1L<<1)
#define XIMHighlight    (1L<<2)
#define XIMPrimary      (1L<<3)
```

Example 5-9. The XIMPreeditDrawCallbackStruct (continued)

```
#define XIMSecondary    (1L<<4)
#define XIMTertiary     (1L<<5)

typedef struct _XIMText {
    unsigned short length;
    XIMFeedback *feedback;
    Bool encoding_is_wchar;
    union {
        char * multi_byte;
        wchar_t * wide_char;
    } string;
} XIMText;

typedef struct _XIMPreeditDrawCallbackStruct {
    int caret;
    int chg_first;
    int chg_length;
    XIMText text;
} XIMPreeditDrawCallbackStruct ;
```

The **XNPreeditDrawCallback** must do the following:

- If **chg_length** is positive, then the application must delete the characters in the pre-edit string between **chg_first** and **chg_first + chg_length–1** inclusive.* Note that manipulations of the pre-edit string are always done on the basis of character positions, so it will generally be most useful to store the pre-edit string in wide-character format.

- If the **text** field is non-NULL, and **text.string** is non-null, the application must insert that string at the position specified by **chg_first**. A position of 0 indicates that the string should be inserted before the first character of the pre-edit string, a position of 1 indicates that the string should be inserted before the second character of the pre-edit string, and so on. If **text.encoding_is_wchar** is TRUE then the string to be inserted is the wide-character string **text.string.wide_char** which is **text.length** characters long. If FALSE, then the string to be inserted is the multi-byte string **text.string.multi_byte**, which is also **text.length** characters (not bytes) long. Since there is no way to request that the IM use either wide-character or multi-byte strings, your application will have to be prepared to handle either case. When passed a multi-byte string, it will probably be easiest to convert it to a wide-character string and operate on it in that representation.

- If there is a string to be inserted, and **text.feedback** is not NULL then **text.feedback** is an array of **XIMFeedback** with **text.length** elements. Each character of the string to be inserted must be drawn with the "feedback style" indicated by the corresponding element of the **text.feedback** array. If the array element is 0 then no special highlighting of the character needs to be done. Otherwise the character must be highlighted in one of the following ways:

  - **XIMReverse** means the character should be drawn with foreground and background colors reversed.

---

*The spec says, "Characters starting from chg_first to chg_first+chg_length must be deleted."

- **XIMUnderline** means that a line should be drawn along the character's baseline.

- **XIMHighlight** means that the character should be drawn highlighted in some style other than the styles used for **XIMReverse** and **XIMUnderline**.*

- **XIMPrimary** means that the character should be drawn in some application defined highlighting style which is not the same as the style used for **XIMSecondary**.

- **XIMSecondary** means that the character should be drawn in some application defined highlighting style which is not the same as the style used for **XIMPrimary**.

- **XIMTertiary** means that the character should be drawn in some application defined highlighting style.

- If **text.feedback** is not NULL, but **text.string** is NULL, then no string needs to be inserted, but the characters between *chg_first* and *chg_first* + *text.length-1* inclusive should be redrawn with the highlight style indicated by *text.feedback*.

- After any insertions and deletions have been performed, the text insertion cursor (called the "caret" in the XIM spec) should be moved to the position specified in the *caret* field. If the position is 0, the cursor should be positioned so that new text will be inserted before the first character of the pre-edit string. If it is 1, the cursor should be positioned so that new text will be inserted before the second character of the pre-edit string, and so on.

5.8.4 The PreeditCaretCallback

This callback is called by the input method when it wants the application to move the current position of the text insertion cursor or to change the way the cursor is displayed. It is called with *call_data* of type **XIMPreeditCaretCallbackStruct** which is shown in Example 5-10.

Example 5-10. The XIMPreeditCaretCallbackStruct

```
typedef enum {
    XIMForwardChar, XIMBackwardChar,
    XIMForwardWord, XIMBackwardWord,
    XIMCaretUp, XIMCaretDown,
    XIMNextLine, XIMPreviousLine,
    XIMLineStart, XIMLineEnd,
    XIMAbsolutePosition,
    XIMDontChange,
} XIMCaretDirection;

typedef enum {
    XIMIsInvisible,
    XIMIsPrimary,
    XIMIsSecondary,
} XIMCaretStyle;
```

*The spec says nothing about the **XIMHighlight** style.

Example 5-10. The XIMPreeditCaretCallbackStruct (continued)

```
typedef struct _XIMPreeditCaretCallbackStruct {
    int position;
    XIMCaretDirection direction;
    XIMCaretStyle style;
} XIMPreeditCaretCallbackStruct;
```

The **XNPreeditCaretCallback** is required to move the cursor as specified in the **direction** field, display it in the style specified in the **style** field, and return the new character position of the cursor by setting the value of the **position** field. The position field must be set by the callback because in some cases the input method will not be able to compute it itself. This is the case when the cursor is moved down a line, for example—the new character position of the cursor will depend on the number of characters in each line, which is a figure known to the application but not to the input method. Note that to correctly implement this callback, the application will have to remember the position of the insertion cursor at all times, and this position will have to be updated by both the **XNPreeditDraw-Callback** and the **XNPreeditCaretCallback**.

The possible values of the **direction** field and their meanings are listed below. Note that in no case should the insertion cursor be moved to a position before the beginning or after the end of the pre-edit string.*

- **XIMForwardChar** means move the cursor forward one character.

- **XIMBackwardChar** means move the cursor backwards one character.

- **XIMForwardWord** means move the cursor forward one word. It is up to the application to decide what constitutes a "word" in a pre-edit string. In many locales, a word will be delimited by characters for which **isspace** returns **True**.

- **XIMBackwardWord** means move the cursor backwards one word.

- **XIMCaretUp** means move the cursor up one line, keeping its position in the line constant if possible.

- **XIMCaretDown** means move the cursor down one line, keeping its position in the line constant if possible.

- **XIMPreviousLine** means move the cursor to the beginning of the previous line of pre-edit text.

- **XIMNextLine** means move the cursor to the beginning of the next line of pre-edit text.

- **XIMLineStart** means move the cursor to the beginning of the line it is currently on.

- **XIMLineEnd** means move the cursor to the end of the line it is currently on.

- **XIMAbsolutePosition** means move the cursor to the absolute character position specified in the **position** field of the **XIMPreeditCallbacksStruct**. If the

---

*The spec does not say what an application should do if a cursor motion request would take the cursor beyond the pre-edit text. You should probably leave the cursor where it is or move it to one end of the text. In either case simply return the new or unchanged position.

position is 0, the cursor should be positioned so that new text will be inserted before the first character of the pre-edit string. If it is 1, the cursor should be positioned so that new text will be inserted before the second character of the pre-edit string, and so on.

- **XIMDontChange** means that the cursor position should not be changed. The current position of the cursor must still be returned in the **position** field, however.

The **XNPreeditCaretCallback** can also be called to request that the insertion cursor become hidden or be drawn in a different style. Different cursor appearances may be used by the input method to indicate different pre-editing modes, insert versus overwrite mode, for example. The possible values of the **style** field and their meanings are as follows:

- **XIMIsInvisible** means that the insertion cursor should not be displayed.

- **XIMIsPrimary** means that the insertion cursor should be displayed in its primary or normal style. The particular style used is up to the application.

- **XIMIsSecondary** means that the insertion cursor should be displayed in its secondary or special style. The particular style used is up to the application.

Note that there is no provision for the handling of mouse clicks (for example, to move the position of the insertion cursor in the pre-edit text) in this interaction style. Since the input method does not know how the pre-edit text is displayed, it cannot interpret mouse clicks over the text, and there is no specified way for the IM to request the application to convert pixel locations to character positions. Furthermore, the application cannot handle mouse clicks on the pre-edit text because it has no way of changing the internal insertion position of the IM. Note that some input methods will allow mouse clicks and drags while pre-editing in the **XIMPreeditPosition** and **XIMPreeditArea** interaction styles; in this case these styles may actually provide a more consistent user interface than the **XIMPreedit-Callbacks** style.

5.8.5 The StatusStartCallback and the StatusDoneCallback

These callbacks are called when an IC gains focus or loses focus (possibly by being destroyed). They give the application the chance to set up or clean up any internal structures for handling status display, and allow the application to provide graphical feedback of the new IC focus state to the user. Both are passed **NULL** *call_data* and neither has any required actions.

5.8.6 The StatusDrawCallback

The input method invokes the **XNStatusDrawCallback** when it wants the application to display a string or a bitmap in the status area. The callback procedure is passed *call_data* of type **XIMStatusDrawCallbackStruct**, which is shown in Example 5-11.

Example 5-11. The XIMStatusDrawCallbackStruct

```
typedef enum {XIMTextType, XIMBitmapType} XIMStatusDataType;

typedef struct _XIMStatusDrawCallbackStruct {
    XIMStatusDataType type;
    union {
        XIMText text;
        Pixmap  bitmap;
    } data;
} XIMStatusDrawCallbackStruct ;
```

If the **type** field is **XIMTextType**, then the callback must display the text described by **data.text** in the status area of the IC. The **XIMText** type is also used by the **XNPreeditDrawCallback**, and is shown and explained in Section 5.8.3. The text may be in multi-byte or wide-character form, so the application must be able to handle either case. Recall that the **length** field of the **XIMText** structure gives the number of characters of text, even when the text is in multi-byte form. The length in bytes of a multi-byte string is required for a call to **XmbDrawImageString**, so when text is passed in multi-byte form, the application will have to use **strlen** to determine its length before displaying it.

If the **type** field is **XIMBitmapType**, then the callback must display the 1-bit deep **Pixmap data.bitmap**.* Notice that the callback does not return the width or height of the pixmap, so these must be obtained with a call to **XGetGeometry** before the pixmap is displayed.

The **XIMStatusCallbacks** interaction style does not allow for any communication between the application and the input method about the maximum size of the status area. Since it can always be passed data to display that is larger than the area it has allocated, the **XNStatusDrawCallback** must be prepared either to clip or provide scrolling for the strings and pixmaps it is passed, or to attempt to enlarge the status area. Resizing the status area requires the main application window to be made larger or other windows to be rearranged or resized. The **XIMStatusCallbacks** interaction style can be useful for an application designed to be used with a single input method which calls the **XNStatusDrawCallback** with well specified values. In general, however, when you don't know what sort of data your application will be asked to display (or the meaning of that data), you won't be able to do anything beyond displaying the data in some rectangular region of your application, which amounts to the same thing as the **XIMStatusArea** interaction style. So in these cases it may make more sense to use **XIMStatusArea** if the input method supports it.

---

*The spec does not say anything about the depth of this **Pixmap**.

5.9 Filtering Events

An input method needs to receive X events other than keystrokes. It must receive expose events when its Preedit or Status areas need refreshing, it needs mouse button events if it is to support full-featured editing of pre-edit text, and it needs mouse motion events if it implements popup menus. The input method needs to get first crack at these events, but will not always be able to intercept them directly from the server, so the application is responsible for passing all events to the input method before processing them itself. This is done with the function **XFilterEvent**. It should be called from the event loop of all internationalized applications, generally right after **XNextEvent**. **XFilterEvent** takes two arguments, the event to filter, and the window to which the event is directed. If the application (or a toolkit used by the application) performs event redirection, this window may not be the same as the window in which the event occurred. If the window argument is **None,** the window of the event will be used. An application cannot know in advance which events the IM will need to filter; it must pass all events to **XFilterEvent**. If **XFilterEvent** returns **True**, it filtered the event the application should dispatch the event no further.

Remember that an input method may be interested in different types of events than the application is. If the application is to pass events to the input method through **XFilterEvent**, the application must have registered interest in receiving those events with **XSelect-Input**. The **XNFilterEvents** input context attribute contains a mask of events that the input method is interested in receiving, and all clients should read this attribute and use it when selecting events. Example 5-12 shows code that does this and an event loop that uses **XFilterEvent**.

Example 5-12. Selecting events for an IM and using XFilterEvent in an event loop

```
long im_event_mask;
      .
      .
      .
XGetICValues(ic, XNFilterEvents, &im_event_mask, NULL);
XSelectInput(dpy, win, ExposureMask | KeyPressMask
             | StructureNotifyMask | im_event_mask);
for(;;) {
    XEvent e;

    XNextEvent(dpy, &e);
    if (XFilterEvent(&e, None)) continue;
    switch (e.type) {
        .
        .   /* dispatch the event here */
        .
    }
}
```

The X11R5 X Toolkit Intrinsics have been modified to make appropriate use of **XFilter-Event** in the function **XtDispatchEvent** called from **XtAppMainLoop**.

5.10 Getting Composed Text

Prior to X11R5, **XLookupString** was used to convert the keycode returned in a KeyPress event into a KeySym and further into a character string that could be passed to the X text drawing functions. Unfortunately, this function only works for the Latin-1 charset. To support internationalization in a limited way, there were alternate **LookupString** functions in the Xmu library: **XmuLookupLatin2, XmuLookupJISX0201, XmuLookupGreek,** etc. In X11R5, these have been superseded by **XmbLookupString** and **XwcLookup-String**. These functions are identical except in the type of string they return: the **Xmb** version returns a multi-byte string of **char**, and **Xwc** version returns a wide-character string of **wchar_t**. In both cases the string will be encoded as appropriate for the locale of the IC.*

Whenever a **KeyPress** event is delivered to an application that is performing internationalized text input, the application should use that event in a call to **XmbLookupString** or **XwcLookupString**. (Note that **KeyRelease** events should not be passed to these functions—they will result in undefined behavior.) The application should not expect that each call to **Xmb/XwcLookupString** will return a string. Depending on the complexity of the input method in use, a user may type many keystrokes before any composed input is ready for the application. Neither should the application expect that **Xmb/XwcLookupString** will return a single character at a time—in some input methods a user may type a phrase, a sentence, or more before hitting the key that triggers the conversion from pre-edit to composed text.

XmbLookupString and **XwcLookupString** take as arguments the IC for which input is to be looked up (which is usually the IC with the focus), the X event that triggered the call, a buffer to return the multi-byte or wide-character string in, a pointer to a location to return a keysym, and a pointer to a location to return a status value. The value returned by both functions is an integer which specifies the number of bytes in the returned multi-byte string or the number of **wchar_t** in the returned wide-character string. There are five status values that these functions return, each of which may require separate processing:

- **XLookupNone** means that the input method does not have any composed input ready to pass to the application, and the application need not do any further processing on the current key event. When this status value is returned, the return value of the function will be 0.

- **XLookupKeySym** means that a keysym, but no string, has been returned. This likely means that the user has struck a special key of some sort (a function key, an arrow key, Delete, etc.). The application should handle the keysym as appropriate. Because no string is returned, the return value of the function is 0. Be careful to capitalize the constant **XLookupKeySym** correctly; Xlib also defines (pre-X11R5) the function **XLookupKeysym**.

---

*As this book goes to press, there is a bug in the Xsi implementation of **XwcLookupString**. It is supposed to return as its value the number of characters in the returned string, but appears, at least in some cases, to return the number of bytes instead.

- **XLookupChars** means that a string, but no keysym, has been returned. The multi-byte or wide-character string is encoded in the codeset of the locale of the IC and is placed in the buffer passed to the function. The return value of the function is the length of the multi-byte string in bytes or the length of the wide-character string in wide characters.

- **XLookupBoth** means that both a string and a keysym are returned. This may indicate that a single keystroke has passed through the input method without any pre-editing, as is common in European input methods, for example. The return value of the function is the length of the string, as described for **XLookupChars** above.

- **XBufferOverflow** means that the string to be returned will not fit in the provided buffer. The return value of the function is the required size of the buffer (in bytes or wide characters), and nothing is returned in the string buffers. The input string remains in the IC, waiting to be looked up. The application should allocate a buffer of the required size and look up the string, or should display an error message and flush the pending input with a call to **XmbResetIC** or **XwcResetIC**. If this return status is ignored, the large input string will remain pending and block any further input on that IC.

Some input method architectures allow the input method to intercept events from the X server before the application ever sees them. If these input methods remove all **KeyPress** events from the input stream, then the application will never be triggered to call **Xmb/wc-LookupString**. If this is the case, the input method will send a synthetic **KeyPress** event to the application when it has composed input ready for lookup. By convention, the keycode in this synthetic event should be 0. Note, though, that these are architectural details and do not affect the structure of an internationalized applications.

Example 5-13 shows code that uses **XwcLookupString** and handles each of the possible return status values.

Example 5-13. Looking up internationalized input

```
XEvent event;
int len;
int buf_len = 10;
wchar_t *buffer = (wchar_t *)malloc(buf_len * sizeof(wchar_t));
KeySym keysym;
Status status;

while(1) {
    XNextEvent(dpy, &event);
    if (XFilterEvent(&event, None))
      continue;

    switch (event.type) {
    case Expose:
        Redraw();
        break;
    case KeyPress:
        len = XwcLookupString(ic, &event, buffer, buf_len,
                              &keysym, &status);
        if (status == XBufferOverflow) {
            buf_len = len;
            buffer = (wchar_t *)realloc(buffer, buf_len*sizeof(wchar_t));
            len = XwcLookupString(ic, &event, buffer, buf_len,
                                  &keysym, &status);
```

Example 5-13. Looking up internationalized input (continued)

```
        }
        switch (status) {
        case XLookupNone:
            break;
        case XLookupKeySym:
        case XLookupBoth:
            /* Handle backspacing */
            if ((keysym == XK_Delete) || (keysym == XK_BackSpace)) {
                Backspace();
                break;
            }
            if (status == XLookupKeySym) break;
        case XLookupChars:
            Insert(buffer, len);
            break;
        }
        break;
    }
}
```

5.11 XIM Programming Checklist

The following list provides useful guidelines when writing an Xlib or Xt application or Xt widget that uses the X11R5 internationalized input mechanisms. It is followed by an example Xlib program that performs simple internationalized text input and implements most of the steps in the list.

- Set the locale with **setlocale**. Use a locale name from a resource, or specify the empty string (" "). In an Xt application do this from the special callback procedure registered with **XtSetLanguageProc**.

- Verify that X supports the locale with **XSupportsLocale**.

- Set the locale modifiers (i.e., the name of the input method to use) from a resource or with the empty string.

- If you want your input method to be customizable with resources, create a database or get a handle to an already created one. In an Xt application, use **XtDatabase**.

- Open a connection to the IM of the locale with **XOpenIM**. Pass a resource database and the name and class the IM should use for looking up its resources in that database. Verify that the IM is successfully opened. If you are writing a widget, you can assume that a valid **XIM** will be passed as a resource, and skip this step.

- Query the IM for its supported interaction styles. Choose one that your application can support based on the value of user-specified resources, or upon some criteria for which will provide the best user interface for your application. In a widget, this should be in the **initialize** method.

- Create an **XFontSet** for use by the IC. The base font name list for the **XFontSet** should be obtained from a resource. In an Xt application, you should use the constant **XtDefaultFontSet** as the default value for this resource. If you are writing a widget, you can assume that a valid **XFontSet** will be passed as a resource.

- Create a **Window** for use by the IC. If you are programming with Xt, create a widget. If you are writing your own widget, the window will be created for you by the **realize** method.

- Create an IC with **XCreateIC**, specifying the interaction style you choose, the **XNEditWindow**, and the **XNFontSet** sub-attribute for both the Preedit and Status Areas. If you are using the **XIMPreeditPosition** style, you must also specify the **XNAreaNeeded** attribute, and if you are using **XIMPreeditCallbacks** or **XIMStatusCallbacks** styles, you must specify values for all the applicable callback attributes. You may also specify any other attributes at this point. If you are writing a widget, create the IC in the **initialize** method, but specify the window in the **realize** method. In a widget, you should provide widget resources which control the setting of IC attributes like **XNLineSpacing** and **XNCursor**.

- Query the value of the **XNFilterEvents** attribute of the IC and augment the event mask for your window with those events. If you are writing an Xt program, call **XtAdd-EventHandler** for the event mask with a no-op procedure. If you are writing a widget, call **XtAddEventHandler** in the same way from the **realize** method.

- If you have selected the **XIMPreeditArea** or the **XIMStatusArea** interaction styles, negotiate a geometry for either or both of those areas using the **XNAreaNeeded** attribute of the IC. Set the geometry you decide on in the **XNArea** attribute. If you are writing a widget, begin the negotiation in the **initialize** method, and set the **XNArea** attribute when the window is created in the **realize** method. Renegotiate geometry whenever your application window changes size.

- If you have selected the **XIMPreeditPosition** interaction style, set the initial location of your insertion cursor in the **XNSpotLocation** attribute, and a region within which pre-editing is allowed in the **XNArea** resource. If you are writing a widget, do this in the **resize** method. In a widget, you may want to implement the Preedit and Status areas as sub-widgets.

- For a simple application that does no focus management, set the focus to your IC with **XSetICFocus**. For more complicated applications, you should set and unset IC focus when you receive **FocusIn** and **FocusOut** events, or whenever your application-internal or toolkit focus changes. In an Xt program or widget, you can use an event handler or a translation and action to track focus changes.

- Use **XFilterEvent** in your event loop before dispatching an event. If it returns **True**, discard the event and wait for another. In Xt programs, this is handled for you by **XtDispatchEvent** in **XtAppMainLoop**.

- When **XFilterEvent** returns an unfiltered **KeyPress** event, use **Xmb/wc-LookupString** to convert it to a KeySym or a string in the encoding of the locale. In Xt programs or widgets, use an event handler or a translation and action to get these events.

- Echo the newly input characters with **Xmb/wcDrawString** or one of the other X11R5 text drawing functions.

- If you are using the **XIMPreeditPosition** interaction style, update the values of the **XNSpotLocation** and **XNArea** attributes of the IC each time you move the insertion cursor.

- If your application supports the **XIMPreeditArea** or **XIMStatusArea** interaction styles, optionally write a **GeometryCallback** procedure to handle requests from the IM to change the size of those areas. If you are writing a composite widget, the **GeometryCallback** and the **geometry_manager** method may be able to share code.

- If your application supports the **XIMPreeditCallbacks** or **XIMStatus-Callbacks** interaction styles, write the required callback procedures to support those styles.

Example 5-14 is the complete code of a program that performs simple internationalized text input. Many of the examples in this chapter and the last are fragments of this program.*

Example 5-14. Performing internationalized text input: a complete program

```
/*
 * This program demonstrates some of the X11R5 internationalized text
 * input functions.  It creates a very simple window, connects to an
 * input method, and displays composed text obtained by calling
 * XwcLookupString.  It backspaces when it receives the Backspace or
 * Delete keysyms.
 *
 * Note that this program contains a work-around for a bug
 * in the Xsi implementation of XwcLookupString.  If you are using
 * the Ximp implementation, or if the bug has been fixed in your Xlib,
 * you will need to undo the workaround.  See the comment below, near
 * the call to XwcLookupString.
 *
```

---

*To run this program successfully, you must have an input method running. Because there are no input methods as part of the core X11R5 distribution, this may be difficult. If your Xlib uses the Xsi implementation of the X11R5 internationalization features, you can use the input method in *contrib/im/Xsi*. In order to run this program, I had to do the following:

- Build everything in *contrib/im/Xsi*.

- Install everything in *contrib/im/Xsi*. This involved installing a number of files under */usr/local/lib/wnn*, and adding a new user "wnn" to the */etc/passwd* file.

- Start the "translation server" *contrib/im/Xsi/Wnn/jserver/jserver*.

- Start the "input manager" *contrib/im/Xsi/Xwnmo/xwnmo/xwnmo* which was also installed in */usr/bin/X11*.

- Set the **XMODIFIERS** environment variable to "**@im=_XWNMO**."

- Set the **LANG** environment variable to something appropriate, **ja_JP.ujis**, for example.

With these steps accomplished, I was able to run the program and type Latin characters, but I was never able to figure out how to actually make use of the input method to input Japanese. Since the Xsi input method is contributed software, it may have been updated since this program was written, and the above list may no longer be correct.

```
 * This program has not been tested with the Ximp implementation.
 */

#include <stdio.h>
#include <malloc.h>
#include <X11/Xlib.h>
#include <X11/keysym.h>
/*
 * include <locale.h> or the non-standard X substitutes
 * depending on the X_LOCALE compilation flag
 */
#include <X11/Xlocale.h>

/*
 * This function chooses the "more desirable" of two input styles.  The
 * style with the more complicated Preedit style is returned, and if the
 * styles have the same Preedit styles, then the style with the more
 * complicated Status style is returned.  There is no "official" way to
 * order interaction styles.  This one makes the most sense to me.
 * This is a long procedure for a simple heuristic.
 */
XIMStyle ChooseBetterStyle(style1,style2)
XIMStyle style1, style2;
{
    XIMStyle s,t;
    XIMStyle preedit = XIMPreeditArea | XIMPreeditCallbacks |
        XIMPreeditPosition | XIMPreeditNothing | XIMPreeditNone;
    XIMStyle status = XIMStatusArea | XIMStatusCallbacks |
        XIMStatusNothing | XIMStatusNone;

    if (style1 == 0) return style2;
    if (style2 == 0) return style1;
    if ((style1 & (preedit | status)) == (style2 & (preedit | status)))
        return style1;

    s = style1 & preedit;
    t = style2 & preedit;
    if (s != t) {
        if (s | t | XIMPreeditCallbacks)
            return (s == XIMPreeditCallbacks)?style1:style2;
        else if (s | t | XIMPreeditPosition)
            return (s == XIMPreeditPosition)?style1:style2;
        else if (s | t | XIMPreeditArea)
            return (s == XIMPreeditArea)?style1:style2;
        else if (s | t | XIMPreeditNothing)
            return (s == XIMPreeditNothing)?style1:style2;
    }
    else { /* if preedit flags are the same, compare status flags */
        s = style1 & status;
        t = style2 & status;
        if (s | t | XIMStatusCallbacks)
            return (s == XIMStatusCallbacks)?style1:style2;
        else if (s | t | XIMStatusArea)
            return (s == XIMStatusArea)?style1:style2;
        else if (s | t | XIMStatusNothing)
            return (s == XIMStatusNothing)?style1:style2;
    }
```

```
}

void GetPreferredGeometry(ic, name, area)
XIC ic;
char *name;            /* XNPreEditAttributes or XNStatusAttributes */
XRectangle *area;      /* the constraints on the area */
{
    XVaNestedList list;

    list = XVaCreateNestedList(0, XNAreaNeeded, area, NULL);

    /* set the constraints */
    XSetICValues(ic, name, list, NULL);

    /* Now query the preferred size */
    /* The Xsi input method, Xwnmo, seems to ignore the constraints, */
    /* but we're not going to try to enforce them here. */
    XGetICValues(ic, name, list, NULL);
    XFree(list);
}

void SetGeometry(ic, name, area)
XIC ic;
char *name;            /* XNPreEditAttributes or XNStatusAttributes */
XRectangle *area;      /* the actual area to set */
{
    XVaNestedList list;

    list = XVaCreateNestedList(0, XNArea, area, NULL);
    XSetICValues(ic, name, list, NULL);
    XFree(list);
}

main(argc, argv)
int argc;
char *argv[ ];
{
    Display *dpy;
    int screen;
    Window win;
    GC gc;
    XGCValues gcv;
    XEvent event;
    XFontSet fontset;
    XIM im;
    XIC ic;
    XIMStyles *im_supported_styles;
    XIMStyle app_supported_styles;
    XIMStyle style;
    XIMStyle best_style;
    XVaNestedList list;
    long im_event_mask;
    XRectangle preedit_area;
    XRectangle status_area;
    char *program_name = argv[ 0 ];
    char **missing_charsets;
    int num_missing_charsets = 0;
    char *default_string;
```

```
wchar_t string[ 200 ];
int str_len = 0;
int i;

/*
 * The error messages in this program are all in English.
 * In a truely internationalized program, they would not
 * be hardcoded; they would be looked up in a database of
 * some sort.
 */
if (setlocale(LC_ALL, "") == NULL) {
    (void) fprintf(stderr, "%s: cannot set locale.\n",program_name);
    exit(1);
}

if ((dpy = XOpenDisplay(NULL)) == NULL) {
    (void) fprintf(stderr, "%s: cannot open Display.\n", program_name);
    exit(1);
}

if (!XSupportsLocale()) {
    (void) fprintf(stderr, "%s: X does not support locale
                    program_name, setlocale(LC_ALL, NULL));
    exit(1);
}

if (XSetLocaleModifiers("") == NULL) {
    (void) fprintf(stderr, "%s: Warning: cannot set locale modifiers.\n",
                        argv[ 0 ]);
}

/*
 * Create the fontset.
 */
fontset = XCreateFontSet(dpy,
                    "-adobe-helvetica-*-r-*-*-*-120-*-*-*-*-*-*,\
                    -misc-fixed-*-r-*-*-*-130-*-*-*-*-*-*",
                    &missing_charsets, &num_missing_charsets,
                    &default_string);

/*
 * if there are charsets for which no fonts can
 * be found, print a warning message.
 */
if (num_missing_charsets > 0) {
    (void)fprintf(stderr, "%s: The following charsets are missing:\n",
                    program_name);
    for(i=0; i < num_missing_charsets; i++)
        (void)fprintf(stderr, "%s:     %s\n", program_name,
                    missing_charsets[i ]);
    XFreeStringList(missing_charsets);

    (void)fprintf(stderr, "%s: The string
                    program_name, default_string);
    (void)fprintf(stderr, "%s: of any characters from those sets.\n",
                    program_name);
}
```

```
screen = DefaultScreen(dpy);

win = XCreateSimpleWindow(dpy, RootWindow(dpy, screen), 0, 0, 400, 100,
                          2, WhitePixel(dpy,screen),BlackPixel(dpy,screen));

gc = XCreateGC(dpy,win,0,&gcv);
XSetForeground(dpy,gc,WhitePixel(dpy,screen));
XSetBackground(dpy,gc,BlackPixel(dpy,screen));

/* Connect to an input method.  */
/* In this example, we don't pass a resource database */
if ((im = XOpenIM(dpy, NULL, NULL, NULL)) == NULL) {
    (void)fprintf(stderr, "Couldn't open input method\n");
    exit(1);
}

/* set flags for the styles our application can support */
app_supported_styles = XIMPreeditNone | XIMPreeditNothing | XIMPreeditArea;
app_supported_styles |= XIMStatusNone | XIMStatusNothing | XIMStatusArea;

/* figure out which styles the IM can support */
XGetIMValues(im, XNQueryInputStyle, &im_supported_styles, NULL);

/*
 * now look at each of the IM supported styles, and
 * chose the "best" one that we can support.
 */
best_style = 0;
for(i=0; i < im_supported_styles->count_styles; i++) {
    style = im_supported_styles->supported_styles[i];
    if ((style & app_supported_styles) == style) /* if we can handle it */
        best_style = ChooseBetterStyle(style, best_style);
}

/* if we couldn't support any of them, print an error and exit */
if (best_style == 0) {
    (void)fprintf(stderr, "%s: application and program do not share a\n",
                  argv[0]);
    (void)fprintf(stderr, "%s: commonly supported interaction style.\n",
                  argv[0]);
    exit(1);
}

XFree(im_supported_styles);

/*
 * Now go create an IC using the style we chose.
 * Also set the window and fontset attributes now.
 */
list = XVaCreateNestedList(0,XNFontSet,fontset,NULL);
ic = XCreateIC(im,
               XNInputStyle, best_style,
               XNClientWindow, win,
               XNPreeditAttributes, list,
               XNStatusAttributes, list,
               NULL);
XFree(list);
if (ic == NULL) {
    (void) fprintf(stderr, "Couldn't create input context\n");
```

```
        exit(1);
    }

    XGetICValues(ic, XNFilterEvents, &im_event_mask, NULL);
    XSelectInput(dpy,win, ExposureMask | KeyPressMask
                 | StructureNotifyMask | im_event_mask);

    XSetICFocus(ic);

    XMapWindow(dpy,win);

    while(1) {
        int buf_len = 10;
        wchar_t *buffer = (wchar_t *)malloc(buf_len * sizeof(wchar_t));
        int len;
        KeySym keysym;
        Status status;
        Bool redraw = False;

        XNextEvent(dpy, &event);
        if (XFilterEvent(&event, None))
            continue;

        switch (event.type) {
        case Expose:
            /* draw the string at a hard-coded location */
            if (event.xexpose.count == 0)
                XwcDrawString(dpy, win, fontset, gc, 10, 50, string, str_len);
            break;
        case KeyPress:
            len = XwcLookupString(ic, &event, buffer, buf_len,
                                  &keysym, &status);
            /*
             * Workaround:  the Xsi implementation of XwcLookupString
             * returns a length that is 4 times too big.  If this bug
             * does not exist in your version of Xlib, remove the
             * following line, and the similar line below.
             */
            len = len / 4;

            if (status == XBufferOverflow) {
                buf_len = len;
                buffer = (wchar_t *)realloc((char *)buffer,
                                           buf_len * sizeof(wchar_t));
                len = XwcLookupString(ic, &event, buffer, buf_len,
                                      &keysym, &status);
                /* Workaround */
                len = len / 4;
            }

            redraw = False;

            switch (status) {
            case XLookupNone:
                break;
            case XLookupKeySym:
            case XLookupBoth:
                /* Handle backspacing, and <Return> to exit */
                if ((keysym == XK_Delete) || (keysym == XK_BackSpace)) {
```

```
                    if (str_len > 0) str_len--;
                    redraw = True;
                    break;
                }
                if (keysym == XK_Return) exit(0);
                if (status == XLookupKeySym) break;
            case XLookupChars:
                for(i=0; i < len; i++)
                    string[ str_len++ ] = buffer[ i ];
                redraw = True;
                break;
            }

            /* do a very simple-minded redraw, if needed */
            if (redraw) {
                XClearWindow(dpy, win);
                XwcDrawString(dpy, win, fontset, gc, 10, 50, string, str_len);
            }
            break;
        case ConfigureNotify:
            /*
             * When the window is resized, we should re-negotiate the
             * geometry of the Preedit and Status area, if they are used
             * in the interaction style.
             */
            if (best_style & XIMPreeditArea) {
                preedit_area.width = event.xconfigure.width*4/5;
                preedit_area.height = 0;
                GetPreferredGeometry(ic, XNPreeditAttributes, &preedit_area);
                preedit_area.x = event.xconfigure.width - preedit_area.width;
                preedit_area.y = event.xconfigure.height - preedit_area.height;
                SetGeometry(ic, XNPreeditAttributes, &preedit_area);
            }
            if (best_style & XIMStatusArea) {
                status_area.width = event.xconfigure.width/5;
                status_area.height = 0;
                GetPreferredGeometry(ic, XNStatusAttributes, &status_area);
                status_area.x = 0;
                status_area.y = event.xconfigure.height - status_area.height;
                SetGeometry(ic, XNStatusAttributes, &status_area);
            }
            break;
        }
    }
}
```

6

Resource Management

The resource management changes described in this chapter affect how resource files are written and organized and where they are installed. A thorough understanding of the X11R5 changes is necessary, particularly for Xt programmers, in order to take full advantage of the new features and provide maximum flexibility to system administrators and end users. Xlib programmers who are developing applications without the high-level resource management features provided by Xt will also be interested in the new Xrm functions.

In This Chapter:

6
Resource Management

Resource management is not new to X11R5, but there have been a number of important changes. The changes include new resource file syntax, per-screen (rather than per-display) resources set by **xrdb**, and the ability to specify customized app-defaults files for an Xt application. Most of the important changes to resource management are part of the X Toolkit. To implement these changes, though, a number of new **Xrm** functions have been added to Xlib.

What's New

X11R5 includes the following changes to resource management:

- The character **?** may be used in resource files to wildcard a single component of a resource name. This allows greater flexibility in the specification of resources.

- Resource files may now include other files with a C-like **#include** syntax.

- Xt now reads resources from a property on the root window of each screen of a display rather than just the default screen. This allows, for example, color resources to be placed on a color screen and monochrome resources to be placed on a monochrome screen.

- **XtResolvePathname** now looks for the value of the **customization** resource and uses this value in a new path substitution (%C) when searching for application defaults and other files. This resource can be used to specify whether an application should read an app-defaults file customized for a color screen or a file customized for a monochrome screen.

- A new "pseudo-resource," **XtNbaseTranslations**, allows an application developer to override items in a widget's default translation table in such a way that the application user can override the resulting translations without losing the application developer's customizations.

- A new function, **XrmSetDatabase**, associates a resource database with a display, and another new function, **XrmGetDatabase**, queries the database of a display. Xt uses these functions, and they may be useful to other applications or toolkits that manipulate multiple displays or multiple databases.

- A function, **XrmLocaleOfDatabase**, returns the locale of a resource database.

- Two new functions, **XrmCombineDatabase** and **XrmCombineFileDatabase**, merge the contents of two resource databases. They are more flexible than the existing **XrmMergeDatabase**.

- A new function, **XrmEnumerateDatabase**, iterates through the items in a resource database.

- Xrm quarks may now be created using permanently-allocated strings, which means that the string-to-quark routine need not make a copy of the string. The X Toolkit takes advantage of this new feature by using permanently-allocated strings in all of its widget meta-classes.

- The procedure followed by the X Toolkit to build the application resource database has changed significantly to accommodate the changes described above. The net result of this procedure remains substantially the same, however.

6.1 New Resource File Syntax

X11R5 introduces two new features to resource files: wildcarding of resource component names, and inclusion of other resource files. They are described in the sections below.

6.1.1 Wildcarding Resource Component Names

X11R5 resource databases allow the character **?** to be used to wildcard a single component (name or class) in a resource specification. Thus the specification:

    xmail.?.?.Background: antique white

sets the background color for all widgets (and only those widgets) that are grandchildren of the top-level shell of the application **xmail**. And the specification:

    xmail.?.?*Background: brick red

sets the background color of the grandchildren of the shell and all of their descendants. It does not set the background color for the child of the top-level shell or for any popup shells. These kinds of specifications simply cannot be done without the **?** wildcard; sometimes the ***** wildcard does not provide the necessary fine-grained control. To set the background of all the grandchildren of an application shell widget without the **?** wildcard, it would be necessary to specify the background for each grandchild individually.

There is one obvious restriction on the use of the **?** wildcard: it cannot be used as the final component in a resource specification—you can wildcard widget names, but not the resource name itself. Also, remember that the wildcard **?** (like the wildcard *****) means a different thing in a resource file than it does on a UNIX command line.

The **?** wildcard is convenient in cases like those above, but it has more subtle uses that have to do with its precedence with respect to the ***** wildcard. First, note the important distinctions between the **?** and the ***** wildcards: a **?** wildcards a single component name or class

and falls between two periods (unless it is the first component in a specification), while the *
indicates a "loose binding" (in the terminology of the resource manager) and falls between
two component names or classes. A **?** does not specify the name or class of a resource component, but does at least specify the existence of a component. The * on the other hand only
specifies that zero or more components have been omitted from the resource.

Recall that in order to look up the value of a resource, an application must provide a fully
specified resource name, i.e., the name and class of each resource component. The returned
value will be from the resource in the database that most closely matches the full resource
specification provided by the application. To determine which resouce matches best, the full
resource specification is scanned from left to right, one component at a time. When there is
more than one possible match for a component name, the following rules are applied:

1. A resource that matches the current component by name, by class, or with the **?** wildcard
    takes precedence over an resource that omits the current component by using a *.

2. A resource that matches the current component by name takes precedence over a resource
    that matches it by class, and both take precedence over a resource that matches it with the
    ? wildcard.

3. A resource in which the current component is preceded by a dot (**.**) takes precedence
    over a resource in which the current component is preceded by a *.

As these rules are applied, component by component, entries in the resource database are
eliminated until there are none remaining or until there is a single matching entry remaining
after the last component has been checked. These rules are not new with X11R5; they have
simply been updated to accomodate the new **?** wildcard.

With these rules of precedence in mind, consider what happens when users specify a line like
*Background: grey in their personal resource files. They would like to set the background of all widgets in all applications to grey, but if the app-defaults file for the application
"xmail" has a specification of the form ***Dialog*Background: peach**, the background of the dialog boxes in the xmail application will be peach-colored, because this second specification is more specific. So if they really don't like those peach dialog boxes,
(pre-X11R5) users will have to add a line like **XMail*Background: grey** to their personal resource files, and will have to add similar lines for any other applications that specify
colors like "xmail" does. The reason this line works is rule 1 above: at the first level of the
resource specification, "XMail" is a closer match than *.

This brings us to the specific reason that the **?** wildcard was introduced: any resource specification that "specifies" an application name with a **?** takes precedence over a specification
that elides the application name with a *, no matter how specific the *rest* of that specification
is. So in X11R5, the frustrated users mentioned above could add the single line:

> **?*Background: grey**

to their personal resource files and achieve the desired result. The sequence **?*** is odd-look-
ing, but correct. The **?** replaces a component name, and the * is resource binding, like a dot
(**.**).

The solution described above relies, of course, on the assumption that no app-defaults files will specify an application name in a more specific way than the user's **?**. If the "xmail" app-defaults file contained one of the following lines:

```
xmail*Dialog*Background: peach
XMail*Background: maroon
```

then the user would be forced to explicitly override them, and the **?** wildcard would not help. To allow for easy customization, programmers should write app-defaults files that do not use the name or class of the application, except in certain critical resources that the user should not be able to trivially or accidentally override. The standard X11R5 clients have app-defaults files written in this way.

6.1.2 Including Files in a Resource File

The Xrm functions that read resources from files, **XrmGetFileDatabase** and **Xrm-CombineFileDatabase** (new in X11R5), recognize a line of the form:

```
#include "filename"
```

as a command to include the named file at that point. The directory of the included file is interpreted relative to the directory of the file in which the include statement occurred. Included files may themselves contain **#include** directives, and there is no specified limit to the depth of this nesting. Note that the C syntax **#include <filename>** is not supported; neither Xlib nor Xt defines a search path for included files.

The ability to include files is useful when producing a special app-defaults file for use on a color screen, for example, you can simply include the monochrome app-defaults file and then set or override the color resources as you desire. This technique is particularly useful when producing app-defaults files for use with the customization resource described below. Example 6-1 shows a hypothetical color resource file for the "xmail" application.

Example 6-1. The resource file

```
! include the basic (monochrome) defaults
#include "XMail"

! and augment them with color
*Background: tan
*Foreground: navy blue
*Command*Foreground: red
*to*Background: grey
*subject*Background: grey
```

Do not confuse this file inclusion syntax with the **#include, #ifdef,** etc. syntax provided by the program *xrdb*. That program invokes the C preprocessor to provide C include, macro, and conditional processing. The include functionality described here is provided directly by Xlib.

Programmer's Supplement for Release 5

6.2 Customized Resource Files

In X11R4, it was possible to install an application with multiple app-defaults files so that users could use the **xnlLanguage** resource to specify what language the application should display itself in. But it was not possible to install one app-defaults file for use on monochrome screens and another for use on color screens and allow the user to specify, through a resource, which file was to be used. Applications are moved between color and monochrome environments far more often than they are ported to other languages, and in X11R5 the X Toolkit allows a user to easily specify which resources should be used.

You may recall that **XtResolvePathname** searches for a file by performing **printf**-type string substitutions on a specified or default directory path. The string "%L" is replaced with the language string (the value of the **xnlLanguage** resource), for example, and the string "%T" is replaced with the type of the file—"app-defaults," "bitmap," "help," etc. In X11R5, **XtResolvePathname** supports a new substitution variable "%C," which is replaced with the value of the application resource named **customization** and of class **Customization**. It is intended that the default or user-provided **XFILESEARCHPATH** will contain filename path components of the form %N%C%S—name, customization, suffix. Then a system administrator could install app-defaults files (which do not have suffixes) like *XMail-color* and *XMail-mono* and a user could run the **xmail** application as follows:

```
xmail -xrm "*customization: -color" &
```

in order to get the app-defaults file with color defaults. (Unfortunately, X11R5 Xt does not define a standard **-customization** command-line option to set the value of this resource.) The system administrator would also have to install an uncustomized app-defaults file, *XMail*, for use when no customization is set. This file could be a symbolic link to the monochrome file, or it could be a base resource file that contains all the resources except those that affect color. Then the customized files could simply include the base file with the new **#include** feature. The hyphen in the customization name (-color) is not part of the Xt specification; it is simply a useful convention that makes for legible customized resource filenames (like *XMail-color*).

The customization resource was designed primarily to allow color customizations, but there are other possibilities as well: app-defaults files with customized translations that work with a single-button mouse might be installed with a **-single-button** customization, or files customized for use within a specific group or department of an organization could be selected by department name. Note, however, that because there is no way to specify multiple customizations with the single **customization** resource, (e.g., users couldn't specify that they wanted both color resources and single button translations) this technique should not be overused. In general, it should be reserved for the color vs. monochrome customization for which it was designed.

A related change in X11R5 is to the Xt specification of the default paths to be used when the environment variables, **XFILESEARCHPATH** and **XUSERFILESEARCHPATH** (on UNIX systems), are not defined. In X11R4, these paths were required to contain specific directories in a specific order. The individual directories in X11R4 had a fixed substitution order: language (optionally), type, name, and suffix. This order meant that an application's auxiliary files (app-default, bitmaps, help text, etc.) had to be installed in scattered locations throughout a file system. In X11R5, the default paths still have a required number of entries in a specified order, but the order in which substitutions appear in these path entries is no longer specified. This means that vendors may choose default paths for their implementations that allow auxiliary files to be installed in a single directory. The MIT implementation retains the substitution order of X11R4, except for the insertion of the "%C" customization substitution between the name and suffix substitutions. When using a vendor-supplied X11R5, be sure to check your documentation for the default file search path. When writing a *Makefile* or *Imakefile* to distribute with an application, bear in mind that app-defaults files, bitmap files, help files, and so on may not be installed in the "usual" places on all systems.

6.3 Screen-specific Resource Strings and Databases

The (pre-X11R5) function, **XResourceManagerString**, returns the contents of the RESOURCE_MANAGER property on the root window of the default screen of the display. This property contains the user's resource customizations in string form, and is usually set with the program **xrdb**. It is read by **XtDisplayInitialize** when creating the resource database to be used by an application. Until X11R5 this single RESOURCE_MANAGER property contained resources for all screens of a display, and there was no way for a user to specify different resources for different screens (for example, color vs. monochrome).

In X11R5, xrdb can set resources in the SCREEN_RESOURCES property on the root window of each screen of a display. **XtDisplayInitialize** reads the SCREEN_RESOURCES specifications and uses them to override the screen-independent RESOURCE_MANAGER specifications. The resource database that is created in this way is the database of the screen, rather than the database of the display. If the same application is executed on different screens of a display, or if a single application creates shell widgets on more than one screen of a display, a resource database will be created for each screen, and the application instances or shell widgets will find resources in them that are appropriate for that screen.

Recall that **XtDisplayInitialize** creates databases using resources from a number of sources other than these window properties, so in many cases resource databases on different screens will contain substantially the same values. Note, however, that the SCREEN_RESOURCES property can be used to set the **customization** resource and thereby cause different app-defaults files to be merged into different screen databases. Screen-specific resource databases are created by Xt only as needed, so an application running exclusively on the default screen of a two-screen system will not have the overhead of maintaining two per-screen databases.

Two new functions support screen-dependent resources and resource databases. The contents of the SCREEN_RESOURCES property on the root window of a screen are returned by the function **XScreenResourceString**. The database of a screen may be obtained with the function **XtScreenDatabase**. The function **XtDatabase**, which prior to X11R5 returned the (single) database of the display, is now specified to return the database of the default screen of the display.

The client **xrdb** has been rewritten for X11R5 to handle the new screen-specific properties. Any load, merge, or query operation can now be performed on the global RESOURCE_MANAGER property, a specific screen property, all screen properties, or all screen properties plus the global property. This last option is the default and "does the right thing"—the input file is processed through the C preprocessor once for each screen, and resource specifications that would appear in all of the per-screen properties are placed in the global property and removed from the screen-specific properties. With this new system, a defaults file which uses `#ifdef COLOR` to separate color from monochrome resource specifications can be used to correctly set the values of the screen-dependent and screen-independent properties for a two-screen monochrome-and-color display. An application can then be run on either screen and find the correct user defaults for that screen. Example 6-2 shows a user default file that takes advantage of the new **xrdb** functionality and the **customization** resource to set different defaults on color and monochrome screens.

Example 6-2. A user defaults file for color and monochrome screens

```
! generic, non-color resources
*Font: -*-courier-medium-r-*-*-*-180-75-75-*-*-iso8859-1
xclock.geometry: -0+0

#ifdef COLOR
! resources for color screens here
*Background: grey
*Foreground: navy blue
XTerm*Foreground: maroon
#else
! resources for monochrome screens here
XTerm*reverseVideo: true
#endif

! set the customization resource to get
! special app-defaults, if they exist.
#ifdef COLOR
*customization: -color
#else
*customization: -mono
#endif
```

When an Xt application creates a shell widget with **XtAppCreateShell**, the value of the **XtNscreen** resource is used to determine what screen the shell should be created on and which screen's resource database should be used to look up the widget's resources. But the value of the **XtNscreen** resource must be looked up itself. The Xt specification resolves this circular problem by stating that the value of the **XtNscreen** resource is looked up first in the argument list passed to **XtAppCreateShell**, and then in the resource database of the default screen of the display. If it is found, then all further resources are looked up in the resource database for that particular screen. If the **XtNscreen** is not found, then the widget is created on the default screen, using the database for that screen.

6.4 The XtNbaseTranslations Resource

Until X11R5, there was an annoying problem with specifying translation tables as resources. Because a translation table is a multi-line resource, it is useful to be able to override or add individual lines to the table rather than always replace the table. Application developers often do this in their application's app-defaults file, using the **#override** or **#augment** directive as part of the **XtNtranslations** resource value. Sometimes, though, users would also like to add or override individual translations, but if they specify a value for the **XtNtranslations** resource in a personal resource file, it will take precedence over the resource in the application's app-defaults file, and the application's customizations will be lost from the database before the widget ever sees them. So until X11R5, users had to duplicate the application's customizations along with their own.

In X11R5, there is a new resource, **XtNbaseTranslations**, that can be used by an application developer to specify a base set of translations that will be correctly overridden, augmented, or replaced by the value of the **XtNtranslations** resource. Note that this is an **Xrm** resource, but is not a widget resource in the usual Xt sense of the word (the Xt specification uses the term "pseudo-resource")—it does not correspond to an instance field in **Core** or any other widget class, and it cannot be set with **XtSetValues** or queried with **XtGetValues**. The value of the **translations** field of the Core widget is handled specially by the Xt resource management code. The final value for a widget's translations are obtained as follows:

1. The default value of a widget instance's translations are obtained from the **Core** widget class field **tm_table**. These translations are specified by the widget writer.

2. When a widget is initialized, the Intrinsics' resource management code looks up the value of the **XtNbaseTranslations** resource for that widget, and if it exists, uses the translations it specifies to replace, override, or augment the widget's default translations. These translations are intended to be specified exclusively by the application developer in the application's app-defaults file.

3. Finally, the value of the **XtNtranslations** resource is looked up for the widget, and if it exists the value is used to replace, override, or augment the widget's translations (which may have once already been replaced, overridden, or augmented). These translations are intended to be specified by the end user of the application.

For maximum flexibility to the user, all X11R5 applications should specify translations in a resource file using the **XtNbaseTranslations** resource rather than with **XtNtranslations**. If the same resource file is to be used by applications compiled under both the X11R5 and X11R4 versions of the Intrinsics, then the resource file should specify the application's translations as the value of both resources. Under X11R4, the **XtNbaseTranslations** resource will be ignored, and under X11R5, any value of the **XtNtranslations** resource specified by the user will override the value specified in the application's app-defaults file.

6.5 New Xrm Functions

There are six new Xrm functions in the X11R5 version of Xlib. Most of these functions were introduced in order to implement the other resource management changes described in this chapter, but they may be useful (to Xlib programmers, at least) in their own right. These new functions are described below, and are thoroughly documented in the reference section at the end of this book.

6.5.1 Combining the Contents of Databases

The pre-X11R5 function `XrmMergeDatabases` combines the contents of a "source" database and a "target" database, using the contents of the source to override the contents of the target. With this function, there is no way to get "augment"-style behavior; i.e., there is no way to combine the two databases so that when source and target contain different values for the same resource specification the value in the target database is left unchanged. The two new functions `XrmCombineDatabase` and `XrmCombineFileDatabase` address this problem. They take a source database and a target database, or the name of a resource file and a target database, and also a `Bool` argument which specifies whether the resource from the source database or the file should override values in the target database. Thus the following two function calls are equivalent:

```
XrmMergeDatabases(source, target);
XrmCombineDatabase(source, target, True);
```

Because the contents of resource files are often merged into databases, the function `Xrm-CombineFileDatabase` was added as a shortcut for a call to `XrmGetFile-Database` followed by a call to `XrmCombineDatabase`. Note that the new X11R5 functions use the singular "Database," while `XrmMergeDatabases` uses the plural.

These functions were added in X11R5 because of a required change in the way the X Toolkit builds up its resource database. Prior to X11R5, that database was built from sources in low-priority to high-priority order, each new source overriding the existing contents of the database, and `XrmMergeDatabases` was sufficient for this purpose. But with the advent of the customization resource in X11R5, it was necessary to build the database in reverse order so that the value of the customization resource could be obtained from any of the other sources before being used to locate the application's app-defaults file. When the order of database creation was reversed, it was necessary to combine databases by augmenting rather than overriding so that the resulting single merged database would be the same. `Xrm-CombineDatabase` and `XrmCombineFileDatabase` were added for precisely this purpose.

6.5.2 Enumerating Database Entries

Prior to X11R5 it was possible to query particular resources in a database or write the contents of a database to a file, but there was no way for a program to individually process each entry of a database. **XrmEnumerateDatabase** fills this need. This function calls a user-supplied procedure once for each entry in a database that matches any completion of a specified partial name and class list. The enumeration can be performed a single level below these name and class prefixes, or for all levels below. The "callback" procedure invoked by this function returns a **Bool** and causes the enumeration to terminate by returning **True**.

The client **appres**, which previously relied on internal knowledge of the opaque **Xrm-Database**, type now uses **XrmEnumerateDatabase**.

6.5.3 Associating a Resource Database with a Display

It is common practice for Xlib applications (and automatic in Xt applications) to build a resource database for each display that is opened, and it is common to talk about the "database of the display." Before X11R5, however, there was no standard way to associate a database with a display for later retrieval. In the MIT Xlib implementation, there is a database field in the **Display** structure, and prior to X11R5 the X Toolkit used this field even though the **Display** structure is supposed to be opaque.

In X11R5, however, there are functions to set and get the database of the display: **XrmSet-Database** and **XrmGetDatabase**. These are simply utility functions; they provide a public interface to fields in an opaque data structure. No Xlib routines use these functions, but **XtDisplayInitialize** sets the database of the display for later use by **Xt-ResolvePathname**. Note that Xlib does not provide a way to associate a display with a screen.

6.5.4 Quarks and Permanently Allocated Strings

Prior to X11R5, the resource manager functions made a copy of all strings when they were registered as quarks. Most strings were widget names, resource names, and resource classes hardcoded into an application's executable, but the copying was required for those few quarks that were created with dynamically-allocated strings. X11R5 contains a new function, **XrmPermStringToQuark**, which behaves like the existing **XrmString-ToQuark** except that it assumes that the passed string is either a string constant hardcoded into the application or at least is in memory that will not be modified or de-allocated for the lifetime of the application. This assumption means that the string need not be copied, and therefore memory is saved. There is no direct connection between **XrmPermString-ToQuark** and **Xpermalloc**. Strings in memory allocated with **Xpermalloc** may be passed to **XrmPerStringToQuark** as long as they will not be changed during the lifetime of the application.

The Xt specification has been changed to require that the resource tables for the `Object` and `Constraint` widget meta-classes have permanently allocated strings for their `resource_name`, `resource_class`, `resource_type`, and `default_type` fields. Also, the `class_name` field of the `Object` class, and the `actions` field of the `Core` class must be permanently allocated. This new restriction should not affect any existing applications but allows run-time memory savings.

6.5.5 Getting the Locale of a Database

As described in Chapter 4, *Internationalization*, every `XrmDatabase` is parsed in the current locale and has that locale associated with it. To return the name of the locale of a database, use the new function `XrmLocaleOfDatabase`.

6.6 The Big Picture: Building the Xt Resource Database

The changes to resource management in X11R5 are numerous, and they have significantly affected the technique used by the X Toolkit to build its resource database or databases. Though the procedure itself has changed, the net result—the contents of the database—is largely the same, except for resources affected by the new `customization` resource or by the new screen-dependent resources.

The list below explains the steps followed by the X Toolkit when building the resource database for a screen. Many of the new features described in this chapter are used in the process. All filenames and environment variables are for a POSIX-based system.

1. A temporary database is created by parsing the resources contained in the `RESOURCE_MANAGER` property on the root window of the default screen of the display. If this property does not exist, the contents of the file $HOME/.Xdefaults are used instead. The contents of the property or file are assumed to be entirely in the X Portable Character Set so that the database can be correctly parsed before the application's locale has been set. (See Chapter 4, *Internationalization*, for information about locale and the X Portable Character Set.)

2. If a language procedure has been set with `XtSetLanguageProc` (see Chapter 4, *Internationalization*, for more information on the language procedure and the internationalization of Xt programs), the application command line is scanned (but not actually parsed into a database) for the **–xnlLanguage** option or an **–xrm** option that specifies the `xnlLanguage` resource. Because the command line is scanned before the locale has been set, the value of this resource must be in the X Portable Character Set. If neither command-line option is found, the temporary database is queried for the value of the `xnlLanguage` resource. The value of this resource, or the empty string if it is not found, is passed to the registered language procedure which sets the locale and returns its name. The return value of the language procedure is associated with the display for future use (for example, by `XtResolvePathname`). All future resource specifications will be parsed in the encoding of this locale, and resource databases will have the locale associated with them. `XrmLocaleOfDatabase` will return the name of the locale.

3. The application command line is parsed, and the resulting resource specifications are stored in a newly created database. This database will be augmented with resources from a number of sources and will become the screen resource database.

4. If a language procedure has not been set, the value of the **xnlLanguage** resource is looked up in the screen database, the temporary database, and the environment variable **LANG**. This language string (or the empty string) is associated with the display for future use.

5. If the **XENVIRONMENT** environment variable is defined, the resource file it points to is merged into the screen database with **XrmCombineFileDatabase**; the new resources do not override existing resource values in the database. If the environment variable does not exist, the file $HOME/.*Xdefaults-hostname* is used, if it exists.

6. The per-screen specifications returned by **XScreenResourceString** are merged into the database. The new resources do not override existing values in the database.

7. The temporary database which was created in step 1, and which contains the per-server **RESOURCE_MANAGER** resources is merged into the screen database. The resources in the temporary database do not override the resources in the screen database.

8. The screen database being built is associated with the display with a call to **XrmSetDatabase**, and the old value of the "display database" is saved so that it can later be restored. The user's application specific app-defaults file is searched for, using **XtResolvePathname** with the path specified by the **XUSERFILESEARCHPATH** environment variable if it exists. If this environment variable does not exist, a default path is used relative to the user's home directory and relative to the value of the **XAPPLRESDIR** environment variable, if that exists. **XtResolvePathname** uses **XrmGetDatabase** to find the current database of the display (which is the screen database created up to this step), and uses that database to look up the value of the **customization** resource for substitution into the path. If a resource file is found in one of these paths, the resource specifications in it are merged into the screen database using **XrmCombineFileDatabase**. The new resources do not override the resources already in the database.

9. The application's app-defaults file is located using **XtResolvePathname** and the path specified in **XFILESEARCHPATH**, or a default path if that environment variable does not exist. As above, **XtResolvePathname** looks up the value of the **customization** resource in the screen database constructed so far. The resources from the app-defaults file are merged into the screen database using **XrmCombineFileDatabase**, and do not override resource values already there. The original "database of the display," which had been stored away in step 8 above, is restored using **XrmSetDatabase**.

10. If no app-defaults file is located in step 9 and the application has registered fallback resources with **XtAppSetFallbackResources**, then those fallback resources are merged into the screen database without overriding the values already there.

7

Other Changes in X11R5

*This chapter contains something for everyone. The section on writing porta-
ble applications explains some simple rules that greatly enhance portablility
to other systems. The Xlib and Xt changes described in the next sections
are minor, but familiarity with them may save frustrations later. If you program with the Athena Widget library, you should read about the new and
changed widgets, and you may also want to know about the new functions in
the Xmu library. The new editres client and protocol will be very useful to
application developers, widget writers, and end users alike, and system
administrators may be interested in the new authorization mechanisms and
the new font formats.*

In This Chapter:

☞

7
Other Changes in X11R5

The preceding chapters have covered the major changes in X11R5: font service, device-independent color, internationalization, and resource management. This chapter describes other changes to Xlib and Xt, as well as all the changes to the Athena Widget library (Xaw) and the Miscellaneous Utilities library (Xmu). It also provides an introduction to new features in X11R5 such as new X header files that help a programmer to write portable applications, the X Input extension, and new authorization protocols.

What's New

Most of the X11R5 changes to Xlib and Xt have been covered in previous chapters. The remaining changes in Release 5 are listed below:

- Substantial effort has been put into the MIT X11R5 implementation to make it comply with ANSI-C and POSIX standards. New standard header files have been defined that make it easier to write portable X applications.

- Miscellaneous minor changes to Xlib and Xt have been made.

- There is a new client, *editres*, which allows a user or programmer to interactively edit the widget resources of any running application that participates in the Editres protocol.

- There are four new Xaw widgets: Panner, Porthole, Repeater, and Tree, and many of the other Xaw widgets have had minor changes or additions. The Xaw VendorShell widget provides support for the Editres protocol for all Xaw applications.

- The Xmu library provides routines to support the Editres protocol, and there have been various other additions to the Xmu library.

- The *X11 Input Device Extension* specification is now a standard of the X Consortium. This extension allows X input from devices other than keyboard and mouse.

- There are two new secure authorization protocols in the MIT implementation of X11R5: **XDM-AUTHORIZATION-1** and **SUN-DES-1**.

- A new format, *pcf*, is used for font files in X11R5. These Portable Compiled Fonts are portable across architectures, which was not the case with the old standard *snf* format.

- The MIT X11R5 distribution contains new fonts in Hebrew, Kanji (Japanese), and Hangul (Korean) charsets.

- There are some new clients shipped with the core MIT X11R5 implementation; other clients have been re-implemented, changed, or replaced.

- A significant amount of work has been done to speed up the MIT X server. The re-implementation of the Xt Translation Manager has resulted in less memory use at run-time.

7.1 Writing Portable Applications with X11R5

A lot of work has been put into making the MIT X11R5 distribution compliant with ANSI-C and POSIX standards, and portable across a variety of platforms. While the goal of the ANSI-C and POSIX standards is portability, many systems do not implement these standards, or do not implement them fully, so the MIT X11R5 distribution defines new header files that attempt to mask the differences between systems. The contents and usage of these header files are described below. None of these files are part of the official X11R5 standard, but they are very useful nevertheless.*

7.1.1 <X11/Xosdefs.h>

The file *<X11/Xosdefs.h>* defines symbols that describe a system's support for ANSI-C and POSIX. Symbols that describe a system's support for other standards may be added in the future. It defines two new symbols, `X_NOT_STDC_ENV` and `X_NOT_POSIX`, for systems that do not have the ANSI-C and POSIX header files, respectively. When standard header files exist, your code should include them. On systems which do not have them, however, attempting to include them would cause a compilation error. The symbols in *<X11/Xosdefs.h>* allow you to write code that takes the right action in either situation. Note that `X_NOT_STDC_ENV` is different from `_STDC_`, which simply indicates whether or not the compiler supports ANSI-C.

An example of using `X_NOT_STDC_ENV` might be to know when the system declares `getenv`:

```
#ifndef X_NOT_STDC_ENV
#include <stdlib.h>
#else
extern char *getenv();
#endif
```

It is convention in the X11R5 code from MIT to put the standard case first using `#ifndef`.

Lack of the symbol `X_NOT_STDC_ENV` does *not* mean that the system has `<stdarg.h>`. This header file is part of ANSI-C, but the X Consortium found it more useful to check for it separately because many systems have all the ANSI-C files except this one. The symbol `_STDC_` is used to control inclusion of this file.

---

*The sections below have been adapted from the X Consortium X11R5 Release Notes.

`X_NOT_POSIX` means the system does not have POSIX.1 header files. Lack of this symbol does *not* mean that the POSIX environment is the default. You may still have to define `_POSIX_SOURCE` before including the header file to get POSIX definitions.

An example of using `X_NOT_POSIX` might be to determine what return type would be declared for `getuid` in *<pwd.h>*:

```
#include <pwd.h>
#ifndef X_NOT_POSIX
    uid_t uid;
#else
    int uid;
    extern int getuid();
#endif
    uid = getuid();
```

Note that both `X_NOT_STDC_ENV` and `X_NOT_POSIX`, when declared, state a noncompliance. This was chosen so that porting to a new, standard platform would be easier. Only non-standard platforms need to add themselves to *<X11/Xosdefs.h>* to turn on the appropriate symbols.

Not all systems for which the X Consortium leaves these symbols undefined strictly adhere to the relevant standards. Thus you will sometimes see checks for a specific operating system near a check for one of the *Xosdefs.h* symbols. The X Consortium found it most useful to label systems as conforming even if they had some holes in their compliance. Presumably these holes will become fewer as time goes on.

<X11/Xosdefs.h> is automatically included by the header *<X11/Xos.h>*.

7.1.2 <X11/Xos.h>

This header file portably defines some of the most commonly used operating system and C library functions, and masks some of the most common system incompatibilities. It should be used instead of *<string.h>*, *<strings.h>*, *<sys/types.h>*, *<sys/file.h>*, *<fcntl.h>*, *<sys/time.h>*, and *<unistd.h>*. Most of these are POSIX standard header files, but are not yet universal. *<X11/Xos.h>* defines any of the four functions `index`, `rindex`, `strchr`, and `strrchr`, which are not defined by the host operating system. It defines `gettimeofday` and `time` as well as all the standard string functions. It also defines the type `caddr_t`, and the constants used by the `open` system call (`O_RDONLY`, `O_RDWR`, etc.) and the constants used by the `fcntl` system call (`R_OK`, `W_OK`, etc.).

Unfortunately, there is not a header file for declaring `malloc` correctly, and it can be a bit tricky. The MIT X11R5 distribution uses lines like the following (from *mit/lib/Xt/Alloc.c*) to declare `malloc` and related functions:

```
#ifndef X_NOT_STDC_ENV
#include <stdlib.h>
#else
    char *malloc(), *realloc(), *calloc();
#endif
#if defined(macII) && !defined(__STDC__)
    char *malloc(), *realloc(), *calloc();
#endif /* macII */
```

Note that because **index** may be a macro declared in this header, you should be sure to avoid this identifier in variable and structure field names.

7.1.3 <X11/Xfuncs.h>

This new header file provides definitions for the BSD functions **bcopy**, **bzero**, and **bcmp**. These are not standard functions, but are widely used in the X source code. Including this header file allows them to be used portably.

7.1.4 <X11/Xfuncproto.h>

This file contains definitions for writing function declarations in a way that is portable between ANSI-C compilers that support function prototypes and pre-ANSI-C compilers that do not support or only partially support function prototypes.

For external header files that might get used from C++, you should wrap all of your function declarations like this:

```
_XFUNCPROTOBEGIN...
...function declarations...
_XFUNCPROTOEND...
```

When in doubt, assume that the header file might get used from C++.

A typical function declaration uses **NeedFunctionPrototypes**, like this:

```
extern Atom XInternAtom(
#if NeedFunctionPrototypes
        Display*                /* display */,
        _Xconst char*           /* atom_name */,
        Bool                    /* only_if_exists */
#endif
);
```

If there are **const** parameters,* use the symbol **_Xconst** instead, as above. This symbol will be defined only if the compiler supports **const** parameters. If it is plausible to pass a string constant to a **char*** parameter, then it is a good idea to declare the parameter with **_Xconst**, so that literals can be passed in C++.

If there are nested function prototypes, use **NeedNestedPrototypes**:

```
extern Bool XCheckIfEvent(
#if NeedFunctionPrototypes
        Display*                /* display */,
        XEvent*                 /* event_return */,
        Bool (*) (
#if NeedNestedPrototypes
        Display*                /* display */,
```

---

*The **const** keyword is new in ANSI-C. It indicates that a partcular variable or function argument will not be changed. A compiler may be able to perform special optimizations on **const** parameters.

```
        XEvent*                /* event */,
        XPointer               /* arg */
#endif
        )                      /* predicate */,
        XPointer               /* arg */
#endif
);
```

If there is a variable argument list, use **NeedVarargsPrototypes**:

```
extern char *XGetIMValues(
#if NeedVarargsPrototypes
    XIM /* im */, ...
#endif
);
```

If you have parameter types in library functions that will widen (be silently cast to a larger type) in traditional C, then you should use **NeedWidePrototypes** so that functions compiled with an ANSI-C compiler may be called from code compiled with a traditional C compiler, and vice versa.

```
extern XModifierKeymap *XDeleteModifiermapEntry(
#if NeedFunctionPrototypes
    XModifierKeymap*     /* modmap */,
#if NeedWidePrototypes
    unsigned int         /* keycode_entry */,
#else
    KeyCode              /* keycode_entry */,
#endif
    int                  /* modifier */
#endif
);
```

If you use **_Xconst, NeedNestedPrototypes, NeedVarargsPrototypes**, or **NeedWidePrototypes**, then your function implementation also has to have a function prototype. For example:

```
#if NeedFunctionPrototypes
Atom XInternAtom (
    Display *dpy,
    _Xconst char *name,
    Bool onlyIfExists)
#else
Atom XInternAtom (dpy, name, onlyIfExists)
    Display *dpy;
    char *name;
    Bool onlyIfExists;
#endif
{
    ...
}
```

Actually, whenever you use a function prototype in a header file, you should use a function prototype in the implementation, as required by ANSI-C.

7.1.5 Other Symbols

Do not use the names **class**, **new**, or **index** as variables or structure members. The names **class** and **new** are reserved words in C++, and you may find your header files used by a C++ program someday. Depending on the system, **index** can be defined as a macro in *<X11/Xos.h>*; this rules out any other use of that name.

The following system-specific symbols are commonly used in X sources where OS dependencies intrude:

USG   Based on System V Release 2.
SYSV   Based on System V Release 3.
SVR4   System V Release 4.

For other system-specific symbols, look at the **StandardDefines** parameters in the *mit/config/*.cf* files.

7.2 Miscellaneous Xlib Changes

A new type, **XPointer**, has been defined to replace **caddr_t**, which is not a standard type and is therefore not necessarily portable. (The type **XtPointer** was added to the X11R4 X Toolkit for the same reason.) An **XPointer** is a **typedef** for a **char ***, and occurs most noticeably in the **XrmValue** and **XrmOptionDescRec** structures.

The X11R5 distribution installs the file **XKeysymDB** in */usr/lib/X11*. This file contains a list of vendor-private keysyms names and their corresponding values. It is required for the correct operation of many Motif applications and any application that wants to make use of vendor-specific keys on a keyboard. This file was in the X11R4 distribution, but was not installed by default.

A new function, **XFlushGC**, forces Xlib to write its cached GC changes to the X server. For efficiency, Xlib combines multiple-client GC changes into a single server request whenever multiple changes to a GC occur before a use of that GC. It is possible for extensions to X to use GCs in ways that Xlib is not aware of, and this can mean that requests made by the extension client library may not operate with the expected contents of the GC. **XFlushGC** is provided to address this problem.

The **XErrorEvent** structure used by Xlib contains only 32 bits of data specific to the error, which is usually used to return a resource ID. This is sufficient for all core X errors, but may not be enough for extensions (notably PEX). This is an Xlib-specific problem: there is plenty of room in the protocol error structure that is transmitted between server and client, but Xlib truncates this information when converting the protocol error into an **XError-Event** structure. Since the **XErrorEvent** structure is smaller than the **XEvent** union of which it is a part, an **XErrorEvent** can be cast into a larger structure with more room for error values, and the workaround provided by X11R5 takes advantage of this fact. X11R5 provides two new functions, **XESetWireToError** and **XESetPrintErrorValues**, which allow an extension library to register a function to convert a protocol error into some type longer than an **XErrorEvent,** and to display an error message that makes use of the additional data in the special error message.

7.3 Miscellaneous Xt Changes

The functions **XtAppInitialize, XtVaAppInitialize, XtOpenDisplay, Xt-DisplayInitialize,** and **XtInitialize** all require a pointer to a number of command line arguments (i.e., **&argc**). In X11R4 these functions expected this argument to be of type **Cardinal *** which, to guarantee portability, required an annoying typecast: **(Cardinal *)&argc.** In X11R5, these functions were changed to expect an argument of type **int *.** This does not affect the binary compatibility of clients, but programs which perform the explicit cast to **Cardinal *** will need to be changed to avoid compilation warnings with the X11R5 Xt header files. The **Cardinal *** type continues to be used in a number of places, including the **XtAppErrorMsg** and **XtAppWarningMsg** functions, type converter functions, and the **initialize** and **set_values** widget methods.

Prior to X11R5, the Xt string constants (the **XtN, XtC,** and **XtR** names) were macros for constant strings. With many compilers, each occurrence of a constant string is compiled into the object file, even when there are multiple instances of the same string. In the X11R5 MIT implementation of Xt, these macros have been changed to pointers into a single large array of characters (with embedded null characters dividing the array into individual strings). Under this new scheme, all of the Xt strings are embedded in every application once, but none more than once. For many applications this will result in an overall memory savings.

Prior to X11R5, the MIT implementation of *<X11/Intrinsic.h>* included the file *<X11/Xos.h>*. This inclusion was a violation of the specification, and the file is no longer included. *<X11/Xos.h>* defines System V and BSD-style string indexing functions (**index** and **strchr**), includes the appropriate time-handling header file, and hides other, more obscure, operating system dependencies. The most likely problem to result from this change in *<X11/Intrinsic.h>* is that programs that unknowingly relied on macro definitions of **index** or **strchr** from *<X11/Xos.h>* will now fail to compile. These programs may be compiled with the **–DXT_BC** flag which will restore the pre-X11R5 behavior. See Section 7.1.2 for more information on the file *<X11/Xos.h>*.

7.4 The Editres Client and Protocol

The *editres* client allows a user to interactively list and set the widget resources of any running application that participates in the editres protocol. It also saves a user's dynamic customizations into a resource file for later use. This can be a tremendous help to users who wish to experiment with resource values and produce a set of personal customizations for an application, to application writers developing an app-defaults file, and to widget writers who wish to test the **set_values** method of a widget. Figure 7-1 shows a screen dump of *editres* displaying a part of its own widget hierarchy. See the *editres* man page in the reference section of this book for full information.

In X11R5, all applications that use the Athena widget set (specifically the Athena Vendor-Shell widget class) automatically participate in the Editres protocol. Xaw applications that do not want to participate in this protocol, or do not want to participate fully, can set the application resource `editresBlock`. The *editres* man page gives details on the values for this resource.

The Xmu library provides an event handler which implements the Editres protocol. An Xt application that is not built with the Athena widgets may easily participate in the protocol by adding this event handler (for ClientMessages) on its shell widget. The Editres protocol is not documented within the X11R5 distribution, but Issue 0 (October 1991) of *The X Resource* (O'Reilly & Associates' X journal) contains documentation on the *editres* client and protocol by Chris Peterson, the author of both.

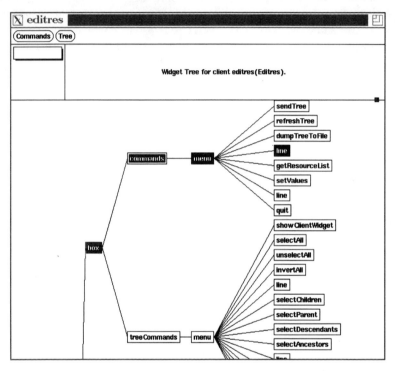

Figure 7-1. The editres application, showing the Panner, Porthole, and Tree widgets

7.5 New and Changed Athena Widgets

There are four new widgets in the Xaw library: Panner, Porthole, Repeater, and Tree.

The Panner widget is conceptually a two-dimensional scrollbar. It displays a rectangle within a rectangle—the inner rectangle represents the visible portion of the larger area represented by the outer rectangle. The size of the inner rectangle represents the size of the visible area relative to the whole, and its position indicates the relative position of the visible area within the whole. The user may drag the inner rectangle with the mouse (or use keyboard arrow keys) to pan through the large diagram or document that is being displayed. A Panner widget is visible in the upper left of the *editres* client, shown in Figure 7-1.

The Porthole widget is designed to be used with the Panner widget. It is a composite widget that maintains a fixed size through which part of its larger child is visible. It supports panning by repositioning its child relative to itself.

The Repeater widget is a subclass of the Command widget. It is a button with "auto repeat" behavior. Clicking on a repeater button causes callbacks on the `XtnstartCallback` list to be invoked once and the callbacks on the `Xtncallback` list to be invoked repeatedly until the mouse button is released. The interval between invocations of the callbacks is specified as a resource. This widget is particularly useful in compound widgets such as scrollbars.

The Tree widget is a constraint widget that lays out its children as nodes in a tree diagram and draws lines between them to indicate the connections between the nodes. The layout of the tree is determined by a constraint resource, `XtNtreeParent`, which, if specified for each child, is sufficient to determine each child's position in the tree. A Tree widget is the main display window of the *editres* client, shown in Figure 7-1.

There is a man page for each of these widgets in the reference section of this book. In addition to these new widgets, there have been a number of minor changes to the existing Athena widgets. Most notably, the Athena VendorShell widget supports the Editres protocol and performs all of an application's communication with the *editres* client. Other changes to the Athena widgets are described in the X11R5 Release Notes; see Appendix A, *Release Notes*.

7.6 New Xmu Functions

The X11R5 Xmu library contains the new Editres protocol event handler as well as ten new functions. These are briefly described below; man pages can be found in the reference section of this book. Additionally, there are a number of Xmu functions which existed prior to X11R5 but which were not documented in any of the existing O'Reilly & Associates X books. They are documented in the reference section of this book.

7.6.1 The Xmu Editres Event Handler

To enable an Xt application that is not built with the Xaw library to participate in the Editres protocol, add the event handler **_XEditResCheckMessages** on each of your top-level shell widgets, as shown in Example 7-1.

Example 7-1. Adding the Xmu Editres protocol event handler to a widget

```
#include <X11/Xmu/Editres.h>
      .
      .
      .
    XtAddEventHandler(shell, (EventMask) 0, True, _XEditResCheckMessages, NULL);
```

The Editres protocol is implemented with **ClientMessage** events. These events are non-maskable, so the event handler should be registered with an event mask of 0 and a *non-maskable* argument of **True**. The event handler requires no additional arguments, so the *client_data* argument should be **NULL**.

7.6.2 New Xmu Converters

The X11R5 Xmu library contains three new string conversion functions for use by the Xt resource manager:

XmuCvtStringToColorCursor
> This is a new-style converter that converts a string to an **X Cursor** using foreground and background colors specified through converter arguments. It recognizes the standard names for the standard cursor font glyphs, names of bitmap files, and also supports a special syntax for specifying glyphs of an arbitrary font.

XmuCvtStringToGravity
> This is an old-style converter that converts a string into one of the window gravity values used in the **XSetWindowAttributes** structure. This function is used by the new Xaw Tree widget.

XmuNewCvtStringToWidget
> This is a new-style converter that performs the same conversion as the existing **XmuCvtStringToWidget**. Since a widget tree may change dynamically, it is usually not safe to cache the results of a name-to-widget conversion, and this new-style converter may be registered with caching explicitly turned off. This converter is used in the X11R5 Xaw Form widget so that constraint resources of type **Widget** can be specified by name from a resource file.

7.6.3 The Xmu Widget Node Functions

The client *listres*, and the new X11R5 client, *viewres*, list and display the class hierarchy of the Athena widget set and the resources and constraint resources provided by each widget class. These clients can be valuable learning and programming tools, but are only useful for the Athena widgets. The X11R5 Xmu library contains four new functions that make it easy to write similar applications for other widget sets. These four functions contain the string **Wn** in their names; it is an abbreviation for "widget node." The descriptions of these functions will be more meaningful if you are familiar with the *listres* or *viewres* clients.

XmuWnInitializeNodes

This function must be called before any of the other widget node functions. It is called with an array of **XmuWidgetNode**, each of which contains a widget name and widget class pointer. It fills in some of the remaining fields of each **XmuWidgetNode** so that they can be passed to the other widget node functions. There will typically be one element in the array for each widget in the set or library. Note that the array must be in alphabetical order by widget name.

XmuWnFetchResources

This function is passed an **XmuWidgetNode** and fills that structure in with the list of resources for that class. Additionally, it is passed another node that is treated as the top of the widget hierarchy when determining where resources come from.

XmuWnCountOwnedResources

This function returns the number of resources or constraint resources of a given widget class that are inherited from a given superclass.

XmuWnNameToNode

This function finds a widget node by name in a list of nodes. The list of nodes must first have been passed to **XmuWnInitializeNodes**.

7.6.4 Other New Xmu Functions

There are three other new Xmu functions:

XmuDistinguishableColors

This function takes an array of **XColor** structures and returns **True** if and only if those colors are all "distinguishable" from one another. There is no formal definition for "distinguishable," and the algorithm used is somewhat arbitrary. Note that this function does not make use of any of the new **Xcms** routines.

`XmuDistinguishablePixels`

This function takes a display, colormap, and an array of colormap cells and returns **True** if and only if those cells contain colors that are "distinguishable." This function is used by the new Xaw Panner widget.

`XmuLocatePixmapFile`

This function is similar to the existing **XmuLocateBitmapFile**, except that it is not restricted to files that contain only a single plane of data.

7.6.5 Newly Documented Xmu Functions

Most of the pre-X11R5 Xmu functions are documented in Appendix J of Volume 2 in the O'Reilly & Associates X series. The functions listed in Table 7-1 are not new in X11R5, but are X Toolkit utilities rather than Xlib utilities, and therefore did not appear in Volume 2. Because they are not currently documented elsewhere in the O'Reilly & Associates X series, they appear in the reference section of this book.

Table 7-1. Previously Undocumented Xmu Functions

`XmuAddInitializer`	`XmuCallInitializers`
`XmuConvertStandardSelection`	`XmuCvtFunctionToCallback`
`XmuCvtStringToBackingStore`	`XmuCvtStringToBitmap`
`XmuCvtStringToCursor`	`XmuCvtStringToJustify`
`XmuCvtStringToLong`	`XmuCvtStringToOrientation`
`XmuCvtStringToShapeStyle`	`XmuCvtStringToWidget`
`XmuReshapeWidget`	

7.7 The Input Device Extension

The *X11 Input Device Extension* has been adopted as a standard of the X Consortium as of X11R5. This extension allows an X application to get input from devices other than the keyboard and mouse (touch screens, bar code readers, foot mice, etc.). It is a large extension to the core X input functionality and includes functions to open and close devices, set and query device state, freeze and thaw device input, and grab and ungrab devices and device buttons and keys. Additionally, it defines new types of input events, and has functions to register interest in receiving those events. It is also possible to use this extension to specify which devices should be used as the default X keyboard and pointer devices handled by the core X input functions. Note that this extension provides a programming interface for the use of multiple input devices, but does not provide support for any particular devices. In order to make use of this extension, you will have to have special hardware (the input device itself), and drivers for that hardware built into your X server.

Documentation for this extension can be found in the X11R5 distribution from MIT in the directories *mit/doc/extensions/xinput* and *mit/hardcopy/extensions/xinput*. The X Input Device Extension will also be documented in a future edition of *The X Resource*, O'Reilly & Associates X journal.

7.8 New Authorization Protocols

In X11R4, there were two ways to control access to an X server: per-host control with *xhost*, and per-user control with the **MIT-MAGIC-COOKIE-1** scheme. The *xhost* mechanism does not provide sufficient granularity for multi-user machines, and **MIT-MAGIC-COOKIE-1** is not secure because it passes its secret key ("cookie") between client and server without encryption.

X11R5 defines, and the MIT release implements, two new mechanisms that can be used for secure access control. **XDM-AUTHORIZATION-1** is similar to **MIT-MAGIC-COOKIE-1**, but uses DES (Data Encryption Standard) encryption to encrypt the authorization data that is passed between client and server. To compile this authorization scheme, you need an implementation of DES in the file *mit/lib/Xdmcp/Wraphelp.c*. Due to U.S. export regulations, this file may not appear in your distribution. If you do not plan to export the file outside of the U.S., you may legally obtain it over the network from the X Consortium. Ftp to the host *export.lcs.mit.edu* and see the file *pub/R5/xdm-auth/README*. Outside the U.S. you may be able to obtain a compatible version of this file from the directory */pub/X11R5* on the machine *ftp.psy.uq.oz.au* (130.102.32.1). If you do have this file, but this security mechanism is not automatically built on your system, you can add the following line to the file *mit/config/site.def* before building X11R5:

```
#define HasXdmAuth YES
```

The other new authorization mechanism is named **SUN-DES-1**, and is based on the public key Sun Secure RPC system included with recent version of SunOS. If your system provides this secure RPC system, then the *.cf* file for your system in *mit/config* should define the variable **HasSecureRPC**, which will cause this security mechanism to be automatically built. The forthcoming (Spring, 1992) *X Window System Administrator's Guide* from O'Reilly & Associates explains the issues of X security and these X11R5 security mechanisms in detail.

Miscellaneous

7.9 New Fonts and the pcf Font File Format

Besides the new scalable fonts described in Chapter 2, *Font Service and Scalable Fonts*, X11R5 provides new fonts in the Latin/Hebrew ISO8859-8 charset, the Kanji (Japanese) JISX208.1983-0 16-bit charset, and the Hangul (Korean) KSC5601.1987-0 16-bit charset. In addition, many of the fonts in the *misc* directory now contain all the Latin-1 characters rather than just the ASCII characters.

The font server and the R5 X server both use a new font format called *pcf* (Portable Compiled Font) that can be read by hosts of any architecture. This means that compiled fonts can be placed in a single NFS directory, for example, and be used by any machine in the network. For compatibility, the R5 X server retains the ability to read the old snf format fonts. Unfortunately, the pcf file format is not documented in the MIT X11R5 distribution.

7.10 New and Changed Clients in X11R5

There are four new clients in X11R5:

editres   This program allows users to graphically view the widget tree of an application, dynamically set resources on those widgets, and save the customizations into a resource file. The application must participate in the Editres protocol.

viewres   This program is a graphical version of *listres*. It uses the new Athena widgets to display the class hierarchy of the Athena widget set as a pannable tree.

xconsole This program displays output directed to */dev/console*. It is an alternative to *xterm -C*.

xcmsdb   This program is a utility for setting the **XDCCC** properties on the root window of a screen. These properties must be set in order for device-independent color to work correctly. *xcmsdb* will typically be run on startup by **xdm**.

The client *xlswins* is no longer in the X11R5 distribution; the **-tree** option to *xwininfo* performs the same function. The clients *muncher* and *plaid* have been moved out of the core distribution and into *contrib/*. There are new demos including several **PEX** clients, a device-independent color demo, and an X server performance test program.

bitmap and *xmag* have been re-implemented; they have new interfaces, more options, and support copy-and-paste. Text selection in *xterm* has been improved. Most notably, wrapped lines may be selected and pasted without embedded newline characters. New items have also been added to the *xterm* fonts menu. *xmh* now uses the **MH** environment variable if it exists. It also has a number of new application resources. In general, most X11R5 clients now participate in the **WM_DELETE_WINDOW** protocol and respond correctly to window manager "delete" commands.

For more information on new and changed clients, see the X11R5 Release Notes in Appendix A, *Release Notes*.

7.11 Performance Changes in X11R5

Considerable effort has been put into improving the performance of the X11R5 server shipped by MIT. The X11R5 Xt Intrinsics make use of permanently-allocated strings for quarks, and a re-implemented Translation Manager saves memory at runtime. The addition of device-independent color and internationalization to Xlib has made this library much larger, and even clients which do not use Xcms or internationalization functions may grow significantly. On systems without shared libraries, this increased size may affect performance by increasing application startup time and causing more frequent swapping to disk.

Reference Pages

This section presents reference pages for the new X11R5 Xlib and Xt functions, the new functions in the Miscellaneous Utilities (Xmu) library, the new Athena widgets, and the new and changed X11R5 clients that are of interest to programmers. It also documents some functions from the Xmu library that are not new in X11R5 but are not covered elsewhere in the O'Reilly & Associates series of X manuals. This section does not contain reference pages for the more obscure Xcms functions. Those can be found in The X Color Management System, forthcoming from O'Reilly & Associates.

The reference pages for functions, widgets, and clients are placed in a single section, alphabetized without regard to case. Note that functions prefixed with Xcms, Xmb, and Xwc are part of Xlib and functions prefixed with Xmu are part of the Xmu library.

Reference

Name

editres – a dynamic resource editor for X Toolkit applications.

Synopsis

```
editres [toolkit options]
```

Availability

Release 5 and later.

Options

editres accepts all standard X Toolkit command line options. The order of the command line options is not important.

Description

editres allows users and application developers to:

- View the full widget hierarchy of any X Toolkit client that speaks the *editres* protocol.

- Construct resource specifications for that client.

- Apply those specifications dynamically to the application.

Once the user is happy with a resource specification *editres* can append it to any resource file.

The *editres* protocol has been built into the Athena Widget set. This allows any application linked against Xaw to speak to *editres*.

editres provides a window consisting of the following four areas:

Menu Bar
Two Pulldown menus (labeled "Command" and "Tree") that allow you full access to *editres*'s features.

Panner
Provides an intuitive way to scroll the application tree display.

Message Area
Displays user instructions, status messages, and error messages.

Application Widget Tree
Displays the selected client's widget tree.

Commands Menu

To begin an *editres* session select the Get Widget Tree menu item from the Command menu. Once you have a widget tree you may now select any command from either menu.

Get Widget Tree

Allows the user to click anywhere on any client that speaks the *editres* protocol and receive its widget tree. If this application understands the *editres* protocol then *editres* displays the client's widget tree in its tree window. If the application does not understand the *editres* protocol, *editres* informs you of this fact in the message area after a few seconds delay.

Refresh Widget Tree

editres only knows about the widgets that existed when Get Widget Tree was most recently invoked. Many applications create and destroy widgets "on-the-fly." Selecting Refresh Widget Tree causes *editres* to ask the application to resend its widget tree, thus updating its information to the new state of the application. Refresh Widget Tree does not require the user to click on the target application.

Dump Widget Tree to a File

Creates a formatted Ascii file consisting of the widget names and classes for all the widgets in the application. This is useful for documenting the widget hierarchy of an application. When this menu item is selected, a popup dialog is activated. Type the name of the file in this dialog, and either select Okay or type <Return> to write the file. To cancel the file dialog select the Cancel button.

Show Resource Box

Pops up a resource box (described in detail below), that allows the user to see and set resources for the currently selected widget in the widget tree display. Only one widget may be currently selected; *editres* otherwise refuses to pop up the resource box and displays an error message in the message area.

Set Resource

Pops up a simple dialog box for setting any single resource on all selected widgets. You must type in the resource name, as well as the value. You can use the Tab key to switch between the resource name field and the resource value field.

Quit

Exits *editres*.

Tree Menu

The Tree menu contains several commands that allow operations to be performed on the widget tree.

Select Widget in Client

This menu item allows you to select a node in the tree by clicking on the desired widget in the target application. *editres* then highlights the corresponding element on the widget tree display. Since some widgets are fully obscured by their children, it is not possible to get to every widget this way, but this mechanism does give very useful feedback between the elements in the widget tree and those visible in the actual client.

Select All

Unselect All

Invert All

These functions allow the user to select, unselect, and invert the selection state of all widgets in the widget tree.

Select Parents

Select Children

These functions select the immediate parents and children of all of the currently selected widgets.

Select Ancestors

Select Descendants

These functions select all ancestors (parents, grandparents ...) and descendants (children, grandchildren ...) of all of the currently selected widgets.

Show Widget Names

Show Class Names

Show Widget IDs

Show Widget Windows

When the widget tree is initially displayed, each widget is labeled with its name. These functions change the labels of *all* widgets in the tree to the class name, widget ID, or window ID associated with each widget. The widget IDs and window IDs are shown as hex numbers.

Flash Active Widgets

This command is the inverse of the Select Widget in Client command. It shows the user each currently selected widget in the widget tree by flashing the corresponding widget in the application `numFlashes` times (three by default) in the `flashColor`.

Accelerators

There are keyboard accelerators for each of the Tree operations. If the input focus is over an individual widget in the tree, then that operation affects only that widget. If the input focus is in the Tree background, then the operation has exactly the same effect as the corresponding menu item.

Key	Action	Corresponding Menu Item
w	`Select(widget)`	Select Widget in Client
s	`Select(all)`	Select All
space	`Select(nothing)`	Unselect All
i	`Select(invert)`	Invert All
p	`Select(parent)`	Select Parents
c	`Select(children)`	Select Children
a	`Select(ancestors)`	Select Ancestors
d	`Select(descendants)`	Select Descendants
N	`Relabel(name)`	Show Widget Names

Key	Action	Corresponding Menu Item
C	Relabel(class)	Show Class Names
I	Relabel(id)	Show Widget IDs
W	Relabel(window)	Show Widget Windows
T	Relabel(toggle)	*No corresponding item*

Clicking button 1 on a widget adds it to the set of selected widgets. Clicking button 2 on a widget deselects all other widgets and then selects just that widget. Clicking button 3 on a widget toggles its label between the widget's instance name and the widget's class name.

Using the Resource Box

The Resource Box allows the user to set the resources of the selected widget in the tree. It is popped up with the Show Resource Box command from the "Commands" menu. The resource box contains five different areas. Each of the areas is discussed as it appears on the screen, from top to bottom.

The Resource Line

The first line of the resource box shows the current resource specification exactly as it would appear if you were to save it to a file or apply it.

The Generalizer

This area, composed of four lines of buttons, allows you to generalize the initial Resource Line so that it applies to more widgets. The first line contains a button for the name of the selected widget and one for each of its ancestors, and one for each dot (**.**) separator. The second line contains buttons for the less specific Class names of each widget, as well as for the less restrictive star (*****) separator. The third line contains a set of buttons called Any Widget that generalize this level to match any single widget by replacing it with a ? in the resource specification. The last line contains a set of buttons called Any Widget Chain that generalize the single level to match zero or more levels by replacing it with a star (*****).

When any of these buttons are clicked, the Resource Line changes and the Tree display changes to reflect which widgets the current Resource Line would affect. A small amount of experimentation makes it clear what each of the Generalizer lines does.

The initial state of the Resource Line is most restrictive, using only resource names and dot separators. By selecting the other buttons in the generalizer you can allow more and more widgets to match the specification. The extreme case is to select all the Any Widget Chain buttons, which match every widget in the application.

Normal and Constraint Resources

The next area lists the normal resources and Constraint resources of the widget you selected when you requested the resource box. Some widgets do not have Constraint resources, in which case that area does not appear.

You can select a resource to set by clicking on the resource name in the list. Note that if you have generalized the Resource Line then some widgets it applies to may not have the resource you select. If this happens, *editres* displays an error message in the Message Area, and no harm is done.

Resource Value

This final area allows you to enter a resource value. This value should be entered exactly as you would type a line into your resource file. Thus it should contain no new-lines unless escaped with two backslashes. As in resource files, you can use \n to indicate a newline and \###, where # is any octal digit, to indicate a single byte containing this octal number. For example, a value containing a null byte can be stored by specifying \000.

Command Area

This area contains the following command buttons:

Set Save File

Select the file to which the Resource Line is to be saved. This button brings up a dialog box that asks you for a filename. Once the filename is entered, either type <Return> or click on the Okay button. To popdown the dialog box without changing the save file, click the Cancel button.

Save

Append the Resource Line to the end of the current save file. If no save file has been set, the Set Save File dialog box pops up to prompt the user for a filename.

Apply

Instructs the application to perform a **XtSetValues** call on all widgets that match the Resource Line. The value specified is passed through the appropriate type converter unless the resource type happens to be String.

Since this feature allows users to put an application in states it may not be expecting to handle, a hook has been provided to allow specific clients to block these SetValues requests (see Blocking *editres* Requests below).

There is no guarantee that the results of an Apply will be the same as what happens when you save the value and restart the application, because not all widgets react the same to resource settings applied at creation as they do to resource settings applied after creation.

Save and Apply

This button combines the Save and Apply actions described above into one button.

Popdown Resource Box

This button removes the resource box from the display.

Blocking editres Requests

While *editres* provides great flexibility, it can also be abused. Any client can set the **editresBlock** application resource on itself to prevent the *editres* protocol handler from divulging information about its internals or from responding to the set values part of the proto-col. The `editresBlock` resource is of class `EditresBlock`, and its legal values are:

`all`

Block all requests. This prevents *editres* from displaying the widget tree or listing or set-ting resources.

`setValues`

Block all SetValues requests. This prevents *editres* from modifying the application in any way.

`none`

Allow all *editres* requests.

Remember that this resource is set on the Xaw client, not *editres*. It allows individual clients to keep all or some of the requests *editres* makes from succeeding.

Application Resources

The available application resources are:

`numFlashes` (Class `NumFlashes`)

Specifies the number of times the widgets in the client application are flashed when the Show Active Widgets command is invoked.

`flashTime` (Class `FlashTime`)

Amount of time between the flashes described above.

`flashColor` (Class `flashColor`)

Specifies the color used to flash client widgets.

`saveResourcesFile` (Class `SaveResourcesFile`)

This is the file to which the Resource Line is appended when the Save button in the resource box is activated.

Files

/usr/lib/X11/app-defaults/Editres - specifies required resources.

Restrictions

This is a prototype. There are lots of nifty features I would love to add, but I hope this gives you some ideas about what a resource editor can do.

Author

Chris D. Peterson, formerly MIT X Consortium

Name

fs – X font server.

Synopsis

fs [**-config** *configuration_file*][**-port** *tcp_port*]

Availability

Release 5 and later.

Description

fs is the X Window System font server. It supplies fonts to X Window System display servers. The server is usually configured by a system administrator, and started via boot files like */etc/rc.local*. Users may also wish to start private font servers for specific sets of fonts.

Options

—config *configuration_file*

> Specifies the configuration file the font server will use.

—ls *listen-socket*

> Specifies a file descriptor which is already set up to be used as the listen socket. This option is only intended to be used by the font server itself when automatically spawning another copy of itself to handle additional connections.

—port *tcp_port*

> Specifies the TCP port number on which the server will listen for connections.

Signals

SIGTERM

> This causes the font server to exit cleanly.

SIGUSR1

> This signal is used to cause the server to re-read its configuration file.

SIGUSR2

> This signal is used to cause the server to flush any cached data it may have.

SIGHUP

> This signal is used to cause the server to reset, closing all active connections and re-reading the configuration file.

Configuration

The configuration language is a list of keyword and value pairs. Each keyword is followed by an '=' and then the desired value. A line beginning with a "#" in the first column is a comment, and is ignored by *fs*. Recognized keywords include:

catalogue

> A comma-separated ordered list of font path element names.

alternate-servers
> A comma-separated list of alternate servers for this font server.

client-limit
> The number of clients this font server will support before refusing service. This is useful for tuning the load on each individual font server.

clone-self
> Whether this font server should attempt to clone itself when it reachs the client-limit. Legal values are on and off.

default-point-size
> The pointsize (in decipoints) to return when the requested font doesn't specify a size.

default-resolutions
> A comma separated list of resolutions the server supports by default. Each resolution is of the form *x-resolution, yresolution*, where each resolution is an integer resolution in dots-per-inch. This information may be used as a hint for pre-rendering, and substituted for scaled fonts which do not specify a resolution.

error-file
> Filename of the error file. All warnings and errors will be logged here.

port
> TCP port on which the server will listen for connections.

use-syslog
> Whether syslog(3) (on supported systems) is to be used for errors. Legal values are on and off.

Example

```
#
# sample font server configuration file
#

# allow a max of 10 clients to connect to this font server
client-limit = 10

# when a font server reaches its limit, start up a new one
clone-self = on

# alternate font servers for clients to use
alternate-servers = hansen:7001,hansen:7002

# where to look for fonts
# the first is a set of Speedo outlines, the second is a set of
# misc bitmaps and the last is a set of 100dpi bitmaps
#
catalogue = /usr/lib/fonts/speedo,
    /usr/lib/X11/ncd/fonts/misc,
    /usr/lib/X11/ncd/fonts/100dpi/
```

```
# in 12 points, decipoints
default-point-size = 120

# 100 x 100 and 75 x 75
default-resolutions = 100,100,75,75
```

Copyright

Copyright 1991, Network Computing Devices, Inc.
Copyright 1991, Massachusetts Institute of Technology
See *X(1)* for a full statement of rights and permissions.

Authors

Dave Lemke, Network Computing Devices, Inc.
Keith Packard, Massachusetts Institute of Technology

Name

Panner widget – a "scrollbar" for two dimensions.

Synopsis

```
#include <X11/StringDefs.h>
#include <X11/Intrinsic.h>
#include <X11/Xaw/Panner.h>
widget = XtCreateWidget(name, pannerWidgetClass,...);
```

Class Hierarchy

Core → Simple → Panner

Availability

Release 5 and later.

Description

The Panner widget is conceptually a two-dimensional scrollbar. It displays a rectangle within a rectangle—the inner rectangle (the "slider") represents the visible portion of a larger area (the "canvas") represented by the outer rectangle. The size of the inner rectangle represents the size of the visible area relative to the whole, and its position indicates the relative position of the visible area within the whole. The user may drag the inner rectangle with the mouse (or use keyboard arrow keys) to pan through the large diagram or document (or whatever) that is being displayed. The Panner widget is typically used with a Porthole widget to scroll a third widget in two dimensions.

When a Panner is created, it is drawn with the slider in a contrasting color. The slider may be moved around the canvas by pressing, dragging, and then releasing Button1. While scrolling is in progress, the application receives notification through callback procedures which it may use to update any associated widgets. Notification may be done either as the slider is dragged, or only when the slider is released.

Resources

When creating a Panner widget instance, the following resources are retrieved from the argument list or from the resource database:

Name	Type	Default	Description
XtNaccelerators	AcceleratorTable	NULL	Accelerators for this widget.
XtNallowOff	Boolean	False	Whether the slider can go beyond the edges.
XtNancestor-Sensitive	Boolean	True	Sensitivity state of the ancestors of this widget.
XtNbackground	Pixel	XtDefault-Background	Window background color.
XtNbackground-Pixmap	Pixmap	XtUnspecified-Pixmap	Window background pixmap.
XtNbackgroundStipple	String	NULL	Background pattern.
XtNbitmap	Pixmap	None	Pixmap to display in place of the label.

Name	Type	Default	Description
XtNborderColor	Pixel	XtDefault– Foreground	Window border color.
XtNborderPixmap	Pixmap	XtUnspecified– Pixmap	Window border pixmap.
XtNborderWidth	Dimension	1	Width of button border.
XtNcanvasHeight	Dimension	0	Height of the canvas to pan.
XtNcanvasWidth	Dimension	0	Width of the canvas to pan.
XtNcolormap	Colormap	Parent's colormap	Colormap that this widget will use.
XtNcursor	Cursor	None	Pointer cursor.
XtNcursorName	String	NULL	A cursor glyph name.
XtNdefaultScale	Dimension	8	Panner size as % of canvas.
XtNdepth	int	Parent's depth	Depth of this widget's window.
XtNdestroy– Callback	XtCallbackList	NULL	Callbacks for XtDestroyWidget.
XtNforeground	Pixel	XtDefaultForeground	Widget foreground color.
XtNheight	Dimension	0	Widget height.
XtNinsensitive– Border	Pixmap	GrayPixmap	Border when not sensitive.
XtNinternalSpace	Dimension	4	Margin around slider.
XtNlineWidth	Dimension	0	Width of rubberband lines.
XtNmappedWhen– Managed	Boolean	TRUE	Whether XtMapWidget is automatic.
XtNpointerColor	Pixel	XtDefaultForeground	Cursor foreground color.
XtNpointerColor– Background	Pixel	XtDefaultBackground	Cursor background color.
XtNreportCallback	XtCallbackList	NULL	Callback for panner motion.
XtNresize	Boolean	True	Whether to resize Panner with canvas.
XtNrubberBand	Boolean	False	Whether to do continuous scrolling.
XtNscreen	Screen	Parent's screen	Screen on which this widget is displayed: this is not a settable resource.
XtNsensitive	Boolean	TRUE	Whether widget receives input.
XtNshadowColor	Pixel	XtDefaultForeground	Color of thumb shadow.
XtNshadowThickness	Dimension	2	Width of thumb shadow.
XtNsliderX	Position	0	X location of thumb.
XtNsliderY	Position	0	Y location of thumb.
XtNsliderHeight	Dimension	0	Thumb height.
XtNsliderWidth	Dimension	0	Thumb width.
XtNtranslations	Translation– Table	See below	Event-to-action translations.
XtNwidth	Dimension	0	Widget width.
XtNx	Position	0	x-coordinate in pixels.
XtNy	Position	0	y-coordinate in pixels.

XtNallowOff
    Whether to allow the edges of the slider to go off the edges of the canvas.

Reference

`XtNbackgroundStipple`
> The name of a bitmap pattern to be used as the background for the area representing the canvas.

`XtNcanvasHeight`
> The height of the canvas.

`XtNcanvasWidth`
> The width of the canvas.

`XtNdefaultScale`
> The percentage size that the Panner widget should have relative to the size of the canvas.

`XtNforeground`
> The slider foreground color.

`XtNinternalSpace`
> The width of internal border in pixels between a slider representing the full size of the canvas and the edge of the Panner widget.

`XtNlineWidth`
> The width of the lines in the rubberbanding rectangle when rubberbanding is in effect instead of continuous scrolling. The default is 0.

`XtNreportCallback`
> All functions on this callback list are called when the slider is moved.

`XtNresize`
> Whether or not to resize the panner whenever the canvas size is changed so that the `Xt-NdefaultScale` is maintained.

`XtNrubberBand`
> Whether or not scrolling should be discrete (only moving a rubberbanded rectangle until the scrolling is done) or continuous (moving the slider itself). This controls whether or not the `move` action procedure also invokes the `notify` action procedure.

`XtNshadowColor`
> The color of the shadow underneath the slider.

`XtNshadowThickness`
> The width of the shadow underneath the slider.

`XtNsliderX`
> The X location of the slider in the coordinates of the canvas.

`XtNsliderY`
> The Y location of the slider in the coordinates of the canvas.

`XtNsliderHeight`
> The height of the slider.

`XtNsliderWidth`
> The width of the slider.

Translations and Actions

The actions supported by the Panner widget are:

start()

This action begins movement of the slider.

stop()

This action ends movement of the slider.

abort()

This action ends movement of the slider and restores it to the position it held when the start action was invoked.

move()

This action moves the outline of the slider (if the **XtNrubberBand** resource is True) or the slider itself (by invoking the notify action procedure).

page(*xamount,yamount*)

This action moves the slider by the specified amounts. The format for the amounts is a signed or unsigned floating-point number (e.g., +1.0 or −.5) followed by either "p" indicating pages (slider sizes), or "c" indicating canvas sizes. A signed number indicates a relative coordinate and an unsigned number indicates an absolute coordinate. Thus, page(+0,+.5p) represents vertical movement down one-half the height of the slider and page(0,0) represents moving to the upper left corner of the canvas. This action causes the callbacks on the **XtNreportCallback** list to be invoked.

notify()

This action informs the application of the slider's current position by invoking the **Xt-NreportCallback** functions registered by the application.

set(*what,value*)

This action changes the behavior of the Panner. The *what* argument must currently be the string "rubberband" and controls the value of the **XtNrubberBand** resource. The *value* argument may have one of the values "on," "off," or "toggle."

The default bindings for Panner are:

```
<Btn1Down>:start( )
<Btn1Motion>:move( )
<Btn1Up>:notify( ) stop( )
<Btn2Down>:abort( )
<Key>KP_Enter:set(rubberband,toggle)
<Key>space:page(+1p,+1p)
<Key>Delete:page(−1p,−1p)
<Key>BackSpace:page(−1p,−1p)
<Key>Left:page(−.5p,+0)
<Key>Right:page(+.5p,+0)
<Key>Up:page(+0,−.5p)
<Key>Down:page(+0,+.5p)
<Key>Home:page(0,0)
```

Callback Structures

The functions registered on the XtNreportCallback list are invoked by the notify action with a *call_data* argument which is a pointer to a structure of type XawPanner-Report:

```
/*
 * XawPannerReport - this structure is used by the reportCallback of the
 * Panner, Porthole, Viewport, and Scrollbar widgets to report its
 * position.  All fields must be filled in, although the changed field
 * may be used as a hint as to which fields have been altered since the
 * last report.
 */
typedef struct {
    unsigned int changed;/* mask, see below */
    Position slider_x, slider_y;/* location of slider within outer */
    Dimension slider_width, slider_height;  /* size of slider */
    Dimension canvas_width, canvas_height;  /* size of canvas */
} XawPannerReport;

#define XawPRSliderX(1 << 0)
#define XawPRSliderY(1 << 1)
#define XawPRSliderWidth(1 << 2)
#define XawPRSliderHeight(1 << 3)
#define XawPRCanvasWidth(1 << 4)
#define XawPRCanvasHeight(1 << 5)
#define XawPRAll(63)/* union of above */
```

Programmatic Interface

- To create a Panner widget instance, use XtCreateWidget and specify the class variable pannerWidgetClass.

- To destroy a Panner widget instance, use XtDestroyWidget and specify the widget ID of the Panner widget.

Related Widgets

Simple, Porthole

Name

Porthole widget – a panable view of a larger child widget.

Synopsis

```
#include <X11/StringDefs.h>
#include <X11/Intrinsic.h>
#include <X11/Xaw/Porthole.h>
widget = XtCreateWidget(name, portholeWidgetClass,...);
```

Class Hierarchy

Core → Composite → Porthole

Availability

Release 5 and later.

Description

The Porthole widget provides geometry management of a list of arbitrary widgets, only one of which may be managed at any particular time. The managed child widget is reparented within the porthole and is moved around by the application (typically under the control of a Panner widget). The Porthole widget allows its managed child to request any size that is as large or larger than the Porthole itself and any location so long as the child still obscures all of the Porthole.

Resources

When creating a Porthole widget instance, the following resources are retrieved from the argument list or from the resource database:

Name	Type	Default	Description
XtNaccelerators	AcceleratorTable	NULL	Accelerators for this widget.
XtNancestorSensitive	Boolean	True	Sensitivity state of the ancestors of this widget.
XtNbackground	Pixel	XtDefaultBackground	Window background color.
XtNbackgroundPixmap	Pixmap	XtUnspecifiedPixmap	Window background pixmap.
XtNborderColor	Pixel	XtDefaultForeground	Window border color.
XtNborderPixmap	Pixmap	XtUnspecifiedPixmap	Window border pixmap.
XtNborderWidth	Dimension	1	Border width on button porthole.
XtNchildren	WidgetList	NULL	List of all this composite widget's current children.
XtNcolormap	Colormap	Parent's colormap	Colormap that this widget will use.
XtNdepth	int	Parent's depth	Depth of this widget's window.
XtNdestroyCallback	XtCallbackList	NULL	Callbacks for XtDestroyWidget
XtNheight	Dimension	See below	Viewing height of inner window.

Name	Type	Default	Description
XtNmappedWhen–Managed	Boolean	TRUE	Whether XtMapWidget is automatic.
XtNnumChildren	Cardinal	0	Number of children in this composite widget.
XtNreportCallback	XtCallbackList	NULL	Called when child moves or resizes.
XtNscreen	Screen	Parent's screen	Screen on which this widget is displayed.
XtNsensitive	Boolean	TRUE	Whether widget receives input.
XtNtranslations	TranslationTable	NULL	Event-to-action translations.
XtNwidth	Dimension	See below	Viewing width of inner window.
XtNx	Position	0	x-coordinate in pixels.
XtNy	Position	0	y-coordinate in pixels.

There is only one new resource (not inherited from a superclasse) associated with the Panner widget:

XtNreportCallback

A list of functions to invoke whenever the managed child widget changes size or position. The *call_data* argument is of type **XawPannerReport** *, shown below.

Callback Structures

The functions registered on the **XtNreportCallback** list are invoked with a call_data argument which is a pointer to a structure of type **XawPannerReport**:

```
/*
 * XawPannerReport - this structure is used by the reportCallback of the
 * Panner, Porthole, Viewport, and Scrollbar widgets to report its
 * position.  All fields must be filled in, although the changed field
 * may be used as a hint as to which fields have been altered since the
 * last report.
 */
typedef struct {
    unsigned int changed;/* mask, see below */
    Position slider_x, slider_y;/* location of slider within outer */
    Dimension slider_width, slider_height;  /* size of slider */
    Dimension canvas_width, canvas_height;  /* size of canvas */
} XawPannerReport;

#define XawPRSliderX(1 << 0)
#define XawPRSliderY(1 << 1)
#define XawPRSliderWidth(1 << 2)
#define XawPRSliderHeight(1 << 3)
#define XawPRCanvasWidth(1 << 4)
#define XawPRCanvasHeight(1 << 5)
#define XawPRAll(63)/* union of above */
```

Programmatic Interface

• To create a Porthole widget instance, use **XtCreateWidget** and specify the class variable **portholeWidgetClass**.

- To add a child to the Porthole, use `XtCreateWidget` and specify the widget ID of the Porthole as the parent of the new widget. Manage the child with `XtManageChild`.

- To remove a child from a Porthole, use `XtUnmanageChild` or `XtDestroyWidget` and specify the widget ID of the child.

- To destroy a Porthole widget instance, use `XtDestroyWidget` and specify the widget ID of the Porthole widget. All the children of this porthole are destroyed automatically at the same time.

Related Widgets

`Composite`, `Panner`

Name

Repeater widget – a Command widget with auto-repeat.

Synopsis

```
#include <X11/StringDefs.h>
#include <X11/Intrinsic.h>
#include <X11/Xaw/Repeater.h>
widget = XtCreateWidget(name, repeaterWidgetClass,...);
```

Class Hierarchy

Core → Simple → Label → Command → Repeater

Availability

Release 5 and later.

Description

The Repeater widget is a version of the Command button that triggers at an increasing rate while it is held down. It is typically used to implement valuators or certain types of scrollbars.

Resources

When creating a Repeater widget instance, the following resources are retrieved from the argument list or from the resource database:

Name	Type	Default	Description
XtNaccelerators	AcceleratorTable	NULL	Accelerators for this widget.
XtNancestor–Sensitive	Boolean	True	Sensitivity state of the ancestors of this widget.
XtNbackground	Pixel	XtDefault–Background	Window background color.
XtNbackground–Pixmap	Pixmap	XtUnspecified–Pixmap	Window background pixmap.
XtNbitmap	Pixmap	None	Pixmap to display in place of the label.
XtNborderColor	Pixel	XtDefault–Foreground	Window border color.
XtNborderPixmap	Pixmap	XtUnspecified–Pixmap	Window border pixmap.
XtNborderWidth	Dimension	1	Width of button border.
XtNcallback	XtCallbackList	NULL	Called for each activation.
XtNcolormap	Colormap	Parent's colormap	Colormap that this widget will use.
XtNcornerRound–Percent	Dimension	25	Radius of rounded corner.
XtNcursor	Cursor	None	Pointer cursor.
XtNcursorName	String	NULL	A cursor glyph name.
XtNdecay	int	5	See below.
XtNdepth	int	Parent's depth	Depth of this widget's window.

Name	Type	Default	Description
XtNdestroy–Callback	XtCallbackList	NULL	Callbacks for XtDestroyWidget.
XtNencoding	unsigned char	XawTextEncoding8bit	8 or 16-bit text.
XtNflash	Boolean	False	Whether to flash on auto-repeat.
XtNfont	XFontStruct*	XtDefaultFont	Label font.
XtNforeground	Pixel	XtDefault–Foreground	Foreground color
XtNheight	Dimension	font height + 2 * XtNinternalHeight	Button height
XtNhighlight–Thickness	Dimension	2	Width of border to be highlighted.
XtNinitialDelay	int	200	See below.
XtNinsensitive–Border	Pixmap	GrayPixmap	Border when not sensitive.
XtNinternal–Height	Dimension	2	Internal border height for highlighting.
XtNinternalWidth	Dimension	4	Internal border width for highlighting.
XtNjustify	XtJustify	XtJustifyCenter	Type of text alignment.
XtNlabel	String	name of widget	Button label.
XtNleftBitmap	Pixmap	None	A bitmap to display to the left of the label.
XtNmappedWhen–Managed	Boolean	TRUE	Whether XtMapWidget is automatic.
XtNminimumDelay	int	10	See below.
XtNpointerColor	Pixel	XtDefaultForeground	Cursor foreground color.
XtNpointerColor–Background	Pixel	XtDefaultBackground	Cursor background color.
XtNrepeatDelay	int	50	See below.
XtNresize	Boolean	TRUE	Whether to auto-resize in SetValues.
XtNscreen	Screen	Parent's screen	Screen on which this widget is displayed: this is not a settable resource.
XtNsensitive	Boolean	TRUE	Whether widget receives input.
XtNshapeStyle	ShapeStyle	XmuShapeRectangle	Shape of button.
XtNstartCallback	XtCallbackList	NULL	Called when button pressed.
XtNstopCallback	XtCallbackList	NULL	Called when button released.
XtNtranslations	Translation–Table	See below	Event-to-action translations.
XtNwidth	Dimension	XtNlabel width + 2* XtNinternalWidth	Button width.

Name	Type	Default	Description
XtNx	Position	0	x-coordinate in pixels.
XtNy	Position	0	y-coordinate in pixels.

The Repeater widget invokes the callbacks on the `XtNstartCallback` and `XtNcallback` lists when it receives a `ButtonDown` event. If the button is held down, it starts a timer for `XtNinitialDelay` milliseconds. If the button is still down when that time has passed, it invokes the functions on the `XtNcallback` list again, and begins to repeat. The second repetition occurs after `XtNrepeatDelay` milliseconds, and subsequent intervals are reduced by `XtNdecay` milliseconds until they reach a minimum of `XtNminimumDelay` milliseconds. When the mouse button is released, the callbacks on the `XtNstopCallback` list are invoked, and all the timers are removed.

The new resources (not inherited from superclasses) associated with the Repeater widget are:

XtNdecay
> The number of milliseconds to subtract from the repeat interval after each repetition. The interval starts at `XtNrepeatDelay` and decreases to `XtNminimumDelay`. The default is 5 milliseconds.

XtNflash
> Whether or not to flash the Repeater button whenever the timer goes off. The default is `False`.

XtNinitialDelay
> The number of milliseconds before the Repeater widget begins to repeat. The default is 200.

XtNminimumDelay
> The minimum time between callbacks in milliseconds. The default is 10.

XtNrepeatDelay
> The number of milliseconds between repetitions, once the `XtNinitialDelay` has elapsed and the widget has begun to repeat. The actual delay interval will have `XtNdecay` milliseconds subtracted from it at each repetition until it reaches `XtNminimumDelay`.

XtNstartCallback
> The list of functions executed from the `start` action (typically when the Repeater button is first pressed). The `call_data` parameter is unused.

XtNstopCallback
> The list of functions executed from the `stop` action (typically when the Repeater button is released). The `call_data` parameter is unused.

Translations and Actions

The Repeater widget supports the following actions beyond those of the Command button:

`start()`

> This invokes the functions on the `XtNstartCallback` and `XtNcallback` lists and sets a timer to go off in `XtNinitialDelay` milliseconds. The timer will cause the `XtNcallback` functions to be invoked with increasing frequency until the `stop` action occurs.

`stop()`

> This invokes the functions on the `XtNstopCallback` list and prevents any further timers from occurring until the next `start` action.

The following are the default translation bindings used by the Repeater widget:

```
<EnterWindow>:highlight( )
<LeaveWindow>:unhighlight( )
<Btn1Down>:set( ) start( )
<Btn1Up>:stop( ) unset( )
```

Programmatic Interface

- To create a Repeater widget instance, use `XtCreateWidget` and specify the class variable `repeaterWidgetClass`.

- To destroy a Repeater widget instance, use `XtDestroyWidget` and specify the widget ID of the Repeater widget.

Related Widgets

Command

Reference

Tree

Name

Tree widget – a constraint widget that arranges its children in a tree.

Synopsis

```
#include <X11/StringDefs.h>
#include <X11/Intrinsic.h>
#include <X11/Xaw/Tree.h>
widget = XtCreateWidget(name, treeWidgetClass,...);
```

Class Hierarchy

Core → Composite → Constraint → Tree

Availability

Release 5 and later.

Description

The Tree widget provides geometry management of arbitrary widgets arranged in a directed, acyclic graph (i.e., a tree). The hierarchy is constructed by attaching a constraint resource called **XtNtreeParent** to each child indicating which other node in the tree should be treated as the child's superior. The structure of the tree is shown by laying out the nodes in the standard format for tree diagrams with lines drawn to connect each node with its children.

The Tree sizes itself according to the needs of its children and is not intended to be resized by its parent. Instead, it should be placed inside another composite widget (such as the Porthole or Viewport) that can be used to scroll around in the tree.

Resources

When creating a Tree widget instance, the following resources are retrieved from the argument list or from the resource database:

Name	Type	Default	Description
XtNaccelerators	AcceleratorTable	NULL	Accelerators for this widget.
XtNancestor-Sensitive	Boolean	True	Sensitivity state of the ancestors of this widget.
XtNautoReconfigure	Boolean	False	Whether to re-layout the tree when each new child is added.
XtNbackground	Pixel	XtDefault-Background	Window background color.
XtNbackground-Pixmap	Pixmap	XtUnspecified-Pixmap	Window background pixmap.
XtNborderColor	Pixel	XtDefault-Foreground	Window border color.
XtNborderPixmap	Pixmap	XtUnspecified-Pixmap	Window border pixmap.
XtNborderWidth	Dimension	1	Width of border in pixels.

Name	Type	Default	Description
XtNchildren	WidgetList	NULL	List of all this composite widget's current children.
XtNcolormap	Colormap	Parent's colormap	Colormap that this widget will use.
XtNdepth	int	Parent's depth	Depth of this widget's window.
XtNdestroy–Callback	XtCallbackList	NULL	Callbacks for XtDestroyWidget.
XtNforeground	Pixel	XtDefaultForeground	Widget foreground color.
XtNgravity	XtGravity	West	Window gravity of widget.
XtNheight	Dimension	Computed at realize	Height of tree.
XtNhSpace	Dimension	20	Horizontal space between children.
XtNlineWidth	Dimension	0	Width of tree lines.
XtNmappedWhen–Managed	Boolean	TRUE	Whether XtMapWidget is automatic.
XtNnumChildren	Cardinal	0	Number of children in this composite widget.
XtNscreen	Screen	Parent's screen	Screen on which this widget is displayed.
XtNsensitive	Boolean	TRUE	Whether widget receives input.
XtNtranslations	TranslationTable	NULL	Event-to-action translations.
XtNvSpace	Dimension	6	Vertical space between children.
XtNwidth	Dimension	Computed at realize	Width of tree.
XtNx	Position	0	x-coordinate in pixels.
XtNy	Position	0	y-coordinate in pixels.

XtNautoReconfigure
> Whether or not to lay out the tree every time a node is added or removed.

XtNforeground
> Foreground color for the widget.

XtNgravity
> Specifies the side of the widget from which the tree should grow. Valid values include `WestGravity`, `NorthGravity`, `EastGravity`, and `SouthGravity`.

XtNhSpace
> The amount of horizontal space, in pixels, to leave between the children. This resource also specifies the amount of space left between the outermost children and the edge of the box.

XtNlineWidth
> The width of the lines drawn between nodes that do not have a `XtNtreeGC` constraint resource and their inferiors in the tree.

XtNvSpace
> The amount of vertical space, in pixels, to leave between the children. This resource also specifies the amount of space left between the outermost children and the edge of the box.

Reference

Constraints

When creating children to be added to a Tree, the following additional resources are retrieved from the argument list or from the resource database. Note that these resources are maintained by the Tree widget even though they are stored in the child.

Name	Type	Default	Description
XtNtreeGC	GC	NULL	GC used to draw lines between the child and its inferiors in the tree.
XtNtreeParent	Widget	NULL	The child's superior node in the tree.

`XtNtreeGC`

This specifies the GC to use when drawing lines between this widget and its inferiors in the tree. If this resource is not specified, the Tree's `XtNforeground` and `XtNlineWidth` will be used.

`XtNtreeParent`

This specifies the superior node in the tree for this widget. The default is for the node to have no superior (and to therefore be at the top of the tree).

The position of each child in the tree hierarchy (as opposed to the widget hierarchy) is determined by the value of the `XtNtreeParent` constraint resource. Each time a child is managed or unmanaged, the Tree widget will attempt to reposition the remaining children to fix the shape of the tree if the `XtNautoReconfigure` resource is set. Children at the root of the tree are drawn at the side specified by the `XtNgravity` resource. After positioning all children, the Tree widget attempts to shrink its own size to the minimum dimensions required for the layout.

Programmatic Interface

- To create a Tree widget instance, use `XtCreateWidget` and specify the class variable `treeWidgetClass`.

- To add a new child to a Tree, use `XtCreateWidget` and specify the widget ID of the previously created Tree as the parent of the child. Use `XtManageChild` to manage the child.

- To remove a child from a Tree, use `XtUnmanageChild` or `XtDestroyWidget` and specify the widget ID of the child widget.

- To destroy a Tree widget instance, use `XtDestroyWidget` and specify the widget ID of the Tree. All children of the Tree are destroyed automatically at the same time.

- To force a Tree widget to re-layout its children (when `XtNautoReconfigure` is `False`, for example), use `XawTreeForceLayout`.

```
void XawTreeForceLayout(w)
    Widget w;
```

w Specifies the Tree widget.

When adding several children to a Tree widget, it is most efficient to set `XtNauto-Reconfigure` to `False` and use this function once all the widgets have been added.

Related Widgets
```
Constraint
```

Name

viewres – graphical class browser for the Athena widget set.

Synopsis

viewres [*options*]

Availability

Release 5 and later.

Description

The *viewres* program displays a tree showing the widget class hierarchy of the Athena widget set. Each node in the tree can be expanded to show the resources that the corresponding class adds (i.e., does not inherit from its parent). This application allows the user to visually examine the class hierarchy and resource inheritance for the Athena Widget Set.

Options

viewres accepts all of the standard toolkit command line options as well as the following:

–top *name*

This option specifies the name of the highest widget in the hierarchy to display. This is typically used to limit the display to a subset of the tree. The default is the Object class.

–variable

This option indicates that the widget variable names (as declared in header files) should be displayed in the nodes rather than the widget class name. This is sometimes useful to distinguish widget classes that share the same name (such as Text).

–vertical

This option indicates that the tree should be displayed top to bottom rather left to right.

View Menu

The way in which the tree is displayed may be changed through the entries in the View menu:

Show Variable Names

This entry causes the node labels to be set to the variable names used to declare the corresponding widget class. This operation may also be performed with the SetLabel-Type(variable) action.

Show Class Names

This entry causes the node labels to be set to the class names used when specifying resources. This operation may also be performed with the SetLabelType(class) action.

Layout Horizontal

This entry causes the tree to be laid out from left to right. This operation may also be performed with the SetOrientation(West) action.

Layout Vertical

This entry causes the tree to be laid out from top to bottom. This operation may also be performed with the SetOrientation(North) action.

Show Resource Boxes

This entry expands the selected nodes (see next section) to show the new widget and constraint resources. This operation may also be performed with the `Resources(on)` action.

Hide Resource Boxes

This entry removes the resource displays from the selected nodes. This operation may also be performed with the `Resources(off)` action.

Select Menu

Resources for a single widget class can be displayed by clicking Button2 on the corresponding node, or by adding the node to the selection list with Button1 and using the Show Resource Boxes entry in the View menu. Button1 actually toggles the selection state of a node; clicking on a selected node will cause it to be removed from the selected list.

Collections of nodes may also be selected through the various entries in the Select menu:

Unselect All

This entry removes all nodes from the selection list. This operation may also be performed with the `Select(nothing)` action.

Select All

This entry adds all nodes to the selection list. This operation may also be performed with the `Select(all)` action.

Invert All

This entry adds unselected nodes to, and removes selected nodes from, the selection list. This operation may also be performed with the `Select(invert)` action.

Select Parent

This entry selects the immediate parents of all selected nodes. This operation may also be performed with the `Select(parent)` action.

Select Ancestors

This entry recursively selects all parents of all selected nodes. This operation may also be performed with the `Select(ancestors)` action.

Select Children

This entry selects the immediate children of all selected nodes. This operation may also be performed with the `Select(children)` action.

Select Descendants

This entry recursively selects all children of all selected nodes. This operation may also be performed with the `Select(descendants)` action.

Select Has Resources

This entry selects all nodes that add new resources (regular or constraint) to their corresponding widget classes. This operation may also be performed with the `Select(resources)` action.

Reference

Select Shown Resource Boxes
> This entry selects all nodes whose resource boxes are currently expanded (usually so that they can be closed with Hide Resource Boxes). This operation may also be performed with the `Select(shown)` action.

Actions

The following application actions are provided:

`Quit()`
> This action causes *viewres* to exit.

`SetLabelType(type)`
> This action sets the node labels to display the widget variable or class names, according to the argument *type*. Legal values for *type* are `variable` and `class`.

`SetOrientation(direction)`
> This action sets the root of the tree to be at one of the four sides of the window. Legal values for *direction* are: `West`, `North`, `East`, or `South`.

`Select(what)`
> This action selects the indicated nodes, as described for the Select menu above. Legal values for *what* are: `nothing`, `invert`, `parent`, `ancestors`, `children`, `descendants`, `resources`, `shown`.

`Resources(op)`
> This action turns on, turns off, or toggles the resource boxes for the selected nodes. The legal values for *op* are: `on`, `off`, and `toggle`. If this action is invoked from within one of the nodes (through the keyboard or pointer), only that node is used.

Widget Hierarchy

The widget hierarchy for *viewres* is shown below. Each line describes a single widget in the application. The widget class is given first, and it is followed by the widget instance name. Indentation indicates the hierarchical structure of the widget tree. The widgets that are children of the Tree widget are named *variable-name* in the example below. When created these widgets are given the widget variable name for the Athena widget class that they represent.

```
Viewres viewres
        Paned pane
                Box buttonbox
                        Command quit
                        MenuButton view
                                SimpleMenu viewMenu
                                        SmeBSB layoutHorizontal
                                        SmeBSB layoutVertical
                                        SmeLine line1
                                        SmeBSB namesVariable
                                        SmeBSB namesClass
                                        SmeLine line2
```

```
                              SmeBSB viewResources
                              SmeBSB viewNoResources
                  MenuButton select
                     SimpleMenu selectMenu
                              SmeBSB unselect
                              SmeBSB selectAll
                              SmeBSB selectInvert
                              SmeLine line1
                              SmeBSB selectParent
                              SmeBSB selectAncestors
                              SmeBSB selectChildren
                              SmeBSB selectDescendants
                              SmeLine line2
                              SmeBSB selectHasResources
                              SmeBSB selectShownResources
            Form treeform
                  Porthole porthole
                     Tree tree
                        Box variable-name
                              Toggle variable-name
                              List variable-name
                  Panner panner
```

Environment Variables

DISPLAY   Specifies the display and screen to use.

Related Commands

xrdb, listres, editres, appres

Copyright

Copyright 1990, Massachusetts Institute of Technology.
See *X(1)* for a full statement of rights and permissions.

Author

Jim Fulton, MIT X Consortium

Name

XBaseFontNameListOfFontSet – get the base font list of a font set.

Synopsis

```
char *XBaseFontNameListOfFontSet(font_set)
    XFontSet font_set;
```

Arguments

font_set   Specifies the font set.

Availability

Release 5 and later.

Description

The `XBaseFontNameListOfFontSet` function returns the original base font name list supplied by the client when the `XFontSet` was created. A null-terminated string containing a list of comma-separated font names is returned as the value of the function. Whitespace may appear immediately on either side of separating commas.

If `XCreateFontSet` obtained an XLFD (X Logical Font Description) name from the font properties for the font specified by a non-XLFD base name, the `XBaseFontNameList-OfFontSet` function will return the XLFD name instead of the non-XLFD base name.

The base font name list is owned by Xlib and should not be modified or freed by the client. It will be freed by a call to `XFreeFontSet` on the associated `XFontSet`. Until freed, its contents will not be modified by Xlib.

Related Commands

XCreateFontSet, XExtentsOfFontSet, XFontsOfFontSet, XLocaleOfFontSet

Name

XCloseIM – close an input method.

Synopsis

```
Status XCloseIM( im )
    XIM im;
```

Arguments

im   Specifies the input method.

Availability

Release 5 and later.

Description

XCloseIM closes the connection to an input method opened with XOpenIM. Once an input method is closed, none of the input contexts associated with that input method may be used.

Related Commands

XCreateIC, XSetICFocus, XSetICValues, XmbResetIC, XOpenIM,
XGetIMValues, XDisplayOfIM, XLocaleOfIM

Reference

XcmsAllocColor

Name

XcmsAllocColor – allocate device-independent color.

Synopsis

```
Status XcmsAllocColor(display, colormap, color_in_out, result_format)
    Display *display;
    Colormap colormap;
    XcmsColor *color_in_out;
    XcmsColorFormat result_format;
```

Arguments

display   Specifies the connection to the X server.

colormap   Specifies the colormap.

color_in_out   Specifies the color to allocate and returns the pixel and color that is actually used in the colormap.

result_format   Specifies the color format for the returned color specification.

Availability

Release 5 and later.

Description

The XcmsAllocColor function is similar to XAllocColor except the color can be specified in any format. The XcmsAllocColor function ultimately calls XAllocColor to allocate a read-only color cell (colormap entry) with the specified color. XcmsAllocColor first converts the color specified to an RGB value and then passes this to XAllocColor. XcmsAllocColor returns the pixel value of the color cell and the color specification actually allocated. This returned color specification is the result of converting the RGB value returned by XAllocColor into the format specified with the *result_format* argument. If there is no interest in a returned color specification, unnecessary computation can be bypassed if *result_format* is set to XcmsRGBFormat. If this routine returns XcmsFailure, the *color_in_out* color specification is left unchanged.

Structures

The XcmsColor and XcmsColorFormat structures are shown on the XcmsColor reference page.

Errors

BadColor   The *colormap* argument does not name a defined Colormap.

Related Commands

XcmsQueryColor, XcmsStoreColor, XcmsAllocNamedColor, XcmsColor

Name

XcmsAllocNamedColor – allocate a named device-independent color.

Synopsis

```
Status XcmsAllocNamedColor(display, colormap, color_string,
        color_screen_return, color_exact_return, result_format)
    Display *display;
    Colormap colormap;
    char *color_string;
    XcmsColor *color_screen_return;
    XcmsColor *color_exact_return;
    XcmsColorFormat result_format;
```

Arguments

display　　　　Specifies the connection to the X server.

colormap　　　Specifies the colormap.

color_string　Specifies the color string whose color definition structure is to be returned.

color_screen_return

　　　　　　　Returns the pixel value of the color cell and color specification that actually is stored for that cell.

color_exact_return

　　　　　　　Returns the color specification parsed from the color string or parsed from the corresponding string found in a color name database.

result_format　Specifies the color format for the returned color specification.

Description

The XcmsAllocNamedColor function is similar to XAllocNamedColor except the color returned can be in any format specified. This function ultimately calls XAllocColor to allocate a read-only color cell with the color specified by a color string. The color string is parsed into an XcmsColor structure, converted to an RGB value, then finally passed to XAlloc-Color.

A color string may be a color name that appears in the client-side color database, or it may be a device-dependent or device-independent color specification in one of the following formats:

RBG:*red*/*green*/*blue*
RGBi:*R*/*G*/*B*
CIEXYZ:*X*/*Y*/*Z*
CIEuvY:*u*/*v*/*Y*
CIExyY:*x*/*y*/*Y*
CIELab:*L*/*a*/*b*
CIELuv:*L*/*u*/*v*
TekHVC:*H*/*V*/*C*

For the RGB color space, the *red*, *green*, and *blue* parameters are hexidecimal strings of one to four digits. For each of the other color spaces, each parameter is a floating-point number in standard string format. In each case, each number specifies a value for one of the parameters of the color space. Old-style RGB color strings beginning with a "#" remain supported for backwards compatiblity. If the color name is not in the Host Portable Character Encoding the result is implementation-dependent. Color names are case-insensitive.

This function returns both the color specification as a result of parsing (exact specification) and the actual color specification stored (screen specification). This screen specification is the result of converting the RGB value returned by XAllocColor into the format specified in *result_format*. If there is no interest in a returned color specification, unnecessary computation can be bypassed if *result_format* is set to XcmsRGBFormat.

Errors
BadColor   The *colormap* argument does not name a defined Colormap.

Structures
The XcmsColor and XcmsColorFormat structures are shown on the XcmsColor reference page.

Related Commands
XcmsQueryColor, XcmsStoreColor, XcmsAllocColor, XcmsColor

Name

XcmsCCCOfColormap – get the color conversion context of a colormap.

Synopsis

```
XcmsCCC XcmsCCCOfColormap(display, colormap)
    Display *display;
    Colormap colormap;
```

Arguments

display   Specifies the connection to the X server.

colormap   Specifies the colormap for which the CCC is to be returned.

Availability

Release 5 and later.

Description

XcmsCCCOfColormap returns the CCC associated with the specified colormap. This CCC is used implicitly when the specified colormap is used as an argument to many Xcms device-independent color functions. XcmsCCCOfColormap returns the CCC so that it can be passed explicitly to color conversion functions that do not take a colormap argument.

Related Commands

XcmsDefaultCCC, XcmsConvertColors

Reference

Name

XcmsColor – Xcms color struture.

Availability

Release 5 and later.

Description

The XcmsColor structure contains a union of substructures, each supporting color specification encoding for a particular color space.

The XcmsColorFormat type is used to indicate which color space the values in an XcmsColor structure belong to. It is also used to indicate which format Xcms routines should return colors in.

Structures

The XcmsColor structure contains:

```
typedef unsigned long XcmsColorFormat;/* Color Specification Format */

#define XcmsUndefinedFormat      (XcmsColorFormat)0x00000000
#define XcmsCIEXYZFormat         (XcmsColorFormat)0x00000001
#define XcmsCIEuvYFormat         (XcmsColorFormat)0x00000002
#define XcmsCIExyYFormat         (XcmsColorFormat)0x00000003
#define XcmsCIELabFormat         (XcmsColorFormat)0x00000004
#define XcmsCIELuvFormat         (XcmsColorFormat)0x00000005
#define XcmsTekHVCFormat         (XcmsColorFormat)0x00000006
#define XcmsRGBFormat            (XcmsColorFormat)0x80000000
#define XcmsRGBiFormat           (XcmsColorFormat)0x80000001

typedef struct {
      union {
              XcmsRGB RGB;
              XcmsRGBi RGBi;
              XcmsCIEXYZ CIEXYZ;
              XcmsCIEuvY CIEuvY;
              XcmsCIExyY CIExyY;
              XcmsCIELab CIELab;
              XcmsCIELuv CIELuv;
              XcmsTekHVC TekHVC;
              XcmsPad Pad;
      } spec;
      XcmsColorFormat format;
      unsigned long pixel;
} XcmsColor;                       /* Xcms Color Structure */

typedef double XcmsFloat;

typedef struct {
      unsigned short red;          /* 0x0000 to 0xffff */
      unsigned short green;        /* 0x0000 to 0xffff */
```

```
        unsigned short blue;        /* 0x0000 to 0xffff */
} XcmsRGB;                          /* RGB Device */

typedef struct {
        XcmsFloat red;              /* 0.0 to 1.0 */
        XcmsFloat green;            /* 0.0 to 1.0 */
        XcmsFloat blue;             /* 0.0 to 1.0 */
} XcmsRGBi;                         /* RGB Intensity */

typedef struct {
        XcmsFloat X;
        XcmsFloat Y;                /* 0.0 to 1.0 */
        XcmsFloat Z;
} XcmsCIEXYZ;                       /* CIE XYZ */

typedef struct {
        XcmsFloat u_prime;          /* 0.0 to ~0.6 */
        XcmsFloat v_prime;          /* 0.0 to ~0.6 */
        XcmsFloat Y;                /* 0.0 to 1.0 */
} XcmsCIEuvY;                       /* CIE u'v'Y */

typedef struct {
        XcmsFloat x;                /* 0.0 to ~.75 */
        XcmsFloat y;                /* 0.0 to ~.85 */
        XcmsFloat Y;                /* 0.0 to 1.0 */
} XcmsCIExyY;                       /* CIE xyY */

typedef struct {
        XcmsFloat L_star;           /* 0.0 to 100.0 */
        XcmsFloat a_star;
        XcmsFloat b_star;
} XcmsCIELab;                       /* CIE L*a*b* */

typedef struct {
        XcmsFloat L_star;           /* 0.0 to 100.0 */
        XcmsFloat u_star;
        XcmsFloat v_star;
} XcmsCIELuv;                       /* CIE L*u*v* */

typedef struct {
        XcmsFloat H;                /* 0.0 to 360.0 */
        XcmsFloat V;                /* 0.0 to 100.0 */
        XcmsFloat C;                /* 0.0 to 100.0 */
} XcmsTekHVC;                       /* TekHVC */

typedef struct {
        XcmsFloat pad0;
        XcmsFloat pad1;
        XcmsFloat pad2;
        XcmsFloat pad3;
```

Reference

```
} XcmsPad;                         /* space reserved for future or */
                                   /* user-defined color spaces    */
```

Related Commands
XcmsAllocColor, XcmsStoreColor, XcmsConvertColors

Name

XcmsConvertColors – convert CCC color specifications.

Synopsis

```
Status XcmsConvertColors(ccc, colors_in_out, ncolors, target_format,
      compression_flags_return)
  XcmsCCC ccc;
  XcmsColor colors_in_out[];
  unsigned int ncolors;
  XcmsColorFormat target_format;
  Bool compression_flags_return[];
```

Arguments

ccc   Specifies the CCC. If Conversion is between device-independent color spaces only (for example, TekHVC to CIELuv), the CCC is necessary only to specify the Client White Point.

colors_in_out   Specifies an array of color specifications. Pixel members are ignored and remain unchanged upon return.

ncolors   Specifies the number of XcmsColor structures in the color specification array.

target_format   Specifies the target color specification format.

compression_flags_return

Specifies an array of *ncolors* Boolean values for returning compression status of each color conversion. If a non-NULL pointer is supplied, each element of the array is set to True if the corresponding color was compressed, and False otherwise. Pass NULL if the compression status is not useful.

Availability

Release 5 and later.

Description

The XcmsConvertColors function converts the color specifications in the specified array of XcmsColor structures from their current format (which may vary from element to element of the array) to a single target format using the specified CCC. If all the conversions succeed without gamut compression, XcmsConvertColors returns XcmsSuccess. If one or more of the conversions required gamut compression, the function returns XcmsSuccessWith-Compression, and sets the appropriate flags in *compression_flags_return* array. If any of the conversions fail, the function returns XcmsFailure and the contents of the color specification array are left unchanged.

Reference

Structures

The XcmsColor and XcmsColorFormat structures are shown on the XcmsColor reference page.

Related Commands

XcmsCCCofColormap, XcmsDefaultCCC

Name

xcmsdb – set screen color characterization data properties.

Synopsis

xcmsdb [*options*] [*filename*]

Availability

Release 5 and later.

Description

xcmsdb is used to load, query, or remove Screen Color Characterization Data stored in properties on the root window of the screen. Screen Color Characterization Data is an integral part of Xlib, necessary for proper conversion between device-independent and device-dependent color specifications. Xlib uses the properties XDCCC_LINEAR_RGB_MATRICES and XDCCC_LINEAR_RGB_CORRECTION to store color characterization data for color monitors. It uses XDCCC_GRAY_SCREENWHITEPOINT and XDCCC_GRAY_CORRECTION properties for gray scale monitors. Because Xlib allows the addition of Screen Color Characterization Function Sets, added function sets may place their Screen Color Characterization Data on other properties. This utility is unaware of these other properties, therefore, you will need to use a similar utility provided with the function set, or use the *xprop* utility.

The ASCII readable contents of *filename* (or the standard input if no input file is given) are appropriately transformed for storage in properties, provided the or options are not specified.

Options

xcmsdb accepts the following options:

—query

This option attempts to read the XDCCC properties off the screen's root window. If successful, it transforms the data into a more readable format, then sends the data to standard out.

—remove

This option attempts to remove the XDCCC properties on the screen's root window.

—color

This option sets the query and remove options to only check for the XDCCC_LINEAR_RGB_MATRICES and XDCCC_LINEAR_RGB_CORRECTION properties. If the **—color** option is not set then the query and remove options check for all the properties.

—format *property_format*

Specifies the property format (the number of bits per entry) for the XDCCC_LINEAR_RGB_CORRECTION property. Legal values are 8, 16, and 32. Precision of encoded floating point values increases with the increase in bits per entry. The default is 32 bits per entry.

Environment Variables

DISPLAY

Specifies the display and screen to use.

Related Commands

xprop

Bugs

Unknown

Copyright

Copyright 1990, Tektronix Inc.

Author

Chuck Adams, Tektronix Inc.

XcmsDefaultCCC

Name

XcmsDefaultCCC – get the default color conversion context for a screen.

Synopsis

```
XcmsCCC XcmsDefaultCCC(display, screen_number)
    Display *display;
    int screen_number;
```

Arguments

display   Specifies the connection to the X server.

screen_number   Specifies the screen number.

Availability

Release 5 and later.

Description

XcmsDefaultCCC returns the default CCC for the specified screen.

Related Commands

XcmsCCCOfColormap, XcmsConvertColors

XcmsLookupColor

Name

XcmsLookupColor – obtain color values.

Synopsis

```
Status XcmsLookupColor(display, colormap, color_string,
        color_exact_return, color_screen_return, result_format)
    Display *display;
    Colormap colormap;
    char *color_string;
    XcmsColor *color_exact_return;
    XcmsColor *color_screen_return;
    XcmsColorFormat result_format;
```

Arguments

display   Specifies the connection to the X server.

colormap   Specifies the colormap.

color_string Specifies the color string.

color_exact_return

       Returns the color specification parsed from the color string or parsed from the corresponding string found in a color name database.

color_screen_return

       Returns the color that can be reproduced on the Screen.

result_format Specifies the color format for the returned color specifications.

Availability

Release 5 and later.

Description

The XcmsLookupColor function looks up the string name of a color with respect to the screen associated with the specified colormap, but does not allocate any color cells in the color map. It returns both the exact color values and the closest values provided by the screen with respect to the visual type of the specified colormap. The values are returned in the format specified by *result_format*.

A color string may be a color name that appears in the client-side color database, or it may be a device-dependent or device-independent color specification in one of the following formats:

```
RBG:red/green/blue
RGBi:R/G/B
CIEXYZ:X/Y/Z
CIEuvY:u/v/Y
CIExyY:x/y/Y
CIELab:L/a/b
CIELuv:L/u/v
TekHVC:H/V/C
```

For the RGB color space, the *red*, *green*, and *blue* parameters are hexidecimal strings of one to four digits. For each of the other color spaces, each parameter is a floating point number in standard string format. In each case, each number specifies a value for one of the parameters of the color space. Old-style RGB color strings beginning with a "#" remain supported for backwards compatiblity. If the color name is not in the Host Portable Character Encoding the result is implementation dependent. Color names are case-insensitive.

If *format* is XcmsUndefinedFormat and the color string contains a numerical color specification, the specification is returned in the format used in that numerical color specification. If *format* is XcmsUndefinedFormat and the color string contains a color name, the specification is returned in the format used to store the color in the database.

XcmsLookupColor returns XcmsSuccess or XcmsSuccessWithCompression if the name is resolved, otherwise it returns XcmsFailure. If XcmsSuccessWith-Compression is returned, then the color specification in *color_screen_return* is the result of gamut compression.

Structures

The XcmsColor and XcmsColorFormat structures are shown on the XcmsColor reference page.

Related Commands

XcmsAllocColor, XcmsStoreColor, XQueryColor, XcmsQueryColor, Xcms-QueryColors, XcmsColor

Name

XcmsQueryBlack – obtain a device-independent specification for RGBi:0.0/0.0/0.0.

Synopsis

```
Status XcmsQueryBlack(ccc, target_format, color_return)
    XcmsCCC ccc;
    XcmsColorFormat target_format;
    XcmsColor *color_return;
```

Arguments

ccc   Specifies the CCC. Note that the CCC's Client White Point and White Point
                Adjustment procedures are ignored.

target_format   Specifies the target color specification format.

color_return   Returns the color specification in the specified target format. The white point
                associated with the returned color specification is the Screen White Point.
                The value returned in the pixel member is undefined.

Availability

Release 5 and later.

Description

The XcmsQueryBlack function returns the color specification in the specified target format
for zero intensity red, green, and blue.

Structures

The XcmsColor and XcmsColorFormat structures are shown on the XcmsColor reference page.

Related Commands

XcmsQueryBlue, XcmsQueryGreen, XcmsQueryRed, XcmsQueryWhite,
XcmsColor

Name

XcmsQueryBlue – obtain a device independent specification for RGBi:0.0/0.0/1.0.

Synopsis

```
Status XcmsQueryBlue(ccc, target_format, color_return)
   XcmsCCC ccc;
   XcmsColorFormat target_format;
   XcmsColor *color_return;
```

Arguments

ccc   Specifies the CCC. Note that the CCC's Client White Point and White Point
                       Adjustment procedures are ignored.

target_format   Specifies the target color specification format.

color_return   Returns the color specification in the specified target format. The white point
                       associated with the returned color specification is the Screen White Point.
                       The value returned in the pixel member is undefined.

Availability

Release 5 and later.

Description

The XcmsQueryBlue function returns the color specification in the specified target format
for full intensity blue and zero intensity red and green.

Structures

The XcmsColor and XcmsColorFormat structures are shown on the XcmsColor reference page.

Related Commands

XcmsQueryBlack, XcmsQueryGreen, XcmsQueryRed, XcmsQueryWhite,
XcmsColor

Reference

Name

XcmsQueryColor – obtain color values.

Synopsis

```
Status XcmsQueryColor(display, colormap, color_in_out, result_format)
    Display *display;
    Colormap colormap;
    XcmsColor *color_in_out;
    XcmsColorFormat result_format;
```

Arguments

display   Specifies the connection to the X server.

colormap   Specifies the colormap.

color_in_out   Specifies the pixel that indicates the color cell to query, and returns the color
                 specification stored for that color cell.

result_format   Specifies the color format for the returned color specifications.

Availability

Release 5 and later.

Description

XcmsQueryColor obtains the RGB value for the colormap cell specified by the *pixel* field
of the specified XcmsColor structure, and then converts the value to the target format specified by the *result_format* argument. If the pixel is not a valid index into the specified
colormap, a BadValue error results.

Errors

BadColor   The *colormap* argument does not name a defined Colormap.

BadValue   The specified pixel does not represent a valid color cell in the specified color-
                 map.

Structures

The XcmsColor and XcmsColorFormat structures are shown on the XcmsColor reference page.

Related Commands

XcmsAllocColor, XcmsStoreColor, XQueryColor, XcmsQueryColors,
XcmsLookupColor, XcmsColor

Name

XcmsQueryColors – obtain color values.

Synopsis

```
Status XcmsQueryColors(display, colormap, colors_in_out, ncolors,
        result_format)
    Display *display;
    Colormap colormap;
    XcmsColor *colors_in_out[];
    unsigned int ncolors;
    XcmsColorFormat result_format;
```

Arguments

display   Specifies the connection to the X server.

colormap   Specifies the colormap.

colors_in_out   Specifies an array of XcmsColor structures, each pixel member indicating the color cell to query. The color specifications for the color cells are returned in these structures.

ncolors   Specifies the number of XcmsColor structures in the colors_in_out array.

result_format   Specifies the color format for the returned color specifications.

Availability

Release 5 and later.

Description

XcmsQueryColors obtains the RGB values for the colors stored in the colormap cells specified by the pixel fields of the specified XcmsColor structures, and then converts the values to the target format specified by the result_format argument. If a pixel is not a valid index into the specified colormap, a BadValue error results. If more than one pixel is in error, the one that gets reported is arbitrary.

Errors

BadColor   The colormap argument does not name a defined Colormap.

BadValue   A specified pixel does not represent a valid color cell in the specified colormap.

Structures

The XcmsColor and XcmsColorFormat structures are shown on the XcmsColor reference page.

Related Commands

XcmsAllocColor, XcmsStoreColor, XQueryColor, XcmsQueryColors, XcmsLookupColor, XcmsColor

XcmsQueryGreen

Name

XcmsQueryGreen – obtain a device-independent specification for RGBi:0.0/1.0/0.0.

Synopsis

```
Status XcmsQueryGreen(ccc, target_format, color_return)
    XcmsCCC ccc;
    XcmsColorFormat target_format;
    XcmsColor *color_return;
```

Arguments

ccc   Specifies the CCC. Note that the CCC's Client White Point and White Point Adjustment procedures are ignored.

target_format   Specifies the target color specification format.

color_return   Returns the color specification in the specified target format. The white point associated with the returned color specification is the Screen White Point. The value returned in the pixel member is undefined.

Availability

Release 5 and later.

Description

The XcmsQueryGreen function returns the color specification in the specified target format for full intensity green and zero intensity red and blue.

Structures

The XcmsColor and XcmsColorFormat structures are shown on the XcmsColor reference page.

Related Commands

XcmsQueryBlack, XcmsQueryBlue, XcmsQueryRed, XcmsQueryWhite, XcmsColor

XcmsQueryRed

Name

XcmsQueryRed – obtain a device-independent specification for RGBi:1.0/0.0/0.0.

Synopsis

```
Status XcmsQueryRed(ccc, target_format, color_return)
    XcmsCCC ccc;
    XcmsColorFormat target_format;
    XcmsColor *color_return;
```

Arguments

ccc   Specifies the CCC. Note that the CCC's Client White Point and White Point
                   Adjustment procedures are ignored.

target_format   Specifies the target color specification format.

color_return   Returns the color specification in the specified target format. The white point
                   associated with the returned color specification is the Screen White Point.
                   The value returned in the pixel member is undefined.

Availability

Release 5 and later.

Description

The XcmsQueryRed function returns the color specification in the specified target format for
full intensity red and zero intensity green and blue.

Structures

The XcmsColor and XcmsColorFormat structures are shown on the XcmsColor reference page.

Related Commands

XcmsQueryBlack, XcmsQueryBlue, XcmsQueryGreen, XcmsQueryWhite,
XcmsColor

XcmsQueryWhite

Name

XcmsQueryWhite – obtain a device-independent specification for RGBi:1.0/1.0/1.0.

Synopsis

```
Status XcmsQueryWhite(ccc, target_format, color_return)
    XcmsCCC ccc;
    XcmsColorFormat target_format;
    XcmsColor *color_return;
```

Arguments

ccc   Specifies the CCC. Note that the CCC's Client White Point and White Point Adjustment procedures are ignored.

target_format Specifies the target color specification format.

color_return   Returns the color specification in the specified target format. The white point associated with the returned color specification is the Screen White Point. The value returned in the pixel member is undefined.

Availability

Release 5 and later.

Description

The XcmsQueryWhite function returns the color specification in the specified target format for full intensity red, green, and blue.

Structures

The XcmsColor and XcmsColorFormat structures are shown on the XcmsColor reference page.

Related Commands

XcmsQueryBlack, XcmsQueryBlue, XcmsQueryGreen, XcmsQueryRed, XcmsColor

Name

XcmsRGB – Xcms color struture.

Structures

The structure for XcmsColor contains:

```
typedef unsigned long XcmsColorFormat;/* Color Specification Format */

typedef struct {
      union {
              XcmsRGB RGB;
              XcmsRGBi RGBi;
              XcmsCIEXYZ CIEXYZ;
              XcmsCIEuvY CIEuvY;
              XcmsCIExyY CIExyY;
              XcmsCIELab CIELab;
              XcmsCIELuv CIELuv;
              XcmsTekHVC TekHVC;
              XcmsPad Pad;
      } spec;
      XcmsColorFormat format;
      unsigned long pixel;
} XcmsColor;                          /* Xcms Color Structure */

typedef double XcmsFloat;

typedef struct {
      unsigned short red;             /* 0x0000 to 0xffff */
      unsigned short green;           /* 0x0000 to 0xffff */
      unsigned short blue;            /* 0x0000 to 0xffff */
} XcmsRGB;                            /* RGB Device */

typedef struct {
      XcmsFloat red;                  /* 0.0 to 1.0 */
      XcmsFloat green;                /* 0.0 to 1.0 */
      XcmsFloat blue;                 /* 0.0 to 1.0 */
} XcmsRGBi;                           /* RGB Intensity */

typedef struct {
      XcmsFloat X;
      XcmsFloat Y;                    /* 0.0 to 1.0 */
      XcmsFloat Z;
} XcmsCIEXYZ;                         /* CIE XYZ */

typedef struct {
      XcmsFloat u_prime;              /* 0.0 to ~0.6 */
      XcmsFloat v_prime;              /* 0.0 to ~0.6 */
      XcmsFloat Y;                    /* 0.0 to 1.0 */
} XcmsCIEuvY;                         /* CIE u'v'Y */
```

Reference

```
typedef struct {
      XcmsFloat x;                    /* 0.0 to ~.75 */
      XcmsFloat y;                    /* 0.0 to ~.85 */
      XcmsFloat Y;                    /* 0.0 to 1.0 */
} XcmsCIExyY;                         /* CIE xyY */

typedef struct {
      XcmsFloat L_star;               /* 0.0 to 100.0 */
      XcmsFloat a_star;
      XcmsFloat b_star;
} XcmsCIELab;                         /* CIE L*a*b* */

typedef struct {
      XcmsFloat L_star;               /* 0.0 to 100.0 */
      XcmsFloat u_star;
      XcmsFloat v_star;
} XcmsCIELuv;                         /* CIE L*u*v* */

typedef struct {
      XcmsFloat H;                    /* 0.0 to 360.0 */
      XcmsFloat V;                    /* 0.0 to 100.0 */
      XcmsFloat C;                    /* 0.0 to 100.0 */
} XcmsTekHVC;                         /* TekHVC */

typedef struct {
      XcmsFloat pad0;
      XcmsFloat pad1;
      XcmsFloat pad2;
      XcmsFloat pad3;
} XcmsPad;                            /* four doubles */
```

Availability

Release 5 and later.

Description

XcmsColor contains a union of substructures, each supporting color specification encoding for a particular color space.

Related Commands

XcmsAllocColor, XcmsStoreColor, XcmsConvertColors,
XcmsColor, XcmsRGB, XcmsCIEXYZ, XcmsCIEuvY,
XcmsCIExyY, XcmsCIELab, XcmsCIELuv, XcmsTekHVC, XcmsPad

Name
XcmsStoreColor – set a device-independent color in a read/write colormap cell.

Synopsis
```
Status XcmsStoreColor(display, colormap, color)
    Display *display;
    Colormap colormap;
    XcmsColor *color;
```

Arguments
display   Specifies the connection to the X server.

colormap   Specifies the colormap.

color   Specifies the color cell and the color to store. Values specified in this Xcms-
              Color structure remain unchanged upon return.

Availability
Release 5 and later.

Description
XcmsStoreColor converts the color specified in the XcmsColor structure into RGB values and then uses this RGB specification in an XColor structure, whose three flags (DoRed, Do-Green, and DoBlue) are set, in a call to XStoreColor to change the color cell specified by the pixel member of the XcmsColor structure. This pixel value must be a valid index for the specified colormap, and the color cell specified by the pixel value must be a read/write cell. If the pixel value is not a valid index, a BadValue error results. If the color cell is unallocated or is allocated read-only, a BadAccess error results. If the colormap is an installed map for its screen, the changes are visible immediately.

XcmsStoreColor returns XcmsSuccess if it succeeded in converting and storing the color. It returns XcmsSuccessWithCompression if it converted the requested device-independent color to the device RGB color space with gamut compression, and it returns XcmsFailure if it could not convert the specified color at all. Note that XStoreColor has no return value; therefore, a XcmsSuccess return value from this function indicates that the conversion to RGB succeeded and the call to XStoreColor was made. To obtain the actual color stored, use XcmsQueryColor. Due to the screen's hardware limitations or gamut compression, the color stored in the colormap may not be identical to the color specified.

Errors
BadAccess   The specified colormap cell was read-only.

BadColor   The colormap argument does not name a defined colormap.

BadValue   The specified pixel does not represent a valid color cell in the specified color-
              map.

Structures

The XcmsColor and XcmsColorFormat structures are shown on the XcmsColor reference page.

Related Commands

XcmsAllocColor, XcmsQueryColor, XcmsStoreColors, XcmsColor

Name

XcmsStoreColors – set device-independent colors in read/write colormap cells.

Synopsis

```
Status XcmsStoreColors(display, colormap, colors, ncolors,
        compression_flags_return)
    Display *display;
    Colormap colormap;
    XcmsColor colors[];
    int ncolors;
    Bool compression_flags_return[];
```

Arguments

display   Specifies the connection to the X server.

colormap   Specifies the colormap.

colors   Specifies an array of XcmsColor structures, each specifying a color cell and
                 the color to store in that cell. Values specified in the array remain unchanged
                 upon return.

ncolors   Specifies the number of XcmsColor structures in the color specification
                 array.

compression_flags_return
                 Specifies an array of ncolors Boolean values for returning compression
                 status. If a non-NULL pointer is supplied, each element of the array is set to
                 True if the corresponding color was compressed, and False otherwise.
                 Pass NULL if the compression status is not useful.

Availability

Release 5 and later.

Description

The XcmsStoreColors function converts the colors specified in the array of XcmsColor
structures into RGB values and then uses these RGB specifications in an XColor structures,
whose three flags (DoRed, DoGreen, and DoBlue) are set, in a call to XStoreColors to
change the color cells specified by the pixel member of the corresponding XcmsColor structure. Each pixel value must be a valid index for the specified colormap, and the color cell
specified by each pixel value must be a read/write cell. If a pixel value is not a valid index, a
BadValue error results. If a color cell is unallocated or is allocated read-only, a BadAccess
error results. If more than one pixel is in error, the one that gets reported is arbitrary. If the
colormap is an installed map for its screen, the changes are visible immediately.

XcmsStoreColors returns XcmsSuccess if it succeeded in converting and storing the
colors. It returns XcmsSuccessWithCompression if one or more of the requested device-
independent colors required gamut compression during conversion to the device RGB color
space, and it returns XcmsFailure if it could not convert one or more of the specified colors
at all. Note that XStoreColors has no return value; therefore, a XcmsSuccess return

value from this function indicates that conversions to RGB succeeded and the call to XStore-Colors was made. To obtain the actual colors stored, use XcmsQueryColors. Due to the screen's hardware limitations or gamut compression, the colors stored in the colormap may not be identical to the colors specified.

Errors

BadAccess   A specified colormap cell was read-only.

BadColor   The *colormap* argument does not name a defined Colormap.

BadValue   The specified pixel does not represent a valid color cell in the specified colormap.

Structures

The XcmsColor and XcmsColorFormat structures are shown on the XcmsColor reference page.

Related Commands

XcmsAllocColor, XcmsQueryColor, XcmsStoreColor, XcmsColor

Name

XcmsTekHVC – Xcms color struture.

Structures

The structure for `XcmsColor` contains:

```
typedef unsigned long XcmsColorFormat;/* Color Specification Format */

typedef struct {
      union {
              XcmsRGB RGB;
              XcmsRGBi RGBi;
              XcmsCIEXYZ CIEXYZ;
              XcmsCIEuvY CIEuvY;
              XcmsCIExyY CIExyY;
              XcmsCIELab CIELab;
              XcmsCIELuv CIELuv;
              XcmsTekHVC TekHVC;
              XcmsPad Pad;
      } spec;
      XcmsColorFormat format;
      unsigned long pixel;
} XcmsColor;                            /* Xcms Color Structure */

typedef double XcmsFloat;

typedef struct {
      unsigned short red;               /* 0x0000 to 0xffff */
      unsigned short green;             /* 0x0000 to 0xffff */
      unsigned short blue;              /* 0x0000 to 0xffff */
} XcmsRGB;                              /* RGB Device */

typedef struct {
      XcmsFloat red;                    /* 0.0 to 1.0 */
      XcmsFloat green;                  /* 0.0 to 1.0 */
      XcmsFloat blue;                   /* 0.0 to 1.0 */
} XcmsRGBi;                             /* RGB Intensity */·

typedef struct {
      XcmsFloat X;
      XcmsFloat Y;                      /* 0.0 to 1.0 */
      XcmsFloat Z;
} XcmsCIEXYZ;                           /* CIE XYZ */

typedef struct {
      XcmsFloat u_prime;                /* 0.0 to ~0.6 */
      XcmsFloat v_prime;                /* 0.0 to ~0.6 */
      XcmsFloat Y;                      /* 0.0 to 1.0 */
} XcmsCIEuvY;                           /* CIE u'v'Y */
```

Reference

```
typedef struct {
      XcmsFloat x;                    /* 0.0 to ~.75 */
      XcmsFloat y;                    /* 0.0 to ~.85 */
      XcmsFloat Y;                    /* 0.0 to 1.0 */
} XcmsCIExyY;                         /* CIE xyY */

typedef struct {
      XcmsFloat L_star;              /* 0.0 to 100.0 */
      XcmsFloat a_star;
      XcmsFloat b_star;
} XcmsCIELab;                         /* CIE L*a*b* */

typedef struct {
      XcmsFloat L_star;              /* 0.0 to 100.0 */
      XcmsFloat u_star;
      XcmsFloat v_star;
} XcmsCIELuv;                         /* CIE L*u*v* */

typedef struct {
      XcmsFloat H;                    /* 0.0 to 360.0 */
      XcmsFloat V;                    /* 0.0 to 100.0 */
      XcmsFloat C;                    /* 0.0 to 100.0 */
} XcmsTekHVC;                         /* TekHVC */

typedef struct {
      XcmsFloat pad0;
      XcmsFloat pad1;
      XcmsFloat pad2;
      XcmsFloat pad3;
} XcmsPad;                            /* four doubles */
```

Availability

Release 5 and later.

Description

The XcmsColor structure contains a union of substructures, each supporting color specification encoding for a particular color space.

Related Commands

XcmsAllocColor, XcmsStoreColor, XcmsConvertColors,
XcmsColor, XcmsRGB, XcmsCIEXYZ, XcmsCIEuvY,
XcmsCIExyY, XcmsCIELab, XcmsCIELuv, XcmsPad

Name

XcmsTekHVCQueryMaxC – find the maximum chroma for a given TekHVC Hue and Value.

Synopsis

```
Status XcmsTekHVCQueryMaxC(ccc, hue, value, color_return)
    XcmsCCC ccc;
    XcmsFloat hue;
    XcmsFloat value;
    XcmsColor *color_return;
```

Arguments

ccc   Specifies the CCC. Note that the CCC's Client White Point and White Point Adjustment procedures are ignored.

hue   Specifies the Hue at which to find the maximum Chroma.

value   Specifies the Value at which to find the maximum Chroma.

color_return Returns the maximum Chroma along with the actual Hue and Value. The white point associated with the returned color specification is the Screen White Point. The value returned in the pixel member is undefined.

Availability

Release 5 and later.

Description

XcmsTekHVCQueryMaxC determines the maximum displayable Chroma for a given a Hue and Value. The maximum Chroma is returned in the *color_return* argument, along with the actual Hue and Value at which it occurs. Note that because of gamut compression or hardware limitations, the returned Hue and Value may differ from those specified by the *hue* and *value* arguments.

Structures

The XcmsColor and XcmsColorFormat structures are shown on the XcmsColor reference page.

Related Commands

XcmsTekHVCQueryMaxV, XcmsTekHVCQueryMaxVC,
XcmsTekHVCQueryMaxVSamples, XcmsTekHVCQueryMinV,
XcmsColor

Name

XcmsTekHVCQueryMaxV – find the maximum Value for a given TekHVC Hue and Chroma.

Synopsis

```
Status XcmsTekHVCQueryMaxV(ccc, hue, chroma, color_return)
    XcmsCCC ccc;
    XcmsFloat hue;
    XcmsFloat chroma;
    XcmsColor *color_return;
```

Arguments

ccc   Specifies the CCC. Note that the CCC's Client White Point and White Point Adjustment procedures are ignored.

hue   Specifies the Hue at which to find the maximum Value.

chroma   Specifies the chroma at which to find maximum Value.

color_return   Returns the maximum Value along with the Hue and Chroma. The white point associated with the returned color specification is the Screen White Point. The value returned in the pixel member is undefined.

Availability

Release 5 and later.

Description

XcmsTekHVCQueryMaxV determines the maximum displayable Value for a given a Hue and Chroma. The maximum Value is returned in the color_return argument along with the actual Hue and Chroma at which it occurs. Note that because of gamut compression or hardware limitations, the returned Hue and Chroma may differ from those specified by the hue and chroma arguments.

Structures

The XcmsColor and XcmsColorFormat structures are shown on the XcmsColor reference page.

Related Commands

XcmsTekHVCQueryMaxC, XcmsTekHVCQueryMaxVC,
XcmsTekHVCQueryMaxVSamples, XcmsTekHVCQueryMinV, XcmsColor

Name

XcmsTekHVCQueryMaxVC – find the maximum Chroma and the Value at which it occurs given a TekHVC Hue.

Synopsis

```
Status XcmsTekHVCQueryMaxVC(ccc, hue, color_return)
    XcmsCCC ccc;
    XcmsFloat hue;
    XcmsColor *color_return;
```

Arguments

ccc   Specifies the CCC. Note that the CCC's Client White Point and White Point Adjustment procedures are ignored.

hue   Specifies the Hue at which to find the maximum Chroma.

color_return   Returns the maximum Chroma, the Value at which that maximum Chroma is reached and actual Hue. The white point associated with the returned color specification is the Screen White Point. The value returned in the pixel member is undefined.

Availability

Release 5 and later.

Description

XcmsTekHVCQueryMaxVC determines the maximum displayable Chroma for a given Hue, and the Value at which that Chroma is reached. The Chroma and Value are returned in the *color_return* argument along with the actual Hue at which they occur. Note that because of gamut compression or hardware limitations, the returned Hue may differ from that specified by the *hue* argument.

Structures

The XcmsColor and XcmsColorFormat structures are shown on the XcmsColor reference page.

Related Commands

XcmsTekHVCQueryMaxC, XcmsTekHVCQueryMaxV,
XcmsTekHVCQueryMaxVSamples, XcmsTekHVCQueryMinV, XcmsColor

XcmsTekHVCQueryMaxVSamples

Name

XcmsTekHVCQueryMaxVSamples – return the boundaries of the TekHVC gamut for a given Hue.

Synopsis

```
Status XcmsTekHVCQueryMaxVSamples(ccc, hue, colors_return, nsamples)
    XcmsCCC ccc;
    XcmsFloat hue;
    XcmsColor colors_return[];
    unsigned int nsamples;
```

Arguments

ccc　　　　　Specifies the CCC. Note that the CCC's Client White Point and White Point Adjustment procedures are ignored.

hue　　　　　Specifies the Hue at which to find the maximum Chroma/Value samples.

colors_return Specifies an array of *nsamples* XcmsColor structures into which the returned color specifications will be stored.

nsamples　　Specifies the number of samples.

Availability

Release 5 and later.

Description

For the specified Hue, XcmsTekHVCQueryMaxVSamples partitions the legal values of Chroma into *nsamples* samples, and queries the maximum Value for the Hue and each Chroma sample. The resulting values are stored into the elements of the *colors_return* array. This function can be used to plot the upper boundary of the TekHVC device gamut for a given Hue.

Structures

The XcmsColor and XcmsColorFormat structures are shown on the XcmsColor reference page.

Related Commands

XcmsTekHVCQueryMaxC, XcmsTekHVCQueryMaxV,
XcmsTekHVCQueryMaxVSamples, XcmsTekHVCQueryMinV, XcmsColor

Name

XcmsTekHVCQueryMinV – obtain the TekHVC coordinates.

Synopsis

```
Status XcmsTekHVCQueryMinV(ccc, hue, chroma, color_return)
    XcmsCCC ccc;
    XcmsFloat hue;
    XcmsFloat chroma;
    XcmsColor *color_return;
```

Arguments

ccc   Specifies the CCC. Note that the CCC's Client White Point and White Point Adjustment procedures are ignored.

hue   Specifies the Hue at which to find the minimum Value.

chroma   Specifies the chroma at which to find the minimum Value.

color_return   Returns the minimum Value and the actual Hue and Chroma. The white point associated with the returned color specification is the Screen White Point. The value returned in the pixel member is undefined.

Availability

Release 5 and later.

Description

XcmsTekHVCQueryMinV determines the minimum displayable Value for a given a Hue and Chroma. The minimum Value is returned in the *color_return* argument along with the actual Hue and Chroma at which it occurs. Note that because of gamut compression or hardware limitations, the returned Hue and Chroma may differ from those specified by the *hue* and *chroma* arguments.

Structures

The XcmsColor and XcmsColorFormat structures are shown on the XcmsColor reference page.

Related Commands

XcmsTekHVCQueryMaxC, XcmsTekHVCQueryMaxV,
XcmsTekHVCQueryMaxVC, XcmsTekHVCQueryMaxVSamples, XcmsColor

Reference

XContextDependentDrawing

Name

XContextDependentDrawing – get a hint about context dependencies in the text of the locale.

Synopsis

```
Bool XContextDependentDrawing( font_set )
    XFontSet font_set;
```

Arguments

font_set   Specifies the font set.

Availability

Release 5 and later.

Description

If XContextDependentDrawing returns True, then text in the locale of the specified font set may contain context dependencies. If it returns False, then text drawn with the font set does not contain context dependencies.

When text contains context dependencies, a character may be rendered with different glyphs in different locations in the string, a single character may be rendered with multiple font glyphs, and multiple characters may be rendered with a single glyph. When there are context dependencies, drawing the characters of a string indivdually may have different results than drawing the string with a single call to one of the internationalized text drawing functions. When changing or inserting characters into an already drawn string, the characters surrounding the change may also need to be redrawn.

Related Commands

XCreateFontSet, XExtentsOfFontSet, XFontsOfFontSet,
XBaseFontNameListOfFontSet, XLocaleOfFontSet

Name

XCreateFontSet – create a font set.

Synopsis

```
XFontSet XCreateFontSet(display, base_font_name_list,
        missing_charset_list_return, missing_charset_count_return,
        def_string_return)
    Display *display;
    char *base_font_name_list;
    char ***missing_charset_list_return;
    int *missing_charset_count_return;
    char **def_string_return;
```

Arguments

display   Specifies the connection to the X server.

base_font_name_list
                    Specifies the base font names.

missing_charset_list_return
                    Returns the missing charsets.

missing_charset_count_return
                    Returns the number of missing charsets.

def_string_return
                    Returns the string drawn for missing charsets.

Availability

Release 5 and later.

Description

XCreateFontSet creates a font set for the specified display. The font set is bound to the current locale when XCreateFontSet is called. The *font_set* may be used in subsequent calls to obtain font and character information, and to image text in the locale of the *font_set*.

The *base_font_name_list* argument is a comma-separated list of base font names which Xlib uses to load the fonts needed for the locale. The string is null-terminated, and is assumed to be in the Host Portable Character Encoding; otherwise, the result is implementation dependent. Whitespace immediately on either side of a separating comma is ignored.

Use of XLFD font names permits Xlib to obtain the fonts needed for a variety of locales from a single locale-independent base font name. When used, this single base font name should name a family of fonts whose members are encoded in the various charsets needed by the locales of interest.

Alternatively, an XLFD base font name can explicitly name a charset needed for the locale. This allows the user to specify an exact font for use with a charset required by a locale, fully controlling the font selection.

If a base font name is not an XLFD name, Xlib will attempt to obtain an XLFD name from the font properties for the font. If this action is successful in obtaining an XLFD name, the `XBaseFontNameListOfFontSet` function will return this XLFD name instead of the client-supplied name.

The following algorithm is used to select the fonts that will be used to display text with the `XFontSet`:

For each font charset required by the locale, the base font name list is searched for the first one of the following cases that names a set of fonts that exist at the server:

1.   The first XLFD-conforming base font name that specifies the required charset or a superset of the required charset in its `CharSetRegistry` and `CharSetEncoding` fields The implementation may use a base font name whose specified charset is a superset of the required charset, for example, an ISO8859-1 font for an ASCII charset.

2.   The first set of one or more XLFD-conforming base font names that specify one or more charsets that can be remapped to support the required charset. The Xlib implementation may recognize various mappings from a required charset to one or more other charsets, and use the fonts for those charsets. For example, JIS Roman is ASCII with tilde and backslash replaced by yen and overbar; Xlib may load an ISO8859-1 font to support this character set, if a JIS Roman font is not available.

3.   The first XLFD-conforming font name, or the first non-XLFD font name for which an XLFD font name can be obtained, combined with the required charset (replacing the `CharSetRegistry` and `CharSetEncoding` fields in the XLFD font name). As in case 1, the implementation may use a charset which is a superset of the required charset.

4.   The first font name that can be mapped in some implementation-dependent manner to one or more fonts that support imaging text in the charset.

For example, assume a locale required the charsets:

```
ISO8859-1
JISX0208.1983
JISX0201.1976
GB2312-1980.0
```

Users could supply a *base_font_name_list* which explicitly specifies the charsets, insuring that specific fonts get used if they exist:

```
"-JIS-Fixed-Medium-R-Normal—26-180-100-100-C-240-JISX0208.1983-0,\
-JIS-Fixed-Medium-R-Normal—26-180-100-100-C-120-JISX0201.1976-0,\
-GB-Fixed-Medium-R-Normal—26-180-100-100-C-240-GB2312-1980.0,\
-Adobe-Courier-Bold-R-Normal—25-180-75-75-M-150-ISO8859-1"
```

Or they could supply a *base_font_name_list* which omits the charsets, letting Xlib select font charsets required for the locale:

```
"-JIS-Fixed-Medium-R-Normal—26-180-100-100-C-240,\
-JIS-Fixed-Medium-R-Normal—26-180-100-100-C-120,\
-GB-Fixed-Medium-R-Normal—26-180-100-100-C-240,\
-Adobe-Courier-Bold-R-Normal—25-180-100-100-M-150"
```

Or they could simply supply a single base font name which allows Xlib to select from all available fonts which meet certain minimum XLFD property requirements:

```
"-*-*-*-R-Normal-*-180-100-100-*-*"
```

If XCreateFontSet is unable to create the font set, either because there is insufficient memory or because the current locale is not supported, XCreateFontSet returns NULL, *missing_charset_list_return* is set to NULL, and *missing_charset_count_return* is set to zero. If fonts exist for all of the charsets required by the current locale, XCreateFontSet returns a valid XFontSet, *missing_charset_list_return* is set to NULL, and *missing_charset_count_return* is set to zero.

If no font exists for one or more of the required charsets, XCreateFontSet sets *missing_charset_list_return* to a list of one or more null-terminated charset names for which no font exists, and sets *missing_charset_count_return* to the number of missing fonts. The charsets are from the list of the required charsets for the encoding of the locale, and do not include any charsets to which Xlib may be able to remap a required charset.

If no font exists for any of the required charsets, or if the locale definition in Xlib requires that a font exist for a particular charset and a font is not found for that charset, XCreateFontSet returns NULL. Otherwise, XCreateFontSet returns a valid XFontSet to *font_set*.

When an Xmb/wc drawing or measuring function is called with an XFontSet that has missing charsets, some characters in the locale will not be drawable. If *def_string_return* is non-NULL, XCreateFontSet returns a pointer to a string which represents the glyph(s) which are drawn with this XFontSet when the charsets of the available fonts do not include all font glyph(s) required to draw a codepoint. The string does not necessarily consist of valid characters in the current locale and is not necessarily drawn with the fonts loaded for the font set, but the client can draw and measure the "default glyphs" by including this string in a string being drawn or measured with the XFontSet.

If the string returned to *def_string_return* is the empty string (" "), no glyphs are drawn, and the escapement is zero. The returned string is null-terminated. It is owned by Xlib and should not be modified or freed by the client. It will be freed by a call to XFreeFontSet with the associated XFontSet. Until freed, its contents will not be modified by Xlib.

The client is responsible for constructing an error message from the missing charset and default string information, and may choose to continue operation in the case that some fonts did not exist.

The returned XFontSet and missing charset list should be freed with XFreeFontSet and XFreeStringList, respectively. The client-supplied *base_font_name_list* may be freed by the client after calling XCreateFontSet.

Related Commands

XExtentsofFontSet, XFontsOfFontSet, XFreeFontSet

Name

XCreateIC – create an input context.

Synopsis

```
XIC XCreateIC(im, ...)
    XIM im;
```

Arguments

im   Specifies the input method.

...   Specifies the variable length argument list to set XIC values.

Availability

Release 5 and later.

Description

XCreateIC creates an input context associated with the specified input method. The first argument to this function is the "parent" input method, and it is followed by a NULL-terminated variable-length argument list of input context attribute name/value pairs. The tables below list the standard attribute names and their types. Note that the XNInputStyle attribute and XNFontSet sub-attribute for the Preedit and Status areas must be specified when the IC is created. XNSpotLocation must be specified for the Preedit area if the pre-edit interaction style is XIMPreeditPosition. All the Preedit and Status callbacks must be specified in the call to XCreateIC if the interaction style is XIMPreeditCallbacks or XIMStatus-Callbacks. Any other attributes may be set with XCreateIC, but are not required.

Input Context Attributes

Name	Type	Notes
XNInputStyle	XIMStyle	Required at IC creation; may not be changed.
XNClientWindow	Window	Must be set before IC use; may not be changed.
XNFocusWindow	Window	Changes may cause geometry negotiation.
XNResourceName	char *	
XNResourceClass	char *	
XNGeometryCallback	XIMCallback *	
XNFilterEvents	unsigned long	Read-only attribute; may not be set.
XNPreeditAttributes	XVaNestedList	See sub-attributes below.
XNStatusAttributes	XVaNestedList	See sub-attributes below.

Preedit and Status Area Sub-attributes

Name	Type	Notes
XNArea	XRectangle *	
XNAreaNeeded	XRectangle *	
XNSpotLocation	XPoint *	Required at IC creation for XIMPreedit-Position style.
XNColormap	Colormap	
XNStdColormap	Atom	
XNForeground	unsigned long	
XNBackground	unsigned long	
XNBackgroundPixmap	Pixmap	
XNFontSet	XFontSet	Required at IC creation; changes may cause geometry negotiation.
XNLineSpacing	int	Changes may cause geometry negotiation.
XNCursor	Cursor	
XNPreeditStartCallback	XIMCallback *	Required at IC creation for XIMPreedit-Callbacks style.
XNPreeditDoneCallback	XIMCallback *	Required at IC creation for XIMPreedit-Callbacks style.
XNPreeditDrawCallback	XIMCallback *	Required at IC creation for XIMPreedit-Callbacks style.
XNPreeditCaretCallback	XIMCallback *	Required at IC creation for XIMPreedit-Callbacks style.
XNStatusStartCallback	XIMCallback *	Required at IC creation for XIMStatus-Callbacks style.
XNStatusDoneCallback	XIMCallback *	Required at IC creation for XIMStatus-Callbacks style.
XNStatusDrawCallback	XIMCallback *	Required at IC creation for XIMStatus-Callbacks style.

In addition to the attribute names above, the special name XNVaNestedList indicates that the following argument is a XVaNestedList of attribute name/value pairs. When a nested list is encountered in an argument list, the contents of the nested list are processed as if they appeared in the original argument list at that point.

XCreateIC returns a NULL value if no input context could be created. A NULL value could be returned for any of the following reasons:

• A required argument was not set.

• A read-only argument was set (for example, XNFilterEvents).

• The argument name is not recognized.

• The input method encountered an implementation-dependent error.

XCreateIC can generate `BadAtom`, `BadColor`, `BadPixmap`, and `BadWindow` errors.

Errors

BadAtom   A value for an Atom argument does not name a defined Atom.

BadColor   A value for a Colormap argument does not name a defined Colormap.

BadPixmap   A value for a Pixmap argument does not name a defined Pixmap.

BadWindow   A value for a Window argument does not name a defined Window.

Related Commands

XOpenIM, XSetICFocus, XSetICValues, XDestroyIC, XIMOfIC,
XmbResetIC, XwcResetIC

Reference

XDefaultString

Name

XDefaultString – return the default string used for text conversion.

Synopsis

```
char *XDefaultString( )
```

Availability

Release 5 and later.

Description

XDefaultString returns the default string used by Xlib for text conversion (for example, in XmbTextListToTextProperty). The default string is the string in the current locale which is output when an unconvertible character is found during text conversion. If the string returned by XDefaultString is the empty string (""), no character is output in the converted text. XDefaultString does not return NULL.

The string returned by XDefaultString is independent of the default string for text drawing; see XCreateFontSet to obtain the default string for an XFontSet.

The returned string is null-terminated. It is owned by Xlib and should not be modified or freed by the client. It may be freed after the current locale is changed. Until freed, it will not be modified by Xlib.

Related Commands

XmbTextListToTextProperty, XwcTextListToTextProperty, XmbTextPropertyToTextList, XwcTextPropertyToTextList, XwcFreeStringList

XDestroyIC

Name

XDestroyIC – destroy an input context.

Synopsis

```
void XDestroyIC(ic)
    XIC ic;
```

Arguments

ic   Specifies the input context.

Availability

Release 5 and later.

Description

XDestroyIC destroys the specified input context. Once destroyed, the input context should no longer be used.

Related Commands

XSetICFocus, XSetICValues, XCreateIC, XIMOfIC, XmbResetIC, XwcResetIC

Name

XDisplayOfIM – get the display of an input method.

Synopsis

```
Display * XDisplayOfIM(im)
    XIM im;
```

Arguments

im   Specifies the input method.

Availability

Release 5 and later.

Description

XDisplayOfIM returns the display associated with the specified input method.

Related Commands

XOpenIM, XCloseIM, XGetIMValues, XLocaleOfIM

Name

_XEditResCheckMessages – event handler for the Editres protocol.

Synopsis

```
#include <X11/Xmu/Editres.h>
XtAddEventHandler(shell, (EventMask) 0, True, _XEditResCheckMessages, NULL);
```

Arguments

shell   Specifies the shell widget which is to participate in the Editres protocol.

Availablity

Release 5 and later.

Description

_XEditResCheckMessages, though misleadingly named, is a public function in the Xmu library. It is an event handler, which, when registered on a shell widget, allows that shell widget to participate in the Editres protocol. Shell widgets which are subclasses of the Athena VendorShell widget have this event handler registered automatically. When registering this event handler with XtAddEventHandler, pass an event mask of 0, specify that non-maskable events should be handled by passing True as the third argument, and pass NULL client data as the last argument.

Related Commands

None

Reference

Name

XExtentsOfFontSet – obtain the maximum extents structure for a font set

Synopsis

```
XFontSetExtents *XExtentsOfFontSet( font_set )
      XFontSet font_set;
```

Arguments

font_set   Specifies the font set.

Availability

Release 5 and later.

Description

The XExtentsOfFontSet function returns an XFontSetExtents structure for the given font set.

The XFontSetExtents structure is owned by Xlib and should not be modified or freed by the client. It will be freed by a call to XFreeFontSet with the associated XFontSet. Until freed, its contents will not be modified by Xlib.

Structures

The XFontSetExtents structure contains:

```
typedef struct {
      XRectangle max_ink_extent;        /*over all drawable characters*/
      XRectangle max_logical_extent;    /*over all drawable characters*/
} XFontSetExtents;
```

The XRectangles used to return font set metrics are the usual Xlib screen-oriented XRectangles, with x, y giving the upper left corner, and width and height always positive.

The max_ink_extent member gives the maximum extent, over all drawable characters, of the rectangles which bound the character glyph image drawn in the foreground color, relative to a constant origin. See XmbTextExtents and XwcTextExtents for detailed semantics.

The max_logical_extent member gives the maximum extent, over all drawable characters, of the rectangles which specify minimum spacing to other graphical features, relative to a constant origin. Other graphical features drawn by the client, for example, a border surrounding the text, should not intersect this rectangle. The max_logical_extent member should be used to compute minimum interline spacing and the minimum area which must be allowed in a text field to draw a given number of arbitrary characters.

Due to context-dependent rendering, appending a given character to a string may increase the string's extent by an amount which exceeds the font's max extent:

```
max possible added extent = (max_extent * <total # chars>) - prev_string_extent
```

Related Commands

XCreateFontSet, XFontsOfFontSet

XFilterEvent

Name

XFilterEvent – filter X events for an input method.

Synopsis

```
Bool XFilterEvent(event, w)
    XEvent *event;
    Window w;
```

Arguments

event   Specifies the event to filter.

w   Specifies the window for which the filter is to be applied.

Availability

Release 5 and later.

Description

XFilterEvent passes the specified event to any event filters registered for the specified window. This allows input methods to intercept and respond to events that they are interested in. Internationalized clients should call XFilterEvent from their event loops, generally directly after calling XNextEvent. If XFilterEvent returns True, then some input method has filtered the event, and the client should not dispatch it any further. If XFilterEvent returns False, the client should continue processing it.

If the window argument is None, XFilterEvent applies the filter to the window specified in the XEvent structure. The window argument is provided so that layers above Xlib that do event redirection can indicate to which window an event has been redirected.

If a grab has occurred in the client, and XFilterEvent returns True, the client should ungrab the keyboard.

Input methods register event filters using a non-public mechanism internal to Xlib.

Related Commands

XNextEvent

XFlushGC

Name

XFlushGC – force cached GC changes to the server.

Synopsis

```
void XFlushGC(display, gc)
    Display *display;
    GC gc;
```

Arguments

display   Specifies the connection to the X server.

gc   Specifies the GC.

Availability

Release 5 and later.

Description

Xlib normally defers sending changes to the components of a GC to the server until a graphics function is actually called with that GC. This permits batching of component changes into a single server request. In some circumstances, however, it may be necessary for the client to explicitly force sending of the changes to the server. An example might be when a protocol extension uses the GC indirectly, in such a way that the extension interface cannot know what GC will be used. In a case like this, the extension library could use XFlushGC to force any cached changes to the GC it will use to be flushed to the server.

Related Commands

None

Name

XFontsOfFontSet – get the list of fonts used by a font set.

Synopsis

```
int XFontsOfFontSet(font_set, font_struct_list_return,
        font_name_list_return)
    XFontSet font_set;
    XFontStruct ***font_struct_list_return;
    char ***font_name_list_return;
```

Arguments

font_set   Specifies the font set.

font_struct_list_return
                Returns the list of font structs.

font_name_list_return
                Returns the list of font names.

Availability

Release 5 and later.

Description

XFontsOfFontSet returns a list of one or more XFontStructs and font names for the fonts used by the given font set. A list of pointers to the XFontStruct structures is returned to *font_struct_list_return*. A list of pointers to null-terminated, fully specified, font name strings in the locale of the font set is returned to *font_name_list_return*. The number of elements in each array is returned as the value of the function. The arrays are in the same order, and their elements correspond to one another.

Because it is not guaranteed that a given character will be imaged using a single font glyph, there is no provision for mapping a character or default string to the font properties, font ID, or direction hint for the font for the character. The client may access the XFontStruct list to obtain these values for all the fonts currently in use.

It is not required that fonts be loaded from the server at the creation of an XFontSet. Xlib may choose to cache font data, loading it only as needed to draw text or compute text dimensions. Therefore, existence of the per_char metrics in the XFontStruct structures in the XFontStructSet is undefined. Also, note that all properties in the XFontStruct structures are in the STRING encoding.

The XFontStruct and font name lists are owned by Xlib and should not be modified or freed by the client. They will be freed by a call to XFreeFontSet on the associated XFontSet. Until freed, their contents will not be modified by Xlib.

Related Commands

XCreateFontSet, XExtentsOfFontSet, XBaseFontNameListOfFontSet,
XLocaleOfFontSet

Name

XFreeFontSet – free a font set.

Synopsis

```
void XFreeFontSet(display, font_set)
    Display *display;
    XFontSet font_set;
```

Arguments

display   Specifies the connection to the X server.

font_set   Specifies the font set.

Availability

Release 5 and later.

Description

XFreeFontSet frees the specified font set. The associated base font name list, font name list, XFontStruct list, and XFontSetExtents, if any, are freed.

Related Commands

XExtentsofFontSet, XFontsOfFontSet, XCreateFontSet

Reference

Name

XGetICValues – get input context attributes.

Synopsis

```
char * XGetICValues(ic, ... )
    XIC ic;
```

Arguments

ic	Specifies the input context.
...	Specifies the variable length argument list to set or get XIC values.

Availability

Release 5 and later.

Description

XGetICValues queries the values of input context attributes. The first argument is the input context, and it is followed by a NULL-terminated variable-length argument list of attribute name/value pairs. The standard attributes and their types are listed in the tables below.

Input Context Attributes

Name	Type	Notes
XNInputStyle	XIMStyle	Required at IC creation; may not be changed.
XNClientWindow	Window	Must be set before IC use; may not be changed.
XNFocusWindow	Window	Changes may cause geometry negotiation.
XNResourceName	char *	
XNResourceClass	char *	
XNGeometryCallback	XIMCallback *	
XNFilterEvents	unsigned long	Read-only attribute; may not be set.
XNPreeditAttributes	XVaNestedList	See sub-attributes below.
XNStatusAttributes	XVaNestedList	See sub-attributes below.

Preedit and Status Area Sub-attributes

Name	Type	Notes
XNArea	XRectangle *	
XNAreaNeeded	XRectangle *	
XNSpotLocation	XPoint *	Required at IC creation for XIMPreeditPosition style.
XNColormap	Colormap	

Preedit and Status Area Sub-attributes (Continued)

Name	Type	Notes
XNStdColormap	Atom	
XNForeground	unsigned long	
XNBackground	unsigned long	
XNBackgroundPixmap	Pixmap	
XNFontSet	XFontSet	Required at IC creation; changes may cause geometry negotiation.
XNLineSpacing	int	Changes may cause geometry negotiation.
XNCursor	Cursor	
XNPreeditStartCallback	XIMCallback *	Required at IC creation for XIMPreedit-Callbacks style.
XNPreeditDoneCallback	XIMCallback *	Required at IC creation for XIMPreedit-Callbacks style.
XNPreeditDrawCallback	XIMCallback *	Required at IC creation for XIMPreedit-Callbacks style.
XNPreeditCaretCallback	XIMCallback *	Required at IC creation for XIMPreedit-Callbacks style.
XNStatusStartCallback	XIMCallback *	Required at IC creation for XIMStatus-Callbacks style.
XNStatusDoneCallback	XIMCallback *	Required at IC creation for XIMStatus-Callbacks style.
XNStatusDrawCallback	XIMCallback *	Required at IC creation for XIMStatus-Callbacks style.

In addition to the attribute names above, the special name XNVaNestedList indicates that the following argument is a XVaNestedList of attribute name/value pairs. When a nested list is encountered in an argument list, the contents of the nested list are processed as if they appeared in the original argument list at that point.

The XGetICValues function returns NULL if no error occurred; otherwise, it returns the name of the first attribute that could not be obtained. An attribute could be not obtained for any of the following reasons:

•   The attribute name is not recognized.

•   The input method encountered an implementation dependent error.

Each attribute value argument to XGetICValues (the argument that follows the attribute name) must be the address of a location into which the value is to be stored. For attributes that are pointer types (XNArea, for example), XGetICValues returns a pointer to a copy of the attribute value. In this case, the client must free the memory allocated for that copy with XFree.

Reference

Related Commands

XCreateIC, XOpenIM, XSetICFocus, XSetICValues, XmbResetIC, XwcResetIC

Name

XGetIMValues – obtain input method information.

Synopsis

```
char * XGetIMValues(im, ...)
    XIM im;
```

Arguments

im   Specifies the input method.

...   Specifies the variable length argument list to get XIM values.

Availability

Release 5 and later.

Description

XGetIMValues queries the values of input method attributes. The first argument is the input method, and it is followed by a NULL-terminated variable-length argument list of attribute name/value pairs. Only one standard attribute is defined by Xlib: XNQueryInputStyle. It is of type XIMStyles * (shown below) and is used to query the input styles supported by the input method. A client should always query the input method to determine which styles are supported. The client should then find an input style it is capable of supporting, and use that style when creating input contexts. If the client cannot find an input style that it can support it should negotiate with the user the continuation of the program (exit, choose another input method, and so on).

The attribute value argument (which follows the attribute name argument) must be the address of a location where the returned value will be stored. For the XNQueryInputStyle attribute, the client must pass the address of a variable of type XIMStyles *, and is responsible for freeing the memory allocated for the XIMStyles data structure with XFree.

XGetIMValues returns NULL if it succeeds. Otherwise it returns the name of the first attribute for which a value could not be obtained.

Structures

```
#define XIMPreeditArea0x0001L
#define XIMPreeditCallbacks0x0002L
#define XIMPreeditPosition0x0004L
#define XIMPreeditNothing0x0008L
#define XIMPreeditNone0x0010L
#define XIMStatusArea0x0100L
#define XIMStatusCallbacks0x0200L
#define XIMStatusNothing0x0400L
#define XIMStatusNone0x0800L

typedef unsigned long XIMStyle;
```

Reference

```
typedef struct {
    unsigned short count_styles;
    XIMStyle *supported_styles;
} XIMStyles;
```

Related Commands
XOpenIM, XCloseIM, XDisplayOfIM, XLocaleOfIM

Name

XIMOfIC – obtain the input method of an input context.

Synopsis

```
XIM XIMOfIC(ic)
    XIC ic;
```

Arguments

ic   Specifies the input context.

Availability

Release 5 and later.

Description

XIMOfIC returns the input method associated with a given input context.

Related Commands

XSetICFocus, XSetICValues, XCreateIC, XDestroyIC, XmbResetIC,
XwcResetIC

Name

XLocaleOfFontSet – get the locale of a font set.

Synopsis

```
char *XLocaleOfFontSet(font_set)
    XFontSet font_set;
```

Arguments

font_set   Specifies the font set.

Availability

Release 5 and later.

Description

The `XLocaleOfFontSet` function returns the name of the locale bound to the specified `XFontSet`, as a null-terminated string.

The returned locale name string is owned by Xlib and should not be modified or freed by the client. It may be freed by a call to `XFreeFontSet` with the associated `XFontSet`. Until freed, it will not be modified by Xlib.

Related Commands

`XCreateFontSet`, `XExtentsOfFontSet`, `XFontsOfFontSet`, `XBaseFontNameListOfFontSet`, `XContextDependentDrawing`

Name

XLocaleOfIM – get the locale of an input method.

Synopsis

```
char * XLocaleOfIM( im )
    XIM im;
```

Arguments

im   Specifies the input method.

Availability

Release 5 and later.

Description

XLocaleOfIM returns the name of the locale associated with the specified input method. The returned string is owned by Xlib and should not be freed by the client.

Related Commands

XOpenIM, XCloseIM, XGetIMValues, XDisplayOfIM

Name

XmbDrawImageString – draw internationalized multi-byte image text.

Synopsis

```
void XmbDrawImageString(display, drawable, font_set, gc, x, y, string,
        num_bytes)
    Display *display;
    Drawable drawable;
    XFontSet font_set;
    GC gc;
    int x, y;
    char *string;
    int num_bytes;
```

Arguments

display	Specifies the connection to the X server.
drawable	Specifies the drawable.
font_set	Specifies the font set.
gc	Specifies the GC.
x, y	Specifies the starting position and baseline of the text, relative to the origin of the specified drawable.
string	Specifies the character string.
num_bytes	Specifies the number of bytes in the string argument.

Availability

Release 5 and later.

Description

XmbDrawImageString fills a destination rectangle with the background pixel defined in the GC and then paints the specified multi-byte text with the foreground pixel. The filled rectangle is the rectangle returned to *overall_logical_return* by XmbTextExtents for the same text and XFontSet.

When the XFontSet has missing charsets, each unavailable character is drawn with the default string returned by XCreateFontSet. The behavior for an invalid codepoint is undefined.

XmbDrawImageString draws with fonts from the font set rather than the font of the GC. For this reason, it may modify the font value of the GC. Except for the font, it uses the same GC components as its pre-X11R5 analog XDrawImageString.

Related Commands

XDrawImageString, XDrawString, XDrawText, XmbDrawString, XmbDrawText, XwcDrawImageString

XmbDrawString

Name

XmbDrawString – draw internationalized multi-byte text.

Synopsis

```
void XmbDrawString(display, drawable, font_set, gc, x, y, string,
        num_bytes)
    Display *display;
    Drawable drawable;
    XFontSet font_set;
    GC gc;
    int x, y;
    char *string;
    int num_bytes;
```

Arguments

display	Specifies the connection to the X server.
drawable	Specifies the drawable.
font_set	Specifies the font set.
gc	Specifies the GC.
x, y	Specifies the starting position and baseline of the text, relative to the origin of the specified drawable.
string	Specifies the character string.
num_bytes	Specifies the number of bytes in the string argument.

Availability

Release 5 and later.

Description

XmbDrawString draws the specified multi-byte text with the foreground pixel. When the XFontSet has missing charsets, each unavailable character is drawn with the default string returned by XCreateFontSet. The behavior for an invalid codepoint is undefined.

XmbDrawString draws with fonts from the font set rather than the font of the GC. For this reason, it may modify the font value of the GC. Except for the font, it uses the same GC components as its pre-X11R5 analog XDrawString

Related Commands

XDrawImageString, XDrawString, XDrawText, XmbDrawImageString, XmbDrawText, XwcDrawString

Reference

XmbDrawText

Name

XmbDrawText – draw internationalized multi-byte text using multiple font sets.

Synopsis

```
void XmbDrawText(display, drawable, gc, x, y, items, nitems)
    Display *display;
    Drawable drawable;
    GC gc;
    int x, y;
    XmbTextItem *items;
    int nitems;
```

Arguments

display   Specifies the connection to the X server.

drawable Specifies the drawable.

gc   Specifies the GC.

x, y   Specifies the starting position and baseline of the text, relative to the origin of the specified drawable.

items   Specifies an array of text items.

nitems   Specifies the number of text items in the array.

Description

XmbDrawText allows complex spacing and font set shifts between internationalized multi-byte text strings. Each text item is processed in turn, with the origin of a text element advanced in the primary draw direction by the escapement of the previous text item. A text item delta specifies an additional escapement of the text item drawing origin in the primary draw direction. A *font_set* member other than None in an item causes the font set to be used for this and subsequent text items in the *items* list. Leading text items with *font_set* member set to None will not be drawn.

XmbDrawText does not perform any context-dependent rendering between text segments. Clients may compute the drawing metrics by passing each text segment to XmbTextExtents or XmbTextPerCharExtents. When the XFontSet has missing charsets, each unavailable character is drawn with the default string returned by XCreateFontSet. The behavior for an invalid codepoint is undefined.

XmbDrawText draws with fonts from the font sets of the *items* list rather than the font of the GC. For this reason, it may modify the font value of the GC. Except for the font, it uses the same GC components as its pre-X11R5 analog XDrawText

Structures

The XmbTextItem structure contains:

```
typedef struct {
        char *chars;                /* pointer to string */
        int nchars;                 /* number of characters */
```

```
        int delta;              /* pixel delta between strings */
        XFontSet font_set;      /* fonts, None means don't change */
} XmbTextItem;
```

Related Commands

XDrawImageString, XDrawString, XDrawText, XmbDrawImageString,
XmbDrawString, XwcDrawText

Name

XmbLookupString – obtain composed multi-byte input from an input method.

Synopsis

```
int XmbLookupString(ic, event, buffer_return, bytes_buffer,
        keysym_return, status_return)
    XIC ic;
    XKeyPressedEvent *event;
    char *buffer_return;
    int bytes_buffer;
    KeySym *keysym_return;
    Status *status_return;
```

Arguments

ic   Specifies the input context.

event
    Specifies the keypress event to be used.

buffer_return
    Returns a multibyte string (if any) from the input method.

bytes_buffer
    Specifies the number of bytes in the return buffer.

keysym_return
    Returns the KeySym computed from the event if this argument is not NULL.

status_return
    Returns a value indicating what kind of data is returned.

Availability

Release 5 and later.

Description

XmbLookupString passes a KeyPress event to an input context, returns composed text in the encoding of the locale of the input context if any is ready, and may return a keysym corresponding to the KeyPress event as well.

There are several possible results of a call to XmbLookupString, and a client should check the value returned in the *status_return* argument to determine which has occured. The possible values are:

XBufferOverflow
    The input string to be returned is too large for the supplied *buffer_return*. The required size in bytes is returned as the value of the function, and the contents of *buffer_return* and *keysym_return* are not modified. The client should re-call the function with the same event and a buffer of adequate size in order to obtain the string.

XLookupNone

> No consistent input has been composed so far. The contents of *buffer_return* and *keysym_return* are not modified, and the function returns zero.

XLookupChars

> Some input characters have been composed. They are placed in the *buffer_return* argument, and the string length is returned as the value of the function. The string is encoded in the locale bound to the input context. The contents of the *keysym_return* argument is not modified.

XLookupKeySym

> A KeySym has been returned instead of a string and is returned in *keysym_return*. The contents of the *buffer_return* argument is not modified, and the function returns zero.

XLookupBoth

> Both a KeySym and a string are returned; XLookupChars and XLookupKeySym occur simultaneously.

When XmbLookupString returns a string, the return value of the function is the length in bytes of that string. The returned string is a multi-byte string in the encoding of the locale of the input context. If that encoding is state-dependent, the string begins in the initial state of the encoding.

When both a keysym and a string are returned, the string does not necessarily correspond to the keysym. An application that is not interested in return keysyms can pass a NULL *keysym_return*.

Note that only KeyPress events should be passed to XmbLookupString. When KeyRelease events are passed, the resulting behavior is undefined. It does not make any difference if the input context passed as an argument to XmbLookupString is the one currently in possession of the focus or not. Input may have been composed within an input context before it lost the focus, and that input may be returned on subsequent calls to XmbLookupString even though it no longer has any more keyboard focus.

Related Commands

XLookupKeysym, XwcLookupString

XmbResetIC

Name

XmbResetIC – reset the state of an input context.

Synopsis

```
char * XmbResetIC(ic)
    XIC ic;
```

Arguments

ic   Specifies the input context.

Availability

Release 5 and later.

Description

XmbResetIC resets an input context to its initial state. Any input pending on that context is deleted. The input method is required to clear the Preedit area, if any, and update the Status area accordingly. Calling this function does not change the input context focus.

The return value of XmbResetIC is implementation dependent. If there was input pending on the input context, XmbResetIC may return composed multi-byte text in the encoding of the locale of the input context, or it may return NULL. If any string is returned, the client is responsible for freeing it by calling XFree.

Related Commands

XCreateIC, XSetICFocus, XSetICValues, XwcResetIC

XmbTextEscapement

Name

XmbTextEscapement – obtain the width of internationalized multi-byte text.

Synopsis

```
int XmbTextEscapement(font_set, string, num_bytes)
    XFontSet font_set;
    char *string;
    int num_bytes;
```

Arguments

font_set   Specifies the font set.

string   Specifies the character string.

num_bytes   Specifies the number of bytes in the string argument.

Availability

Release 5 and later.

Description

XmbTextEscapement returns the escapement in pixels of the specified multi-byte string using the fonts loaded for the specified font set. The escapement is the distance in pixels in the primary draw direction from the drawing origin to the origin of the next character to be drawn, assuming that the rendering of the next character is not dependent on the supplied string.

The escapement is always positive, regardless of the character rendering order.

Related Commands

XmbTextExtents, XmbTextPerCharExtents, XwcTextEscapement

Reference

Name

XmbTextExtents – compute the extents of internationalized multi-byte text.

Synopsis

```
int XmbTextExtents(font_set, string, num_bytes, overall_ink_return,
        overall_logical_return)
    XFontSet font_set;
    char *string;
    int num_bytes;
    XRectangle *overall_ink_return;
    XRectangle *overall_logical_return;
```

Arguments

font_set   Specifies the font set.

string   Specifies the character string.

num_bytes   Specifies the number of bytes in the string argument.

overall_ink_return
      Returns the overall ink dimensions.

overall_logical_return
      Returns the overall logical dimensions.

Availability

Release 5 and later.

Description

XmbTextExtents sets the components of the specified *overall_ink_return* and *overall_logical_return* arguments to the overall bounding box of the string's image, and the overall logical bounding box of the string's image plus inter-line and inter-character spacing. It returns the value returned by XmbTextEscapement. The returned metrics are relative to the drawing origin of the string, using the fonts loaded for the specified font set.

If the *overall_ink_return* argument is non-NULL, it is set to the bounding box of the string's character ink. Note that the *overall_ink_return* for a non-descending horizontally drawn Latin character is conventionally entirely above the baseline, that is, *overall_ink_return.height* <= -*overall_ink_return.y*. The *overall_ink_return* for a nonkerned character is entirely at and to the right of the origin, that is, *overall_ink_return.x* >= 0. A character consisting of a single pixel at the origin would have *overall_ink_return* fields $y = 0$, $x = 0$, $width = 1$, and $height = 1$.

If the *overall_logical_return* argument is non-NULL, it is set to the bounding box which provides minimum spacing to other graphical features for the string. Other graphical features, for example, a border surrounding the text, should not intersect this rectangle.

When the XFontSet has missing charsets, metrics for each unavailable character are taken from the default string returned by XCreateFontSet so that the metrics represent the text as it will actually be drawn. The behavior for an invalid codepoint is undefined.

Structures

```
typedef struct {
    short x, y;
    unsigned short width, height;
} XRectangle;
```

Related Commands

XmbTextEscapement, XmbTextPerCharExtents, XwcTextExtents

Name

XmbTextListToTextProperty – convert an internationalized multi-byte text list to a text property structure.

Synopsis

```
int XmbTextListToTextProperty(display, list, count, style,
        text_prop_return)
    Display *display;
    char **list;
    int count;
    XICCEncodingStyle style;
    XTextProperty *text_prop_return;
```

Arguments

display	Specifies the connection to the X server.
list	Specifies an array of null-terminated multi-byte strings.
count	Specifies the number of strings specified.
style	Specifies the manner in which the property is encoded.

text_prop_return

Returns the **XTextProperty** structure.

Availability

Release 5 and later.

Description

XmbTextListToTextProperty sets the specified **XTextProperty** value to a set of null-separated elements representing the concatenation of the specified list of null-terminated text strings. A final terminating null is stored at the end of the *value* field of *text_prop_return* but is not included in the *nitems* field.

XmbTextListToTextProperty sets the encoding field of *text_prop_return* to an Atom (for the specified display), which names the encoding specified by *style*, and converts the specified text list to this encoding for storage in the value field of *text_prop_return*. If the style **XStringStyle** or **XCompoundTextStyle** is specified, this encoding is STRING or COMPOUND_TEXT, respectively. If the style **XTextStyle** is specified, this encoding is the encoding of the current locale. If the style **XStdICCTextStyle** is specified, this encoding is STRING if the text is fully convertible to STRING, otherwise it is COMPOUND_TEXT.

If insufficient memory is available for the new value string, **XmbTextListToText-Property** returns XNoMemory. If the current locale is not supported, it returns XLocale-NotSupported. In both of these error cases, it does not set *text_prop_return*. **Xmb-TextListToTextProperty** will not return **XLocaleNotSupported** if XSupports-Locale has returned **True** for the current locale.

If the supplied text is not fully convertible to the specified encoding, `XmbTextListToText-Property` returns the number of unconvertible characters. Each unconvertible character is converted to an implementation-defined and encoding-specific default string. If the text is fully convertible, `XmbTextListToTextProperty` returns `Success`. Note that full convertibility to all styles except `XStringStyle` is guaranteed. If the supplied text contains bytes that are not valid characters in the encoding of the locale ("invalid codepoints"), the result is undefined.

`XmbTextListToTextProperty` allocates memory for the *value* field of the `XText-Property`. The client is responsible for freeing this memory by calling `XFree`.

Structures

The `XTextProperty` structure contains:

```
typedef struct {
    unsigned char *value;  /* property data */
    Atom encoding;         /* type of property */
    int format;            /* 8, 16, or 32 */
    unsigned long items;   /* number of items in value */
} XTextProperty;
```

The `XICCEncodingStyle` structure contains:

```
typedef enum    {
    XStringStyle,          /* STRING */
    XCompoundTextStyle,    /* COMPOUND_TEXT */
    XTextStyle,            /* text in owner's encoding (current locale) */
    XStdICCTextStyle       /* STRING, else COMPOUND_TEXT */
} XICCEncodingStyle;
```

The possible return values of this function are as follows:

```
#define    XNoMemory                    −1
#define    XLocaleNotSupported          −2
#define    XConverterNotFound           −3
```

Related Commands

XSetTextProperty, XStringListToTextProperty,
XwcTextListToTextProperty, XmbTextPropertyToTextList,
XwcTextPropertyToTextList, XwcFreeStringList, XDefaultString

Name

XmbTextPerCharExtents – obtain per-character measurements of an internationalized multi-byte text string.

Synopsis

```
Status XmbTextPerCharExtents(font_set, string, num_bytes,
        ink_array_return, logical_array_return, array_size,
        num_chars_return, overall_ink_return, overall_logical_return)
    XFontSet font_set;
    char *string;
    int num_bytes;
    XRectangle *ink_array_return;
    XRectangle *logical_array_return;
    int array_size;
    int *num_chars_return;
    XRectangle *overall_ink_return;
    XRectangle *overall_logical_return;
```

Arguments

font_set   Specifies the font set.

string   Specifies the character string.

num_bytes   Specifies the number of bytes in the string argument.

ink_array_return
                Returns the ink dimensions for each character.

logical_array_return
                Returns the logical dimensions for each character.

array_size   Specifies the size of *ink_array_return* and *logical_array_return*. Note that the caller must pass in arrays of this size.

num_chars_return
                Returns the number characters in the string argument.

overall_ink_return
                Returns the overall ink extents of the entire string.

overall_logical_return
                Returns the overall logical extents of the entire string.

Availability

Release 5 and later.

Description

XmbTextPerCharExtents returns the text dimensions of each character of the specified text, using the fonts loaded for the specified font set. Each element of *ink_array_return* and *logical_array_return* is set to the corresponding character's drawn metrics, relative to the drawing origin of the string. The number of elements of *ink_array_return* and *logical_array_return* that have been set is returned in *num_chars_return*.

Each element of *ink_array_return* is set to the bounding box of the corresponding character's drawn foreground color. Each element of *logical_array_return* is set to the bounding box which provides minimum spacing to other graphical features for the corresponding character. Other graphical features should not intersect any of the *logical_array_return* rectangles.

Note that an XRectangle represents the effective drawing dimensions of the character, regardless of the number of font glyphs that are used to draw the character, or the direction in which the character is drawn. If multiple characters map to a single character glyph, the dimensions of all the XRectangles of those characters are the same.

When the XFontSet has missing charsets, metrics for each unavailable character are taken from the default string returned by XCreateFontSet, so that the metrics represent the text as it will actually be drawn. The behavior for an invalid codepoint is undefined.

If the *array_size* is too small for the number of characters in the supplied text, the function returns zero and *num_chars_return* is set to the number of rectangles required. Otherwise, it returns a non-zero value.

If the *overall_ink_return* or *overall_logical_return* argument is non-NULL, XmbTextPerCharExtents returns the maximum extent of the string's metrics to *overall_ink_return* or *overall_logical_return*, as is done by XmbTextExtents.

Structures

```
typedef struct {
    short x, y;
    unsigned short width, height;
} XRectangle;
```

Related Commands

XmbTextEscapement, XmbTextExtents, XwcTextPerCharExtents

Reference

Name

XmbTextPropertyToTextList – convert an internationalized text property to a list of multi-byte strings.

Synopsis

```
int XmbTextPropertyToTextList(display, text_prop, list_return,
        count_return)
    Display *display;
    XTextProperty *text_prop;
    char ***list_return;
    int *count_return;
```

Arguments

display   Specifies the connection to the X server.

text_prop   Specifies the **XTextProperty** structure to be used.

list_return   Returns a list of null-terminated character strings.

count_return   Returns the number of strings.

Availability

Release 5 and later.

Description

XmbTextPropertyToTextList returns a list of multi-byte text strings encoded in the current locale representing the null-separated elements of the specified **XTextProperty** structure. The data in *text_prop* must be format 8.

Multiple elements of the property (for example, the strings in a disjoint text selection) are separated by a null byte. The contents of the property are not required to be null-terminated; any terminating null should not be included in *text_prop.nitems*.

If insufficient memory is available for the list and its elements, **XmbTextPropertyToTextList** returns XNoMemory. If the current locale is not supported, it returns XLocaleNotSupported. If the encoding field of *text_prop* is not convertible to the encoding of the current locale, it returns XConverterNotFound. For supported locales, existence of a converter from COMPOUND_TEXT, STRING, or the encoding of the current locale is guaranteed although the actual text may contain unconvertible characters. Conversion of other encodings is implementation-dependent. In all of these error cases, the function does not set any return values.

Otherwise, **XmbTextPropertyToTextList** returns the list of null-terminated text strings to *list_return*, and the number of text strings to *count_return*.

If the *value* field of *text_prop* is not fully convertible to the encoding of the current locale, the function returns the number of unconvertible characters. Each unconvertible character is converted to a string in the current locale that is specific to the current locale. To obtain the value of this string, use **XDefaultString**. If all characters are convertible, **XmbTextPropertyToTextList** returns **Success**. If the text property contains "invalid codepoints" or bytes that are not valid characters in the encoding of the property, the result is undefined.

To free the storage for the list and its contents returned by XmbTextPropertyToText-List, use XFreeStringList.

Structures

The XTextProperty structure contains:

```
typedef struct              {
      unsigned char *value;      /* property data */
      Atom encoding;             /* type of property */
      int format;                /* 8, 16, or 32 */
      unsigned long nitems;      /* number of items in value */
} XTextProperty;
```

The possible return values of this function are as follows:

```
#define    XNoMemory                 -1
#define    XLocaleNotSupported       -2
#define    XConverterNotFound        -3
```

Related Commands

XSetTextProperty, XStringListToTextProperty, XDefaultString,
XmbTextListToTextProperty, XwcFreeStringList,
XwcTextListToTextProperty, XwcTextPropertyToTextList

XmuAddInitializer

Name

XmuAddInitializer – register an application context initialization procedure.

Synopsis

```
#include <X11/Xmu/Initer.h>
void XmuAddInitializer(func, data)
    void (*func)();
    caddr_t data;
```

Arguments

func   Specifies the procedure to register.

data   Specifies private data to be passed to the procedure.

Description

XmuAddInitializer registers a procedure that will be invoked the first time the function XmuCallInitializers is invoked on a given application context. The procedure will be called with two arguments, the application context and the private data registered with the procedure.

Related Commands

XmuCallInitializers

Name

XmuCallInitializers – call all registered initializer functions for an application context.

Synopsis

```
#include <X11/Xmu/Initer.h>
void XmuCallInitializers(app_context)
    XtAppContext app_context;
```

Arguments

app_context   Specifies the application context for which the initializer functions should be called.

Description

If this is the first time it has been called for the given application context, XmuCall-Initializers invokes each of the functions registered with XmuAddInitializer. Each function is called with two arguments, the application context and the private data that was registered with the function. XmuCallInitializers will never call these functions more than once for any application context.

Related Commands

XmuAddInitializer

Reference

XmuConvertStandardSelection

Name

XmuConvertStandardSelection – convert to standard selection target types.

Synopsis

```
#include <X11/Xmu/StdSel.h>
Boolean XmuConvertStandardSelection(w, time, selection, target, type,
        value, length, format)
    Widget w;
    Time time;
    Atom *selection, *target, *type;
    caddr_t *value;
    unsigned long *length;
    int *format;
```

Arguments

w   Specifies the widget which currently owns the selection.

time   Specifies the time at which the selection was established.

selection   This argument is unused.

target   Specifies the target type for the conversion.

type   Returns the property type of the converted value.

value   Returns the converted value.

length   Returns the number of elements in the converted value.

format   Returns the size in bits of the elements of the converted value.

Description

XmuConvertStandardSelection converts the selection to the following standard targets: CLASS, CLIENT_WINDOW, DECNET_ADDRESS, HOSTNAME, IP_ADDRESS, NAME, OWNER_OS, TARGETS, TIMESTAMP, and USER. It returns True if the conversion was successful, or False if it failed.

XmuConvertStandardSelection converts to the "housekeeping" target types that do not have anything to do with the acutal value of the selection. It is particularly useful within an XtConvertSelectionProc registered with a call to XtOwnSelection. The returned type, value, length, and format can be used directly by that conversion procedure. Note that when this function is used to convert the TARGETS target, it returns only the list of targets that it supports itself. The selection conversion procedure that called it will have to append its own supported targets to this list.

XmuConvertStandardSelection allocates memory for the returned value. The client should free this memory by calling XtFree.

Related Commands

XtOwnSelection, XtConvertSelectionProc

Name

XmuCvtFunctionToCallback – convert a function pointer to an XtCallbackList.

Synopsis

```
#include <X11/Xmu/Converters.h>
XtAddConverter(XtRCallProc, XtRCallback, XmuCvtFunctionToCallback,
               NULL, 0);
```

Description

XmuCvtFunctionToCallback is an old-style converter function that converts a function pointer to an XtCallbackList containing that function and NULL *call_data*.

Related Commands

XtAddConverter, XtAppAddConverter, XmuCvtStringTo*,
XmuNewCvtStringToWidget

Name

XmuCvtStringTo* – convert strings to various types.

Synopsis

```
#include <X11/Xmu/Converters.h>

XtAddConverter(XtRString, XtRBackingStore, XmuCvtStringToBackingStore, NULL, 0);
XtAddConverter(XtRString, XtRGravity, XmuCvtStringToGravity, NULL, 0);
XtAddConverter(XtRString, XtRJustify, XmuCvtStringToJustify, NULL, 0);
XtAddConverter(XtRString, XtRLong, XmuCvtStringToLong, NULL, 0);
XtAddConverter(XtRString, XtROrientation, XmuCvtStringToOrientation, NULL, 0);
XtSetTypeConverter(XtRString, XtRShapeStyle,XmuCvtStringToShapeStyle,
                 NULL, 0, XtCacheNone, NULL);

static XtConvertArgRec screenConvertArg[ ] = {
  {XtBaseOffset, (XtPointer)XtOffset(Widget, core.screen), sizeof(Screen *)}
};
XtAddConverter(XtRString, XtRBitmap, XmuCvtStringToBitmap,
             screenConvertArg, XtNumber(screenConvertArg));
XtAddConverter(XtRString, XtRCursor, XmuCvtStringToCursor,
             screenConvertArg, XtNumber(screenConvertArg));

static XtConvertArgRec parentCvtArg[ ] = {
  {XtBaseOffset, (XtPointer)XtOffset(Widget, core.parent), sizeof(Widget)},
};
XtAddConverter(XtRString, XtRWidget, XmuCvtStringToWidget,
             parentCvtArg, XtNumber(parentCvtArg));

static XtConvertArgRec colorCursorConvertArgs[ ] = {
  {XtWidgetBaseOffset, (XtPointer) XtOffsetOf(WidgetRec, core.screen),
   sizeof(Screen *)},
  {XtResourceString, (XtPointer) XtNpointerColor,sizeof(Pixel)},
  {XtResourceString, (XtPointer) XtNpointerColorBackground, sizeof(Pixel)},
  {XtWidgetBaseOffset, (XtPointer) XtOffsetOf(WidgetRec,core.colormap),
    sizeof(Colormap)}
};
XtSetTypeConverter(XtRString, XtRColorCursor, XmuCvtStringToColorCursor,
                 colorCursorConvertArgs, XtNumber(colorCursorConvertArgs),
                 XtCacheByDisplay, NULL);
```

Availability

XmuCvtStringToColorCursor and XmuCvtStringToGravity are new in Release 5.

Description

These functions are type converters that convert from strings to various resource types. Some
require additional arguments, but most may be registered without any arguments. Two of these
functions are X11R4 "new-style" converters registered with XtSetTypeConverter; the
rest are "old-style" converters registered with XtAddConverter or XtAppAdd-
Converter.

`XmuCvtStringToBackingStore` converts a string to a backing-store integer as defined in *<X11/X.h>*. The string "notUseful" converts to `NotUseful`, "whenMapped" converts to `WhenMapped`, and "always" converts to `Always`. The string "default" converts to the value `Always + WhenMapped + NotUseful`. The case of the string does not matter.

`XmuCvtStringToGravity` converts a string to an `XtGravity` enumeration value. The string "forget" or a NULL value convert to `ForgetGravity`, "NorthWestGravity" converts to `NorthWestGravity`, the strings "NorthGravity" and "top" convert to `NorthGravity`, "NorthEastGravity" converts to `NorthEastGravity`, the strings "West" and "left" convert to `WestGravity`, "CenterGravity" converts to `CenterGravity`, "EastGravity" and "right" convert to `EastGravity`, "SouthWestGravity" converts to `SouthWestGravity`, "South-Gravity" and "bottom" convert to `SouthGravity`, "SouthEastGravity" converts to `SouthEastGravity`, "StaticGravity" converts to `StaticGravity`, and "UnmapGravity" converts to `UnmapGravity`. The case of the string does not matter.

`XmuCvtStringToJustify` converts a string to an `XtJustify` enumeration value. The string "left" converts to `XtJustifyLeft`, "center" converts to `XtJustifyCenter`, and "right" converts to `XtJustifyRight`. The case of the string does not matter.

`XmuCvtStringToLong` converts a string to an integer of type long. It parses the string using `sscanf` with a format of "%ld."

`XmuCvtStringToOrientation` converts a string to an `XtOrientation` enumeration value. The string "horizontal" converts to `XtorientHorizontal` and "vertical" converts to `XtorientVertical`. The case of the string does not matter.

`XmuCvtStringToShapeStyle` converts a string to an integer shape style. The string "rectangle" converts to `XmuShapeRectangle`, "oval" converts to `XmuShapeOval`, "ellipse" converts to `XmuShapeEllipse`, and "roundedRectangle" converts to `XmuShapeRoundedRectangle`. The case of the string does not matter.

`XmuCvtStringToBitmap` creates a bitmap (a Pixmap of depth one) suitable for window manager icons. The string argument is the name of a file in standard bitmap file format. For the possible filename specifications, see the reference page for `XmuLocateBitmapFile`.

`XmuCvtStringToCursor` converts a string to a `Cursor`. The string can either be a standard cursor name formed by removing the XC_ prefix from any of the cursor defines listed in Appendix I of Volume Two, a font name and glyph index in decimal of the form "FONT fontname index [[font] index]," or a bitmap filename acceptable to `XmuLocateBitmapFile`.

`XmuCvtStringToWidget` converts a string to an immediate child widget of the parent widget passed as an argument. Note that this converter only works for child widgets that have already been created; there is no lazy evaluation. The string is first compared against the names of the normal and popup children, and if a match is found the corresponding child is returned. If no match is found, the string is compared against the classes of the normal and popup children, and if a match is found the corresponding child is returned. The case of the string is significant. The converter `XmuNewConvertStringToWidget` performs the same conversion, but allows greater control over the type of caching that will be done on the result of the conversion. Because widget trees are often dynamic in an application, it is usually inappropriate to cache string-to-widget conversion results as is done with `XmuCvtStringToWidget`.

`XmuCvtStringToColorCursor` converts a string to a `Cursor` with the foreground and background pixels specified by the conversion arguments. The string can either be a standard cursor name formed by removing the XC_ prefix from any of the cursor defines listed in Appendix I of Volume Two, a font name and glyph index (in base 10) of the form "FONT fontname index [[font] index]," or a bitmap filename acceptable to `XmuLocateBitmapFile`.

Related Commands

`XtAddConverter, XtAppAddConverter, XtSetTypeConverter,`
`XmuCvtFunctionToCallback, XmuNewCvtStringToWidget,`
`XmuLocateBitmapFile`

Name
XmuDistinguishableColors – determine if colors are visibly different.

Synopsis
```
Bool XmuDistinguishableColors(colors, count)
    XColor *colors;
    int count;
```

Arguments
colors   An array of XColor structures to be tested for distinguishability.

count   The number of elements in the *colors* array.

Availability
Release 5 and later.

Description
This function returns True if and only if all the colors in the passed array are "distinguishable" from one another. There is no formal definition for "distinguishable," and this function does not make use of device independent color, so the algorithm used is somewhat arbitrary. Note that there is no Xmu header file that declares this function, so the declaration should be done explictly.

Related Commands
XmuDistinguishablePixels

XmuDistinguishablePixels

Name

XmuDistinguishablePixels – determine if colormap cells contain visibly different colors.

Synopsis

```
Bool XmuDistinguishablePixels(dpy, cmap, pixels, count)
    Display *dpy;
    Colormap cmap;
    unsigned long *pixels;
    int count;
```

Arguments

dpy   Specifies the display.

cmap   Specifies the colormap.

pixels   An array of colormap cells to be tested for distinguishablity.

count   The number of cells in the *pixels* array.

Availability

Release 5 and later.

Description

This function returns `True` if and only if the colors in the colormap cells specified by the *pixels* array are "distinguishable" from one another. There is no formal definition for "distinguishable," and this function does not make use of device independent color, so the algorithm used is somewhat arbitrary. Note that there is no Xmu header file that declares this function, so the declaration should be done explictly.

Related Commands

XmuDistinguishableColors

XmuLocatePixmapFile

Name

XmuLocatePixmapFile – create a pixmap from a file in a standard location.

Synopsis

```
#include <X11/Xmu/Drawing.h>
Pixmap XmuLocatePixmapFile (screen, name, fore, back, depth, srcname,
        srcnamelen, widthp, heightp, xhotp, yhotp)
    Screen *screen;
    char *name;
    unsigned long fore, back;
    unsigned int depth;
    char *srcname;
    int srcnamelen;
    int *widthp, *heightp, *xhotp, *yhotp;
```

Arguments

screen	Specifies the screen.
name	Specifies the pixmap filename.
fore, back	Specify the foreground and background colors of the pixmap.
depth	Specifies the depth of the pixmap.
srcname	Returns the absolute filename of the pixmap.
srcnamelen	Specifies the length of the srcname buffer.
widthp, heightp	Return the width and height of the pixmap.
xhotp, yhotp	Return the x and y coordinates of the pixmap hotspot.

Availability

Release 5 and later.

Description

This function reads a file in standard bitmap file format, using `XmuReadBitmapDataFrom-File` and creates a pixmap with the specified foreground and background colors and specified depth using `XCreatePixmapFromBitmapData`. The filename may be absolute, or relative to the global resource named `bitmapFilePath` with class `BitmapFilePath`. If the resource is not defined, the default value is */usr/include/X11/bitmaps*. If `srcnamelen` is greater than zero and `srcname` is not NULL, the null-terminated filename will be copied into `srcname`. The size and hotspot of the bitmap are also returned.

Related Commands

`XmuLocateBitmapFile`, `XmuCreatePixmapFromBitmap`, `XmuReadBitmapData`, `XmuReadBitmapDataFromFile`, `XCreatePixmapFromBitmapData`

Reference

Name

XmuNewCvtStringToWidget – convert string to widget without caching.

Synopsis

```
#include <X11/Xmu/Converters>
static XtConvertArgRec parentCvtArg[ ] = {
    {XtWidgetBaseOffset, (XtPointer)XtOffsetOf(WidgetRec,core.parent),
     sizeof(Widget)}
};
XtSetTypeConverter(XtRString, XtRWidget, XmuNewCvtStringToWidget,
              parentCvtArg, XtNumber(parentCvtArg), XtCacheNone, NULL);
```

Availability

Release 5 and later.

Description

This converter is identical in functionality to `XmuCvtStringToWidget`, except that it is a new-style converter, allowing the specification of a cache type at the time of registration. Most widgets will not cache the conversion results, as the application may dynamically create and destroy widgets, which would cause cached values to become illegal.

Related Commands

XtSetTypeConverter, XmuCvtFunctionToCallback, XmuCvtStringTo*

Name

XmuReshapeWidget – change the shape of a widget's Window.

Synopsis

```
#include <X11/Xmu/Converters.h>
Boolean XmuReshapeWidget(w, shape_style, corner_width, corner_height)
    Widget w;
    int shape_style;
    int corner_width, corner_height;
```

Arguments

w   Specifies the widget to reshape.

shape_style   Specifies the new shape.

corner_width   Specifies the width of the rounded corner for a *shape_style* of
                   XmuShapeRoundedRectangle.

corner_height   Specifies the height of the rounded corner for a *shape_style* of
                   XmuShapeRoundedRectangle.

Availability

Release 4 and later. This function will only work on servers that support the Shape extension.

Description

XmuReshapeWidget uses the Shape extension to the X protocol to change the shape of the specified widget's window. The shape is specified by the *shape_style* parameter which can have one of the following arguments: XmuShapeRectangle, XmuShapeOval, Xmu-ShapeEllipse, or XmuShapeRoundedRectangle. If the shape is XmuShape-RoundedRectangle, the *corner_width* and *corner_height* parameters specify the bounding box of the rounded part of the corner. These arguments are ignored for any other shape styles. Note that this function does not change the nominal width and height of the widget's window, nor the widget's position within it's parent.

XmuReshapeWidget returns False if it is passed and unsupported value as the *shape_style* argument. Otherwise it returns True.

Related Commands

XmuFillRoundedRectangle, XmuCvtStringToShapeStyle

Reference

Name

XmuWnCountOwnedResources – determine the number of resources that a widget class inherits from one of its superclasses.

Synopsis

```
#include <X11/Xmu/WidgetNode.h>
int XmuWnCountOwnedResources(node, owner_node, constraints)
    XmuWidgetNode *node;
    XmuWidgetNode *owner_node;
    Bool constraints;
```

Arguments

node   Specifies the widget class whose resources are being examined.

owner_node   Specifies the superclass of *node* which is to have its resources counted.

constraints   Specifies whether constraint resources or normal resources should be counted.

Availability

Release 5 and later.

Description

This function returns the number of resources of the widget class *node* which are "contributed" or "owned" by the superclass *owner_node*. If *constraints* is False, XmuCountOwnedResources counts normal resources; otherwise it counts constraint resources. *node* and *owner_node* must have been passed to XmuWnInitializeNodes before being used in this function, and *node* must have been passed to XmuWnFetchResources.

Related Commands

XmuWnFetchResources, XmuWnInitializeNodes, XmuWnNameToNode

Name

XmuWnFetchResources – get the resource list of a widget class.

Synopsis

```
#include <X11/Xmu/WidgetNode.h>
void XmuWnFetchResources(node, toplevel, top_node)
    XmuWidgetNode *node;
    Widget toplevel;
    XmuWidgetNode *top_node;
```

Arguments

node   Specifies the widget class for which the resource list should be obtained.

toplevel   Specifies a widget which can be used as the parent for a dummy instance of
              the specified widget class. A top-level shell widget is suitable, for example.

top_node   Specifies the widget class that should be treated as the top of the widget class
              hierarchy when determining which superclass contributed which resources to
              the widget class node.

Availability

Release 5 and later.

Description

This function obtains a resource list for the normal resources and the constraint resources of a
widget class. For each resource it also obtains a pointer to the widget class that "contributed"
that resource. XmuWnFetchResources creates and destroys a dummy widget instance of
the specified class. The argument *toplevel* is a widget which may be used as the parent of
that dummy widget; a toplevel shell widget is suitable. The *top_node* argument is used to
specify the top of the widget hierarchy for the purposes of determining "ownership" of
resources. The XmuWidgetNode for the Core class could be used, for example if the programmer were not interested in considering the Object and RectObj widget classes separately.

XmuWnFetchResources does not return a value; the resource lists it obtains are stored in its
node argument, which is of type XmuWidgetNode *. This structure is shown below. The
fields *resources* and *constraints* are the normal and constraint resource lists for the
widget class, and the fields *nresources*, and *nconstraints* specify the number of elements in each list. Additionally, the fields *resourcewn* and *constraintwn* are arrays of
XmuWidgetNode * whose elements point to the widget structure of the widget node class
that "owns" the corresponding resource in the resource lists.

The widget nodes passed to XmuWnFetchResources must first have been initialized in a
call to XmuWnInitializeNodes.

Structures

```
typedef struct _XmuWidgetNode {
    char *label;                                    /* mixed case name */
    WidgetClass *widget_class_ptr;                  /* addr of widget class */
    struct _XmuWidgetNode *superclass;      /* superclass of widget_class */
```

```
    struct _XmuWidgetNode *children, *siblings;        /* subclass links */
    char *lowered_label;                    /* lowercase version of label */
    char *lowered_classname;        /* lowercase version of class_name */
    Bool have_resources;                 /* resources have been fetched */
    XtResourceList resources;            /* extracted resource database */
    struct _XmuWidgetNode **resourcewn;    /* where resources come from */
    Cardinal nresources;                       /* number of resources */
    XtResourceList constraints;        /* extracted constraint resources */
    struct _XmuWidgetNode **constraintwn; /* where constraints come from */
    Cardinal nconstraints;             /* number of constraint resources */
    XtPointer data;                              /* extra data */
} XmuWidgetNode;
```

Related Commands

XmuWnCountOwnedResources, XmuWnInitializeNodes, XmuWnNameToNode

XmuWnInitializeNodes

Name

XmuWnInitializeNodes – initialize an array of widget nodes.

Synopsis

```
#include <X11/Xmu/WidgetNode.h>
void XmuWnInitializeNodes(node_array, num_nodes)
    XmuWidgeNode *node_array;
    int num_nodes;
```

Arguments

node_array   Specifies an array of widget nodes in alphabetical order.

num_nodes   Specifies the number of nodes in the array.

Availability

Release 5 and later.

Description

XmuWnInitializeNodes initializes an array of XmuWidgetNode. It must be called before any of the other Xmu widget node functions. The *node_array* argument is typically a statically initialized array of XmuWidgetNode (shown below) in which only the first two fields of each node are specified. XmuWnInitializeNodes initializes the superclass and subclass links in each XmuWidgetNode structure, and sets the resource fields to NULL. These resource list fields are filled in by the function XmuWnFetchResources. Note that the array of widget nodes must be in alphabetical order by the value of the *label* field, which needn't be the same as the widget class name.

Structures

```
typedef struct _XmuWidgetNode {
    char *label;                              /* mixed case name */
    WidgetClass *widget_class_ptr;            /* addr of widget class */
    struct _XmuWidgetNode *superclass;        /* superclass of widget_class */
    struct _XmuWidgetNode *children, *siblings;   /* subclass links */
    char *lowered_label;                      /* lowercase version of label */
    char *lowered_classname;                  /* lowercase version of class_name */
    Bool have_resources;                      /* resources have been fetched */
    XtResourceList resources;                 /* extracted resource database */
    struct _XmuWidgetNode **resourcewn;       /* where resources come from */
    Cardinal nresources;                      /* number of resources */
    XtResourceList constraints;               /* extracted constraint resources */
    struct _XmuWidgetNode **constraintwn;     /* where constraints come from */
    Cardinal nconstraints;                    /* number of constraint resources */
    XtPointer data;                           /* extra data */
} XmuWidgetNode;
```

Reference

Related Commands

XmuWnCountOwnedResource, XmuWnFetchResources, XmuWnNameToNode

Name

XmuWnNameToNode — look up a widget node by name.

Synopsis

```
#include <X11/Xmu/WidgetNode.h>
XmuWidgetNode *XmuWnNameToNode(node_list, num_nodes, name)
    XmuWidgetNode *node_list;
    int num_nodes;
    char *name;
```

Arguments

node_list   Specifies the array of widget nodes to search.

num_nodes   Specifies the number of nodes in the array.

name   Specifies the name to search for.

Availability

Release 5 and later.

Description

XmuWnNameToNode searches the specified array of **XmuWidgetNode** for a node with *label* field or widget class name which matches the specified *name*. It returns the matching node or NULL is none was found. The comparison used is case insensitive.

Related Commands

XmuWnCountOwnedResource, XmuWnFetchResources, XmuWnInitializeNodes

XOpenIM

Name

XOpenIM – open input method.

Synopsis

```
XIM XOpenIM(display, db, res_name, res_class)
    Display *display;
    XrmDataBase db;
    char *res_name;
    char *res_class;
```

Arguments

display	Specifies the connection to the X server.
db	Specifies a pointer to the resource database.
res_name	Specifies the full resource name of the application.
res_class	Specifies the full class name of the application.

Availability

Release 5 and later.

Description

XOpenIM opens an input method. The current locale and modifiers are bound to the input method when it is opened. The locale associated with an input method cannot be changed dynamically. This implies the strings returned by XmbLookupString or XwcLookup-String, for any input context affiliated with a given input method, will be encoded in the locale that was current at the time the input method was opened.

The specific input method to which this call will be routed is identified on the basis of the current locale. XOpenIM will identify a default input method corresponding to the current locale. That default can be modified using XSetLocaleModifiers with the input method ("im") modifier.

The db argument is the resource database to be used by the input method for looking up resources that are private to the input method. It is not intended that this database be used to look up values that can be set as IC values in an input context. If db is NULL, no data base is passed to the input method.

The res_name and res_class arguments specify the resource name and class of the application. They are intended to be used as prefixes by the input method when looking up resources that are common to all input contexts that may be created for this input method. The characters used for resource names and classes must be in the X portable character set. The resources looked up are not fully specified if res_name or res_class is NULL.

The res_name and res_class arguments are not assumed to exist beyond the call to XOpenIM. The specified resource database is assumed to exist for the lifetime of the input method.

XOpenIM returns NULL if no input method could be opened.

Related Commands

XCloseIM, XGetIMValues, XDisplayOfIM, XLocaleOfIM

Name

xrdb – X server resource database utility.

Synopsis

xrdb [*options*] [*filename*]

Availability

Per-screen resource support is only available in Release 5 and later.

Description

xrdb is used to get or set the contents of the RESOURCE_MANAGER property on the root window of screen 0, or the SCREEN_RESOURCES property on the root window of any or all screens, or everything combined. You would normally run this program from your X startup file.

Most X clients use the RESOURCE_MANAGER and SCREEN_RESOURCES properties to get user preferences about color, fonts, and so on for applications. Having this information in the server (where it is available to all clients) instead of on disk, solves the problem in previous versions of X that required you to maintain defaults files on every machine that you might use. It also allows for dynamic changing of defaults without editing files.

The RESOURCE_MANAGER property is used for resources that apply to all screens of the display. The SCREEN_RESOURCES property on each screen specifies additional (or overriding) resources to be used for that screen. (When there is only one screen, SCREEN_RESOURCES is normally not used, all resources are just placed in the RESOURCE_MANAGER property.)

The file specified by *filename* (or the standard input if a "-" or no filename is specified) is optionally passed through the C preprocessor with the following symbols defined, based on the capabilities of the server being used:

BITS_PER_RGB=*num*

the number of significant bits in an RGB color specification. This is the log base 2 of the number of distinct shades of each primary that the hardware can generate. Note that it usually is not related to PLANES.

CLASS=*visualclass*

one of `StaticGray`, `GrayScale`, `StaticColor`, `PseudoColor`, `TrueColor`, `DirectColor`. This is the visual class of the root window of the default screen.

COLOR

defined only if CLASS is one of `StaticColor`, `PseudoColor`, `TrueColor`, or `DirectColor`.

HEIGHT=*num*

the height of the default screen in pixels.

SERVERHOST=*hostname*

the hostname portion of the display to which you are connected.

HOST=*hostname*
> the same as SERVERHOST.

CLIENTHOST=*hostname*
> the name of the host on which

PLANES=*num*
> the number of bit planes (the depth) of the root window of the default screen.

RELEASE=*num*
> the vendor release number for the server. The interpretation of this number will vary depending on VENDOR.

REVISION=*num*
> the X protocol minor version supported by this server (currently 0).

VERSION=*num*
> the X protocol major version supported by this server (should always be 11).

VENDOR=*vendor*
> a string specifying the vendor of the server.

WIDTH=*num*
> the width of the default screen in pixels.

X_RESOLUTION=*num*
> the x resolution of the default screen in pixels per meter.

Y_RESOLUTION=*num*
> the y resolution of the default screen in pixels per meter.

Lines that begin with an exclamation mark (!) are ignored and may be used as comments.

Note that since *xrdb* can read from standard input, it can be used to the change the contents of properties directly from a terminal or from a shell script.

Options

xrdb accepts the following options:

−help
> This option (or any unsupported option) will cause a brief description of the allowable options and parameters to be printed.

−display *display*
> This option specifies the X server to be used. It also specifies the screen to use for the −screen option, and it specifies the screen from which preprocessor symbols are derived for the −global option.

−all
> This option indicates that operation should be performed on the screen-independent resource property (RESOURCE_MANAGER), as well as the screen-specific property (SCREEN_RESOURCES) on every screen of the display. For example, when used in conjunction with −query, the contents of all properties are output. For −load and −merge,

the input file is processed once for each screen. The resources which occur in common in the output for every screen are collected, and these are applied as the screen-independent resources. The remaining resources are applied for each individual per-screen property. This the default mode of operation.

−global

This option indicates that the operation should only be performed on the screen-independent RESOURCE_MANAGER property.

−screen

This option indicates that the operation should only be performed on the SCREEN_RESOURCES property of the default screen of the display.

−screens

This option indicates that the operation should be performed on the SCREEN_RESOURCES property of each screen of the display. For −load and −merge, the input file is processed for each screen.

−n This option indicates that changes to the specified properties (when used with −load or −merge) or to the resource file (when used with −edit) should be shown on the standard output, but should not be performed.

−quiet

This option indicates that warning about duplicate entries should not be displayed.

−cpp *filename*

This option specifies the pathname of the C preprocessor program to be used. Although *xrdb* was designed to use CPP, any program that acts as a filter and accepts the -D, -I, and -U options may be used.

−nocpp

This option indicates that *xrdb* should not run the input file through a preprocessor before loading it into properties.

−symbols

This option indicates that the symbols that are defined for the preprocessor should be printed onto the standard output.

−query

This option indicates that the current contents of the specified properties should be printed onto the standard output. Note that since preprocessor commands in the input resource file are part of the input file, not part of the property, they won't appear in the output from this option. The −edit option can be used to merge the contents of properties back into the input resource file without damaging preprocessor commands.

−load

> This option indicates that the input should be loaded as the new value of the specified properties, replacing whatever was there (i.e. the old contents are removed). This is the default action.

−merge

> This option indicates that the input should be merged with, instead of replacing, the current contents of the specified properties. Note that this option does a lexicographic sorted merge of the two inputs, which is almost certainly not what you want, but remains for backward compatibility.

−remove

> This option indicates that the specified properties should be removed from the server.

−retain

> This option indicates that the server should be instructed not to reset if *xrdb* is the first client. This should never be necessary under normal conditions, since *xdm* and *xinit* always act as the first client.

−edit *filename*

> This option indicates that the contents of the specified properties should be edited into the given file, replacing any values already listed there. This allows you to put changes that you have made to your defaults back into your resource file, preserving any comments or preprocessor lines.

−backup *string*

> This option specifies a suffix to be appended to the filename used with −edit to generate a backup file.

−D*name*[=*value*]

> This option is passed through to the preprocessor and is used to define symbols for use with conditionals such as *#ifdef.*

−U*name*

> This option is passed through to the preprocessor and is used to remove any definitions of this symbol.

−I*directory*

> This option is passed through to the preprocessor and is used to specify a directory to search for files that are referenced with *#include.*

Files

> Generalizes ˜/.*Xdefaults* files.

Environment Variables

> DISPLAY   Specifies which display and screen to use.

Reference

Bugs

The default for no arguments should be to query, not to overwrite, so that it is consistent with other programs.

Copyright

Copyright 1991, Digital Equipment Corporation and MIT.

Authors

Bob Scheifler, Phil Karlton, rewritten from the original by Jim Gettys.

Name

XResourceManagerString – obtain server resource properties.

Synopsis

```
char *XResourceManagerString(display)
    Display *display;
```

Arguments

display   Specifies the connection to the X server.

Description

XResourceManagerString returns the RESOURCE_MANAGER property from the root window of screen zero, which was returned when the connection was opened using XOpen-Display. The property is converted from type STRING to the current locale. The conversion is identical to that produced by XmbTextPropertyToTextList for a singleton STRING property. The returned string is owned by Xlib, and should not be freed by the client. Note that the property value must be in a format that is acceptable to XrmGetStringDatabase. If no property exists, NULL is returned.

Related Commands

XScreenResourceString

Name

XrmEnumerateDatabase – enumerate resource database entries.

Synopsis

```
Bool XrmEnumerateDatabase(database, name_prefix, class_prefix, mode,
        proc, arg)
    XrmDatabase database;
    XrmNameList name_prefix;
    XrmClassList class_prefix;
    int mode;
    Bool (*proc)();
    XPointer arg;
```

Arguments

database   Specifies the resource database.

name_prefix   Specifies the resource name prefix.

class_prefix   Specifies the resource class prefix.

mode   Specifies the number of levels to enumerate.

proc   Specifies the procedure that is to be called for each matching entry.

arg   Specifies the user-supplied argument that will be passed to the procedure.

Availability

Release 5 and later.

Description

The `XrmEnumerateDatabase` function calls the specified procedure for each resource in the database that would match some completion of the given name/class resource prefix. The order in which resources are found is implementation-dependent. If *mode* is `XrmEnumOne-Level`, then a resource must match the given name/class prefix with just a single name and class appended. If *mode* is `XrmEnumAllLevels`, the resource must match the given name/class prefix with one or more names and classes appended. If the procedure returns `True`, the enumeration terminates and the function returns `True`. If the procedure always returns `False`, all matching resources are enumerated and the function returns `False`.

The procedure is called with the following arguments:

```
(*proc)(database, bindings, quarks, type, value, arg)
      XrmDatabase *database;
      XrmBindingList bindings;
      XrmQuarkList quarks;
      XrmRepresentation *type;
      XrmValue *value;
      XPointer closure;
```

The bindings and quarks lists are terminated by NULLQUARK. Note that pointers to the database and type are passed, but these values should not be modified.

Structures

```
#define     XrmEnumAllLevels          0
#define     XrmEnumOneLevel           1
```

Related Commands

XrmGetResource, XrmInitialize, XrmPutResource

XrmGetDatabase

Name

XrmGetDatabase – retrieve the resource database associated with a display.

Synopsis

```
XrmDatabase XrmGetDatabase(display)
    Display *display;
```

Arguments

display   Specifies the connection to the X server.

Availability

Release 5 and later.

Description

The XrmGetDatabase function returns the database associated with the specified display. It returns NULL if a database has not yet been set with XrmSetDatabase.

Related Commands

XrmSetDatabase

XrmLocaleOfDatabase

Name

XrmLocaleOfDatabase – return the locale of a resource database.

Synopsis

```
char *XrmLocaleOfDatabase(database)
    XrmDatabase database;
```

Arguments

database   Specifies the database that is to be used.

Availability

Release 5 and later.

Description

XrmLocaleOfDatabase returns the name of the locale bound to the specified database, as a null-terminated string. The returned locale name string is owned by Xlib and should not be modified or freed by the client. Xlib is not permitted to free the string until the database is destroyed. Until the string is freed, it will not be modified by Xlib.

Related Commands

XrmGetFileDatabase, XrmGetStringDatabase, XrmDestroyDatabase

Reference

Name

XrmSetDatabase – associate a resource database with a display.

Synopsis

```
void XrmSetDatabase(display, database)
    Display *display;
    XrmDatabase database;
```

Arguments

display   Specifies the connection to the X server.

database   Specifies the resource database.

Availability

Release 5 and later.

Description

The **XrmSetDatabase** function associates the specified resource database (or NULL) with the specified display. The database previously associated with the display (if any) is not destroyed. A client or toolkit may find this function convenient for retaining a database once it is constructed.

Related Commands

XrmGetDatabase

XScreenResourceString

Name

XScreenResourceString – obtain server resource properties.

Synopsis

```
char *XScreenResourceString(screen)
    Screen *screen;
```

Arguments

screen   Specifies the screen.

Availability

Release 5 and later.

Description

The `XScreenResourceString` returns the SCREEN_RESOURCES property from the root window of the specified screen. The property is converted from type STRING to the current locale. The conversion is identical to that produced by `XmbTextPropertyToTextList` for a singleton STRING property. Note that the property value must be in a format that is acceptable to `XrmGetStringDatabase`. If no property exists, NULL is returned. The caller is responsible for freeing the returned string, using `XFree`.

`XScreenResourceString` reads the window property each time it is requested. This differs from the behavior of `XResourceManagerString` which simply returns the value of the property as it was defined when the connection with the X server was established.

Related Commands

`XResourceManagerString`

XSetICFocus

Name

XSetICFocus – set input context focus.

Synopsis

```
void XSetICFocus(ic)
    XIC ic;
```

Arguments

ic   Specifies the input context.

Availability

Release 5 and later.

Description

The XSetICFocus function allows a client to notify an input method that the focus window attached to the specified input context has received keyboard focus. The input method should take action to provide appropriate feedback.

Related Commands

XCreateIC, XSetICValues, XmbResetIC, XwcResetIC, XUnsetICFocus

Name

XSetICValues – set input context attributes.

Synopsis

```
char * XSetICValues(ic, ...)
    XIC ic;
```

Arguments

ic   Specifies the input context.

...   Specifies the variable length argument list to set or get XIC values.

Availability

Release 5 and later.

Description

XSetICValues sets the values of input context attributes. The first argument is the input context, and it is followed by a NULL-terminated variable-length argument list of attribute name/value pairs. The standard attributes and their types are listed in the tables below.

Input Context Attributes

Name	Type	Notes
XNInputStyle	XIMStyle	Required at IC creation; may not be changed.
XNClientWindow	Window	Must be set before IC use; may not be changed.
XNFocusWindow	Window	Changes may cause geometry negotiation.
XNResourceName	char *	
XNResourceClass	char *	
XNGeometryCallback	XIMCallback *	
XNFilterEvents	unsigned long	Read-only attribute; may not be set.
XNPreeditAttributes	XVaNestedList	See sub-attributes below.
XNStatusAttributes	XVaNestedList	See sub-attributes below.

Preedit and Status Area Sub-attributes

Name	Type	Notes
XNArea	XRectangle *	
XNAreaNeeded	XRectangle *	
XNSpotLocation	XPoint *	Required at IC creation for XIMPreeditPosition style.
XNColormap	Colormap	
XNStdColormap	Atom	

Reference

Preedit and Status Area Sub-attributes (Continued)

Name	Type	Notes
XNForeground	unsigned long	
XNBackground	unsigned long	
XNBackgroundPixmap	Pixmap	
XNFontSet	XFontSet	Required at IC creation; changes may cause geometry negotiation.
XNLineSpacing	int	Changes may cause geometry negotiation.
XNCursor	Cursor	
XNPreeditStartCallback	XIMCallback *	Required at IC creation for XIMPreedit-Callbacks style.
XNPreeditDoneCallback	XIMCallback *	Required at IC creation for XIMPreedit-Callbacks style.
XNPreeditDrawCallback	XIMCallback *	Required at IC creation for XIMPreedit-Callbacks style.
XNPreeditCaretCallback	XIMCallback *	Required at IC creation for XIMPreedit-Callbacks style.
XNStatusStartCallback	XIMCallback *	Required at IC creation for XIMStatus-Callbacks style.
XNStatusDoneCallback	XIMCallback *	Required at IC creation for XIMStatus-Callbacks style.
XNStatusDrawCallback	XIMCallback *	Required at IC creation for XIMStatus-Callbacks style.

In addition to the attribute names above, the special name `XNVaNestedList` indicates that the following argument is a `XVaNestedList` of attribute name/value pairs. When a nested list is encountered in an argument list, the contents of the nested list are processed as if they appeared in the original argument list at that point.

`XSetICValues` returns `NULL` if no error occurred; otherwise, it returns the name of the first attribute that could not be set. An attribute could be not set for any of the following reasons:

• A read-only attribute was set (for example, `XNFilterEvents`).

• The attribute name is not recognized.

• The input method encountered an input method implementation dependent error.

Each value to be set must match the type of the attribute.

The `XSetICValues` can generate `BadAtom`, `BadColor`, `BadCursor`, `BadPixmap`, and `BadWindow` errors.

Errors

BadAtom A value for an Atom argument does not name a defined Atom.

BadColor A value for a Colormap argument does not name a defined Colormap.

`BadCursor`   A value for a Cursor argument does not name a defined Cursor.

`BadPixmap`   A value for a Pixmap argument does not name a defined Pixmap.

`BadWindow`   A value for a Window argument does not name a defined Window.

Related Commands
`XCreateIC, XSetICFocus, XmbResetIC, XwcResetIC, XGetICValues`

XSetLocaleModifiers

Name

XSetLocaleModifiers – configure locale modifiers.

Synopsis

```
char *XSetLocaleModifiers(modifier_list)
    char *modifier_list;
```

Arguments

modifier_list   Specifies the modifiers.

Availability

Release 5 and later.

Description

XSetLocaleModifiers sets or queries the X modifiers for the current locale setting. If the *modifier_list* argument is NULL, XSetLocaleModifiers returns the current settings of the X modifiers without modifying them. Otherwise, the *modifier_list* argument is the empty string or a string of the form "{@*category*=*value*}", that is, having zero or more concatenated "@*category*=*value*" entries where *category* is a category name and *value* is the (possibly empty) setting for that category. The values are encoded in the current locale. Category names are restricted to the POSIX Portable Filename Character Set.

The local host X locale modifiers announcer (on POSIX-compliant systems, the XMODIFIERS environment variable) is appended to the *modifier_list* to provide default values on the local host. If a given category appears more than once in the list, the first setting in the list is used. If a given category is not included in the full modifier list, the category is set to an implementation-dependent default for the current locale. An empty value for a category explicitly specifies the implementation-dependent default.

If XSetLocaleModifiers is successful, it returns a string of the current locale modifiers obtained from the *modifier_list* argument and the XMODIFIERS environment variable. This string is formatted so that it may be passed in a subsequent call to XSetLocale-Modifiers to restore the state of the X modifiers. When the current modifiers are queried with a NULL *modifier_list* argument, the returned string is also in this format.

If invalid values are given for one or more modifier categories supported by the locale, a NULL pointer is returned, and none of the current modifiers are changed.

At program startup the modifiers that are in effect are unspecified until the first successful call to set them. Whenever the locale is changed, the modifiers that are in effect become unspecified until the next successful call to set them. Clients should always call XSetLocale-Modifiers with a non-NULL *modifier_list* after setting the locale, before they call any locale-dependent Xlib routine.

The only standard modifier category currently defined is "im," which identifies the desired input method. The values for this category are not standardized. A single locale may use multiple input methods, switching input method under user control. The modifier may specify the initial input method in effect, or an ordered list of input methods. Multiple input methods may be specified in a single im value string in an implementation-dependent manner.

The returned modifiers string is owned by Xlib and should not be modified or freed by the client. It may be freed by Xlib after the current locale or modifiers is changed. Until freed, it will not be modified by Xlib.

Related Commands
XSupportsLocale

XSupportsLocale

Xlib - Locale Management

Name

XSupportsLocale – determine locale support.

Synopsis

```
Bool XSupportsLocale( )
```

Availability

Release 5 and later.

Description

XSupportsLocale returns True if Xlib functions are capable of operating under the current locale. If XSupportsLocale returns False, the client should usually switch to a supported locale or exit. When the current locale is not supported, some Xlib routines will return the status XLocaleNotSupported, and others will silently operate in the default C locale.

Related Commands

XSetLocaleModifiers

Name

XtLanguageProc – prototype procedure to set locale.

Synopsis

```
typedef String (*XtLanguageProc)(Display*, String, XtPointer);
      Display *display;
      String language;
      XtPointer client_data;
```

Arguments

display   Specifies the connection to the X server.

language   Specifies the initial language value obtained from the command line or server
               per-display resource specifications.

client_data   Specifies the additional data registered with the function.

Availability

Release 5 and later.

Description

The procedure registered with **XtSetLanguageProc** and called by **XtDisplay-Initialize** is of type **XtLanguageProc**.

A language procedure is passed the language string, if any, from the application command line or per-display resources, and should use that string to localize the application appropriately. Generally, this will mean calling **setlocale**, **XSupportsLocale**, and **XSetLocale-Modifiers**. The language procedure returns a string which will be copied by **XtDisplay-Initialize** and associated with the display for subsequent use in the language path substitiutions of **XtResolvePathname**. This string will generally be the string returned from the call to **setlocale**.

Related Commands

XtSetLanguageProc

Name

XtSetLanguageProc – register the language procedure that will be called to set the locale.

Synopsis

```
XtLanguageProc XtSetLanguageProc(app_context, proc, client_data)
    XtAppContext app_context;
    XtLanguageProc proc;
    XtPointer client_data;
```

Arguments

app_context   Specifies the application context in which the language procedure is to be used, or NULL.

proc   Specifies the language procedure.

client_data   Specifies additional data to be passed to the language procedure when it is called.

Availability

Release 5 and later.

Description

XtSetLanguageProc sets the language procedure that will be called from XtDisplay-Initialize for all subsequent displays initialized in the specified application context. If *app_context* is NULL, the specified language procedure is registered in all application contexts created by the calling process, including any future application contexts that may be created. If *proc* is NULL a default language procedure is registered. XtSetLanguageProc returns the previously registered language procedure. If a language procedure has not yet been registered, the return value is unspecified but if it is used in a subsequent call to XtSet-LanguageProc, it will cause the default language procedure to be registered.

The default language procedure does the following:

• Sets the locale according to the environment. On ANSI C-based systems this is done by calling setlocale (LC_ALL , *language*). If an error is encountered a warning message is issued with XtWarning .

• Calls XSupportsLocale to verify that the current locale is supported. If the locale is not supported, a warning message is issued with XtWarning and the locale is set to "C."

• Calls XSetLocaleModifiers specifying the empty string.

• Returns the value of the current locale. On ANSI C-based systems this is the return value from a final call to setlocale (LC_ALL, NULL).

A client wishing to use this default procedure to establish locale can do so as in following example:

```
Widget top;
XtSetLanguageProc(NULL, NULL, NULL);
top = XtAppInitialize( ... );
```

Related Commands
`XtLanguageProc, XtDisplayInitialize`

XUnsetICFocus

Name

XUnsetICFocus – set and unset input context focus.

Synopsis

```
void XUnsetICFocus(ic)
   XIC ic;
```

Arguments

ic   Specifies the input context.

Availability

Release 5 and later.

Description

The `XUnsetICFocus` function allows a client to notify an input method that the specified input context has lost the keyboard focus and that no more input is expected on the focus window attached to that input context. The input method should take action to provide appropriate feedback.

Related Commands

XCreateIC, XSetICValues, XmbResetIC, XwcResetIC, XSetICFocus

Name

XVaCreateNestedList – allocate a nested variable argument list.

Synopsis

```
typedef void * XVaNestedList;
XVaNestedList XVaCreateNestedList(dummy, ...)
    int dummy;
```

Arguments

dummy   Unused argument (required by ANSI C).

...   Specifies the variable length argument list.

Availability

Release 5 and later.

Description

XVaCreateNestedList creates a nested argument list of type XVaNestedList. The first argument is an integer value which is unused but required because ANSI-C does not allow variable-length argument lists which do not have any "non-variable" arguments. This first argument is followed by a NULL-terminated variable-length argument list. Generally, the arguments will be input method or input context attribute name/value pairs.

Nested lists created in this way may be used in any of the input method and input context functions which require a variable-length argument list. Also, the XNPreeditAttributes and XNStatusAttributes input context attributes are of this type XVaNestedList.

XVaCreateNestedList allocates memory and copies its arguments into a single list pointer which may be used as value for arguments requiring a list value. Any entries are copied as specified. Data passed by reference is not copied; the caller must ensure that data remains valid for the lifetime of the nested list. The list should be freed using XFree when it is no longer needed.

Related Commands

XCreateIC, XSetICValues, XGetICValues

Reference

Name

XwcDrawImageString – draw internationalized wide-character image text.

Synopsis

```
void XwcDrawImageString(display, drawable, font_set, gc, x, y, string,
        num_wchars)
    Display *display;
    Drawable drawable;
    XFontSet font_set;
    GC gc;
    int x, y;
    wchar_t *string;
    int num_wchars;
```

Arguments

display	Specifies the connection to the X server.
drawable	Specifies the drawable.
font_set	Specifies the font set.
gc	Specifies the GC.
x, y	Specifies the starting position and baseline of the text, relative to the origin of the specified drawable.
string	Specifies the character string.
num_wchars	Specifies the number of characters in the string argument.

Availability

Release 5 and later.

Description

XwcDrawImageString fills a destination rectangle with the background pixel defined in the GC and then paints the specified wide-character text with the foreground pixel. The filled rectangle is the rectangle returned to *overall_logical_return* by XmbTextExtents or XwcTextExtents for the same text and XFontSet.

When the XFontSet has missing charsets, each unavailable character is drawn with the default string returned by XCreateFontSet. The behavior for an invalid codepoint is undefined.

XwcDrawImageString draws with fonts from the font set rather than the font of the GC. For this reason, it may modify the font value of the GC. Except for the font, it uses the same GC components as its pre-X11R5 analog XDrawImageString.

Related Commands

XDrawImageString, XDrawString, XDrawText, XwcDrawString, XwcDrawText, XmbDrawImageString

Name

XwcDrawString – draw internationalized wide-character text.

Synopsis

```
void XwcDrawString(display, drawable, font_set, gc, x, y, string,
        num_wchars)
    Display *display;
    Drawable drawable;
    XFontSet font_set;
    GC gc;
    int x, y;
    wchar_t *string;
    int num_wchars;
```

Arguments

display	Specifies the connection to the X server.
drawable	Specifies the drawable.
font_set	Specifies the font set.
gc	Specifies the GC.
x, y	Specifies the starting position and baseline of the text, relative to the origin of the specified drawable.
string	Specifies the character string.
num_wchars	Specifies the number of characters in the string argument.

Availability

Release 5 and later.

Description

XwcDrawString draws the specified wide-character text with the foreground pixel. When the XFontSet has missing charsets, each unavailable character is drawn with the default string returned by XCreateFontSet. The behavior for an invalid codepoint is undefined.

XwcDrawString draws with fonts from the font set rather than the font of the GC. For this reason, it may modify the font value of the GC. Except for the font, it uses the same GC components as its pre-X11R5 analog XDrawString.

Related Commands

XDrawImageString, XDrawString, XDrawText, XwcDrawImageString,
XwcDrawText, XmbDrawString

Reference

Name

XwcDrawText – draw internationalized wide-character text using multiple font sets.

Synopsis

```
void XwcDrawText(display, drawable, gc, x, y, items, nitems)
    Display *display;
    Drawable drawable;
    GC gc;
    int x, y;
    XwcTextItem *items;
    int nitems;
```

Arguments

display   Specifies the connection to the X server.

drawable   Specifies the drawable.

gc   Specifies the GC.

x, y   Specifies the starting position and baseline of the text, relative to the origin of the specified drawable.

items   Specifies an array of text items.

nitems   Specifies the number of text items in the array.

Availability

Release 5 and later.

Description

XwcDrawText allows complex spacing and font set shifts between wide-character text strings. Each text item is processed in turn, with the origin of a text element advanced in the primary draw direction by the escapement of the previous text item. A text item delta specifies an additional escapement of the text item drawing origin in the primary draw direction. A *font_set* member other than None in an item causes the font set to be used for this and subsequent text items in the *items* list. Leading text items with *font_set* member set to None will not be drawn.

XwcDrawText does not perform any context-dependent rendering between text segments. Clients may compute the drawing metrics by passing each text segment to XwcTextExtents or XmbTextPerCharExtents. When the XFontSet has missing charsets, each unavailable character is drawn with the default string returned by XCreateFontSet. The behavior for an invalid codepoint is undefined.

XwcDrawText draws with fonts from the font sets of the *items* list rather than the font of the GC. For this reason, it may modify the font value of the GC. Except for the font, it uses the same GC components as its pre-X11R5 analog XDrawText

Structures

The XwcTextItem structure contains:

```
typedef struct {
        wchar_t *chars;                 /* pointer to wide char string */
        int nchars;                     /* number of wide characters */
        int delta;                      /* pixel delta between strings */
        XFontSet font_set;              /* fonts, None means don't change */
} XwcTextItem;
```

Related Commands

XDrawImageString, XDrawString, XDrawText, XwcDrawImageString,
XwcDrawString, XmbDrawText

Name

XwcFreeStringList – free memory allocated by **XwcTextPropertyToTextList**.

Synopsis

```
void XwcFreeStringList(list)
   wchar_t **list;
```

Arguments

list   Specifies the list of strings to be freed.

Availability

Release 5 and later.

Description

XwcFreeStringList frees the string list and component strings allocated by **XwcText-PropertyToTextList**.

Related Commands

XwcTextPropertyToTextList

Name

XwcLookupString – obtain composed wide-character input from an input method.

Synopsis

```
int XwcLookupString(ic, event, buffer_return, bytes_buffer,
        keysym_return, status_return)
    XIC ic;
    XKeyPressedEvent *event;
    wchar_t *buffer_return;
    int wchars_buffer;
    KeySym *keysym_return;
    Status *status_return;
```

Arguments

ic	Specifies the input context.
event	Specifies the keypress event to be used.
buffer_return	Returns a wide-character string (if any) from the input method.
wchars_buffer	Specifies the number of wide-characters in return buffer.
keysym_return	Returns the KeySym computed from the event if this argument is not NULL.
status_return	Returns a value indicating what kind of data is returned.

Availability

Release 5 and later.

Description

XmbLookupString passes a **KeyPress** event to an input context, returns composed text in the encoding of the locale of the input context if any is ready, and may return a keysym corresponding to the **KeyPress** event as well.

There are several possible results of a call to XmbLookupString, and a client should check the value returned in the *status_return* argument to determine which has occured. The possible values are:

XBufferOverflow

The input string to be returned is too large for the supplied *buffer_return*. The required size in characters is returned as the value of the function, and the contents of *buffer_return* and *keysym_return* are not modified. The client should re-call the function with the same event and a buffer of adequate size in order to obtain the string.

XLookupNone

No consistent input has been composed so far. The contents of *buffer_return* and *keysym_return* are not modified, and the function returns zero.

Reference

XLookupChars

> Some input characters have been composed. They are placed in the *buffer_return* argument, and the string length is returned as the value of the function. The string is encoded in the locale bound to the input context. The contents of the *keysym_return* argument is not modified.

XLookupKeySym

> A KeySym has been returned instead of a string and is returned in *keysym_return*. The contents of the *buffer_return* argument is not modified, and the function returns zero.

XLookupBoth

> Both a KeySym and a string are returned; XLookupChars and XLookupKeySym occur simultaneously.

When XmbLookupString returns a string, the return value of the function is the length in bytes of that string. The returned string is a multi-byte string in the encoding of the locale of the input context. If that encoding is state-dependent, the string begins in the initial state of the encoding.

When both a keysym and a string are returned, the string does not necessarily correspond to the keysym. An application that is not interested in return keysyms can pass a NULL *keysym_return*

Note that only **KeyPress** events should be passed to XmbLookupString. When Key-Release events are passed, the resulting behavior is undefined. It does not make any difference if the input context passed as an argument to XmbLookupString and XwcLookupString is the one currently in possession of the focus or not. Input may have been composed within an input context before it lost the focus, and that input may be returned on subsequent calls to XmbLookupString or XwcLookupString, even though it no longer has any more keyboard focus.

Related Commands

XLookupKeysym, XmbLookupString

Name

XwcResetIC – reset the state of an input context.

Synopsis

```
wchar_t * XwcResetIC(ic)
    XIC ic;
```

Arguments

ic   Specifies the input context.

Availability

Release 5 and later.

Description

XwcResetIC resets an input context to its initial state. Any input pending on that context is deleted. The input method is required to clear the Preedit area, if any, and update the Status area accordingly. Calling this function does not change the input context focus.

The return value of XwcResetIC is implementation dependent. If there was input pending on the input context, XwcResetIC may return composed wide-character text in the encoding of the locale of the input context, or it may return NULL. If any string is returned, the client is responsible for freeing it by calling XFree.

Related Commands

XCreateIC, XSetICFocus, XSetICValues, XmbResetIC

XwcTextEscapement

Name

XwcTextEscapement – obtain the width of internationalized wide-character text.

Synopsis

```
int XwcTextEscapement(font_set, string, num_wchars)
    XFontSet font_set;
    wchar_t *string;
    int num_wchars;
```

Arguments

font_set   Specifies the font set.

string   Specifies the character string.

num_wchars   Specifies the number of characters in the string argument.

Availability

Release 5 and later.

Description

XwcTextEscapement returns the escapement in pixels of the specified wide-character string using the fonts loaded for the specified font set. The escapement is the distance in pixels in the primary draw direction from the drawing origin to the origin of the next character to be drawn, assuming that the rendering of the next character is not dependent on the supplied string.

The escapement is always positive, regardless of the character rendering order.

Related Commands

XwcTextExtents, XwcTextPerCharExtents, XmbTextEscapement

XwcTextExtents

Name

XwcTextExtents – compute the extents of internationalized wide-character text.

Synopsis

```
int XwcTextExtents(font_set, string, num_wchars, overall_ink_return,
        overall_logical_return)
   XFontSet font_set;
   wchar_t *string;
   int num_wchars;
   XRectangle *overall_ink_return;
   XRectangle *overall_logical_return;
```

Arguments

font_set   Specifies the font set.

string   Specifies the character string.

num_wchars   Specifies the number of characters in the string argument.

overall_ink_return
                  Returns the overall ink dimensions.

overall_logical_return
                  Returns the overall logical dimensions.

Availability

Release 5 and later.

Description

XwcTextExtents sets the components of the specified overall_ink_return and overall_logical_return arguments to the overall bounding box of the string's image, and the overall logical bounding box of the string's image plus inter-line and inter-character spacing. It returns the value returned by XwcTextEscapement. The returned metrics are relative to the drawing origin of the string, using the fonts loaded for the specified font set.

If the overall_ink_return argument is non-NULL, it is set to the bounding box of the string's character ink. Note that the overall_ink_return for a non-descending horizontally drawn Latin character is conventionally entirely above the baseline, that is, overall_ink_return.height <= -overall_ink_return.y. The overall_ink_return for a nonkerned character is entirely at and to the right of the origin, that is, overall_ink_return.x >= 0. A character consisting of a single pixel at the origin would have overall_ink_return fields $y = 0$, $x = 0$, $width = 1$, and $height = 1$.

If the overall_logical_return argument is non-NULL, it is set to the bounding box which provides minimum spacing to other graphical features for the string. Other graphical features, for example, a border surrounding the text, should not intersect this rectangle.

When the XFontSet has missing charsets, metrics for each unavailable character are taken from the default string returned by XCreateFontSet so that the metrics represent the text as it will actually be drawn. The behavior for an invalid codepoint is undefined.

Structures
```
typedef struct {
    short x, y;
    unsigned short width, height;
} XRectangle;
```

Related Commands
XwcTextEscapement, XwcTextPerCharExtents, XmbTextExtents

Name

XwcTextListToTextProperty – convert an internationalized wide-character text list to a text property structure.

Synopsis

```
int XwcTextListToTextProperty(display, list, count, style,
        text_prop_return)
    Display *display;
    wchar_t **list;
    int count;
    XICCEncodingStyle style;
    XTextProperty *text_prop_return;
```

Arguments

display   Specifies the connection to the X server.

list   Specifies an array of null-terminated wide-character strings.

count   Specifies the number of strings specified.

style   Specifies the manner in which the property is encoded.

text_prop_return
        Returns the XTextProperty structure.

Availability

Release 5 and later.

Description

XwcTextListToTextProperty sets the specified XTextProperty value to a set of null-separated elements representing the concatenation of the specified list of null-terminated text strings. A final terminating null is stored at the end of the value field of text_prop_return but is not included in the nitems field.

XwcTextListToTextProperty sets the encoding field of text_prop_return to an Atom (for the specified display), which names the encoding specified by style, and converts the specified text list to this encoding for storage in the value field of text_prop_return. If the style XStringStyle or XCompoundTextStyle is specified, this encoding is STRING or COMPOUND_TEXT, respectively. If the style XTextStyle is specified, this encoding is the encoding of the current locale. If the style XStdICCTextStyle is specified, this encoding is STRING if the text is fully convertible to STRING, otherwise it is COMPOUND_TEXT.

If insufficient memory is available for the new value string, XwcTextListToText-Property returns XNoMemory. If the current locale is not supported, it returns XLocale-NotSupported. In both of these error cases, it does not set text_prop_return. Xmb-TextListToTextProperty will not return XLocaleNotSupported if XSupports-Locale has returned True for the current locale.

To determine if the functions are guaranteed not to return `XLocaleNotSupported`, use `XSupportsLocale`.

If the supplied text is not fully convertible to the specified encoding, `XwcTextListToText-Property` returns the number of unconvertible characters. Each unconvertible character is converted to an implementation-defined and encoding-specific default string. If the text is fully convertible, `XwcTextListToTextProperty` returns `Success`. Note that full convertibility to all styles except `XStringStyle` is guaranteed. If the supplied text contains bytes that are not valid characters in the encoding of the locale ("invalid codepoints"), the result is undefined.

`XwcTextListToTextProperty` allocates memory for the *value* field of the `XText-Property`. The client is responsible for freeing this memory by calling `XFree`.

Structures

The `XTextProperty` structure contains:

```
typedef struct   {
    unsigned char *value;    /* property data */
    Atom encoding;           /* type of property */
    int format;              /* 8, 16, or 32 */
    unsigned long nitems;    /* number of items in value */
} XTextProperty;
```

The `XICCEncodingStyle` structure contains:

```
typedef enum    {
    XStringStyle,           /* STRING */
    XCompoundTextStyle,     /* COMPOUND_TEXT */
    XTextStyle,             /* text in owner's encoding (current locale) */
    XStdICCTextStyle        /* STRING, else COMPOUND_TEXT */
} XICCEncodingStyle;
```

The possible return values of this function are as follows:

```
#define   XNoMemory              −1
#define   XLocaleNotSupported    −2
#define   XConverterNotFound     −3
```

Related Commands

XSetTextProperty, XStringListToTextProperty, XDefaultString,
XmbTextListToTextProperty, XmbTextPropertyToTextList,
XwcTextPropertyToTextList, XwcFreeStringList

Name

XwcTextPerCharExtents – obtain per-character measurements of an internationalized wide-
character text string.

Synopsis

```
Status XwcTextPerCharExtents(font_set, string, num_wchars,
        ink_array_return, logical_array_return, array_size,
        num_chars_return, overall_ink_return, overall_logical_return)
    XFontSet font_set;
    wchar_t *string;
    int num_wchars;
    XRectangle *ink_array_return;
    XRectangle *logical_array_return;
    int array_size;
    int *num_chars_return;
    XRectangle *overall_ink_return;
    XRectangle *overall_logical_return;
```

Arguments

font_set   Specifies the font set.

string   Specifies the character string.

num_wchars   Specifies the number of characters in the string argument.

ink_array_return
                  Returns the ink dimensions for each character.

logical_array_return
                  Returns the logical dimensions for each character.

array_size   Specifies the size of *ink_array_return* and the size of
                  logical_array_return. The caller must pass in arrays of this size.

num_chars_return
                  Returns the number characters in the string argument.

overall_ink_return
                  Returns the overall ink extents of the entire string.

overall_logical_return
                  Returns the overall logical extents of the entire string.

Availability

Release 5 and later.

Description

XwcTextPerCharExtents returns the text dimensions of each character of the specified
text, using the fonts loaded for the specified font set. Each element of *ink_array_return*
and *logical_array_return* is set to the corresponding character's drawn metrics, rela-

tive to the drawing origin of the string. The number of elements of *ink_array_return* and *logical_array_return* that have been set is returned in *num_chars_return*.

Each element of *ink_array_return* is set to the bounding box of the corresponding character's drawn foreground color. Each element of *logical_array_return* is set to the bounding box which provides minimum spacing to other graphical features for the corresponding character. Other graphical features should not intersect any of the *logical_array_return* rectangles.

Note that an XRectangle represents the effective drawing dimensions of the character, regardless of the number of font glyphs that are used to draw the character, or the direction in which the character is drawn. If multiple characters map to a single character glyph, the dimensions of all the XRectangles of those characters are the same.

When the XFontSet has missing charsets, metrics for each unavailable character are taken from the default string returned by XCreateFontSet, so that the metrics represent the text as it will actually be drawn. The behavior for an invalid codepoint is undefined.

If the *array_size* is too small for the number of characters in the supplied text, the function returns zero and *num_chars_return* is set to the number of rectangles required. Otherwise, it returns a non-zero value.

If the *overall_ink_return* or *overall_logical_return* argument is non-NULL, XwcTextPerCharExtents returns the maximum extent of the string's metrics to *overall_ink_return* or *overall_logical_return*, as is done by XwcTextExtents.

Structures
```
typedef struct {
    short x, y;
    unsigned short width, height;
} XRectangle;
```

Related Commands
XwcTextEscapement, XwcTextExtents, XmbTextPerCharExtents

Name

XwcTextPropertyToTextList – convert an internationalized text property to a list of wide-character strings.

Synopsis

```
int XwcTextPropertyToTextList(display, text_prop, list_return,
        count_return)
    Display *display;
    XTextProperty *text_prop;
    wchar_t ***list_return;
    int *count_return;
```

Arguments

display   Specifies the connection to the X server.

text_prop   Specifies the XTextProperty structure to be used.

list_return   Returns a list of null-terminated character strings.

count_return   Returns the number of strings.

Availability

Release 5 and later.

Description

XwcTextPropertyToTextList return a list of wide-character text strings encoded in the current locale representing the null-separated elements of the specified XTextProperty structure. The data in text_prop must be format 8.

Multiple elements of the property (for example, the strings in a disjoint text selection) are separated by a null byte. The contents of the property are not required to be null-terminated; any terminating null should not be included in text_prop.nitems.

If insufficient memory is available for the list and its elements, XwcTextPropertyTo-TextList returns XNoMemory. If the current locale is not supported, it returns XLocale-NotSupported. If the encoding field of text_prop is not convertible to the encoding of the current locale, it returns XConverterNotFound. For supported locales, existence of a converter from COMPOUND_TEXT, STRING, or the encoding of the current locale is guaranteed although the actual text may contain unconvertible characters. Conversion of other encodings is implementation-dependent. In all of these error cases, the function does not set any return values.

Otherwise, XwcTextPropertyToTextList returns the list of null-terminated text strings to list_return, and the number of text strings to count_return.

If the value field of text_prop is not fully convertible to the encoding of the current locale, the functions return the number of unconvertible characters. Each unconvertible character is converted to a string in the current locale that is specific to the current locale. To obtain the value of this string, use XDefaultString. If all characters are convertible, XwcText-PropertyToTextList returns Success. If the text property contains "invalid codepoints" or bytes that are not valid characters in the encoding of the property, the result is undefined.

Structures

The XTextProperty structure contains:

```
typedef struct                    {
        unsigned char *value;     /* property data */
        Atom encoding;            /* type of property */
        int format;               /* 8, 16, or 32 */
        unsigned long nitems;     /* number of items in value */
} XTextProperty;
```

The possible return values of this function are as follows:

```
#define    XNoMemory                  -1
#define    XLocaleNotSupported        -2
#define    XConverterNotFound         -3
```

Related Commands

XSetTextProperty, XStringListToTextProperty, XDefaultString,
XmbTextListToTextProperty, XmbTextPropertyToTextList,
XwcFreeStringList, XwcTextListToTextProperty

A

Release Notes

This appendix reprints the release notes that accompany the MIT X11R5 distribution, X Window System, Version 11, Release 5, Release Notes *by the MIT X Consortium Staff. It contains information on building X11R5, configuring the release to build on new systems, reporting bugs, obtaining patches, and so on. It also details the various bug fixes in X11R5 clients and widgets. Some sections of the original MIT release notes have been omitted here because they are thoroughly covered in the chapters of this book. For this reason, section numbers in this appendix do not correspond to section numbers in the original release notes.*

In This Chapter:

A
Release Notes

This document describes how to build, install, and get started with Release 5 of the X Window System from MIT and gives a brief overview of the contents of the release.

A.1 Brief Overview of the Distribution

(If you want, you can skip to the next section first, and get your build started. While it is compiling, you will have plenty of time to read the rest of the release notes.)

There are two parts to the Release 5 distribution: MIT software and documentation, and user-contributed software and documentation. The MIT part contains:

X Consortium Standards
> The MIT X Consortium produces standards: documents which define network protocols, programming interfaces, and other aspects of the X environment. See the *XStandards* man page for a list of standards. See the *XConsortium* man page for information about the X Consortium.

Sample Implementations
> For most of our standards, we provide *sample* implementations to demonstrate proof of concept. These are not *reference* implementations; the written specifications define the standards.

Fonts
> A collection of bitmap and outline fonts are included in the distribution, contributed by various individuals and companies.

Utility Libraries
> A number of libraries, such as the *Athena Widget Set*, are included. These are not standards, but are used in building MIT applications and may be useful in building other applications.

Sample Programs
> We also provide a number of application programs. A few of these programs, such as *xdm*, should be considered essential in almost all environments. The rest of the applications carry no special status, they are simply programs that have been developed and/or maintained by MIT X Consortium staff. In some cases, you will find better substitutes for these programs in the user-contributed software.

The user-contributed part contains whatever people contribute. You find a variety of software and documentation here, including application programs, demos, examples, libraries, Asian input methods, and X server extensions.

A.1.1 Structure of the MIT Sources

All of the MIT sources are under a single directory, *mit*. Sources are organized into the following subdirectories:

clients This directory contains most of the sample applications. See the program man pages for details.

config This directory contains configuration files and the *imake* program used to build the release. Details are covered in other sections below.

demos This directory contains a small collection of graphics demonstration programs, a few utility/test programs, and some performance demonstration programs. These are by no means the "best" demo programs around, they just happen to be ones we try to maintain.

doc This directory contains *troff* sources to X Consortium standards, server internals documentation, documentation for various utility libraries, and some useful tutorial material.

extensions This directory contains implementations of X server extensions, both the server internals and the application programming libraries, and some test programs. Of particular note here, new in Release 5, is PEX, the PHIGS Extension to X used for 3-D graphics, and the PHIGS programming library, which interfaces to the PEX protocol.

fonts This directory contains bitmap fonts in source form, some outline fonts, a sample font server, a utility font library used by the X server and font server, a client font library for interacting with the font server, and programs for building fonts and querying the font server.

hardcopy This directory contains pregenerated PostScript files for the client man pages and for most of the documentation found in the *doc* directory. The files are compressed with *compress* to save disk space. If you do not have *compress* on your system, you will find a version in the *mit/util/compress* directory.

include This directory contains various library-independent C header files and a collection of bitmap files.

lib This directory contains programming libraries and support files. Of note are Xlib (the lowest-level C programming interface to X), Xt (the X Toolkit Intrinsics), Xmu (an eclectic set of utility functions), Xaw (the Athena Widget Set), and CLX (a Common LISP interface to X).

man This directory contains a few top-level man pages about the release (general information, server access control mechanisms, the X Consortium, and X Consortium standards), and man pages for some of the programming libraries.

rgb　　　　This directory contains a program to generate the color database used by the X server and sample databases.

server　　This directory contains the X server sources, both device-independent (*dix*) and device-dependent (*ddx*). In this release, there is support for building the following servers: DECstation 2100/3100 monochrome and color displays. DECstation 5000 CX and MX displays. IBM RS/6000 skyway adapter. Apple Macintosh monochrome and color displays. MIPS monochrome and color displays. OMRON LUNA monochrome displays (color displays operate in monochrome). Tektronix 4319 color display. VAXstation QVSS and QDSS displays. Sun monochrome and 8-bit color displays (with GX support). Various VGA displays under System V/386.

If your favorite hardware is not listed above, please do not blame us at MIT; we ship what Consortium members provide. Only in a few cases do we try to maintain device-specific software for our own development needs.

util　　　This directory contains miscellaneous utility programs and shell scripts used to build, maintain, and install the release.

A.2 Building the Release

The core distribution (code under the *mit* directory) has been built and tested at MIT on the following systems:

> AIX 3.1.5, on IBM RS/6000
> Apollo SR10.3 (very minimal testing, bsd4.3 only)
> AT&T Unix System V Release 4 V2, on AT&T WGS6386
> A/UX 2.0.1
> HP-UX 7.0, on HP9000/s300
> IRIX 4.0
> Mach 2.5 Version 1.13, on OMRON Luna 88k
> NEWS-OS 4.1, on Sony NWS-1850
> NEWS-OS 5.0U, on Sony NWS-3710
> SunOS 4.1.1, on Sun 3, Sparc 1, and Sparc 2
> Ultrix-32 4.2, VAX and RISC
> UNICOS 5.1
> UTek 4.0
> VAX 4.3bsd (with unknown local changes)

In some cases, we have not used the most recent version of the operating system (sorry). Support for earlier versions of the operating systems listed is not claimed, and not guaranteed.

In addition to the previously-mentioned systems, support has been provided by vendors for:

> AIX 2.2 and AOS 4.3, on IBM RT
> AIX 1.2.1, on IBM PS/2
> ConvexOS V9.0
> DG/UX 4.32
> INTERACTIVE UNIX Version 2.2.1
> Mach 2.5 Version 1.40, on OMRON Luna 68k
> Motorola R32V2/R3V6.2 and R40V1
> RISCOS 4.50
> UNIOS-B 4.3BSD UNIX: 2.00
> UNIX System V/386 Release 3.2, on ESIX, SCO, and AT&T ("work in progress")
> UNIX System V/386 Release 4.0, on DELL

A.2.1 Unpacking the Distribution

The distribution normally comes as multiple *tar* files, either on tape or across a network. Create a directory to hold the distribution, *cd* to it, and *untar* everything from that directory. For example:

```
mkdir sourcedir
cd sourcedir
tar xfp tar-file-or-tape-device
```

If you have obtained compressed and split *tar* files over the network, then the sequence for each part of the *mit* directory might be:

```
cd ftp-dir/mit-N
cat mit-N.?? | uncompress | (cd sourcedir; tar xfp -)
```

The sequence for each part of the `contrib` directory might be:

```
cd ftp-dir/contrib-N
cat contrib-N.?? | uncompress | (cd sourcedir; tar xfp -)
```

The *sourcedir* directory you choose can be anywhere in any of your filesystems that is convenient to you. After extracting the release, you should end up with an *mit* subdirectory, and a *contrib* subdirectory if you unpack user-contributed software. You will need about 100 megabytes of disk space to unpack the *mit* directory contents; building it will of course require more disk space.

A.2.2 Symbolic Link Trees

If you expect to build the distribution on more than one machine using a shared source tree, or you just want to keep the source tree pure, you may want to use the shell script *mit/util/scripts/lndir.sh* to create a symbolic link tree on each build machine. This is fairly expensive in disk space, however. To do this, create a directory for the build, *cd* to it, and type:

```
sourcedir/mit/util/scripts/lndir.sh sourcedir
```

where *sourcedir* is the pathname of the directory where you stored the sources. All of the build instructions given below should then be done in the build directory on each machine, rather than in the source directory.

The shell script is reasonably portable but quite slow to execute. If you want, you can instead try compiling a similar C program, but it is slightly tricky to do before the distribution is built; *cd* to the directory *mit/util/progs* and try typing:

```
ln -s ../../include X11
cc -o lndir -I. lndir.c
```

If it compiles and links, it will probably work; otherwise you can try typing:

```
cc -o lndir -I. -DNOSTDHDRS lndir.c
```

If it still fails, use the shell script.

A.2.3 Setting Configuration Parameters

You will notice that few if any of the subdirectories under *mit* contain a *Makefile*, but they do contain an *Imakefile*. The *Imakefile* is a template file used to create a *Makefile* containing build rules and variables appropriate for the target machine. The *Makefile* is generated by the program *imake*. Most of the configuration work prior to building the release is to set parameters so that *imake* will generate correct files.

The directory *mit/config* contains configuration files that control how the distribution is built. On systems directly supported by this distribution, only minimal editing of these files should be necessary. If your system is not supported by the distribution but conforms to ANSI-C and POSIX.1 and has socket-style networking, then you should be able to build a new configuration file relatively easily. Otherwise, edits to many files throughout the system may be necessary. We only deal with minor editing for supported systems here.

The main files to be concerned with in the *mit/config* directory are *site.def* and one of the *<vendor>.cf* files. The *site.def* file should be used for most site-specific configuration customizations. The *.cf* file should normally only need to be edited if you are using a different release of the operating system.

Release Notes

The vendor.cf File

The following is a list of the *.cf* filenames for various operating systems:

AIX	ibm.cf
AOS	ibm.cf
Apollo	apollo.cf
AT&T UNIX SVR4	att.cf
A/UX	macII.cf
BSD	bsd.cf
ConvexOS	convex.cf
DG/UX	DGUX.cf
HP-UX	hp.cf
INTERACTIVE	x386.cf
IRIX	sgi.cf
Mach (Luna)	luna.cf
Motorola	moto.cf
NEWS-OS	sony.cf
RISCOS	Mips.cf
SunOS	sun.cf
Ultrix	ultrix.cf
UNICOS	cray.cf
UTek	pegasus.cf
UNIOS-B	luna.cf
UNIX System V/386u	x386.cf

Look through the *.cf* file, and check the **OSMajorVersion** and **OSMinorVersion** values. The numbers have been preset to what was tested at MIT or what was supplied by the vendor. If the version numbers match the operating system you are currently running, all is well. If they do not, you will need to edit the file to make them correct. In a few cases (specifically changing UNICOS from 5.1 to 6.0) there should not be a problem in moving the version numbers forward to a newer release. However, if you are moving the version numbers backward, or moving forward to a version that hasn't been pretested, you may have problems, and you may have to edit other parts of the file (and possibly other files) to get things to work.

You can browse through the rest of the items in the *.cf* file, but most of them you should not need to edit.

The site.def File

There are two main variables to set in the *site.def* file: **HasGcc** and **ProjectRoot**. If you are going to compile the distribution with *gcc*, find the line that looks like:

```
/* #define HasGcc YES */
```

and remove the comment markers, turning it into:

```
#define HasGcc YES
```

If you are sharing a single *site.def* across multiple systems, you can do something more complicated. For example, if you only want to use *gcc* on a Sun 3 (but not on Sparcs), you might use this:

```
#ifdef SunArchitecture
#define HasGcc mc68000
#endif
```

The most common error when using *gcc* is to fail to run the *fixincludes* script (from the *gcc* distribution) when installing *gcc*. Make sure you have done this before compiling the release. Another common error is likely to be using *gcc* ANSI-C include files when the vendor operating system supplies correct ones. The *gcc* include files *assert.h*, *limits.h*, and *stddef.h* are prime candidates for not installing.

The `ProjectRoot` variable controls where the software will eventually be installed. The default as distributed for most systems is to install into "system" directories: */usr/bin/X11*, */usr/include/X11*, */usr/lib*, and */usr/man* (this is the behavior when `ProjectRoot` is not defined). If you prefer to install into alternate directories, the simplest thing to do is to set `ProjectRoot`. Find the four `ProjectRoot` lines in the *site.def* file, and again remove the "/*" and "*/" comment markers that surround them. You will see a default choice for `ProjectRoot` of */usr/X11R5*; if you don't like that one, replace it with another. Assuming you have set the variable to some value */path*, files will be installed into */path*/bin, */path*/include/X11, */path*/lib, and */path*/man.

Note that in a few cases (*ibm.cf* and *x386.cf*) the vendor-supplied *.cf* file supplies a `ProjectRoot` by default. If you want to accept this one, do not uncomment the one in *site.def*; otherwise the one you place in *site.def* will override the default setting.

The directories where the software will be installed are compiled into various programs and files during the build process, so it is important that you get the configuration correct at the outset. If you change your mind later, you will want to do a "make Everything" to rebuild correctly.

Notice that the *site.def* file was two parts, one protected with "#ifdef BeforeVendorCF" and one with "#ifdef AfterVendorCF." The file is actually processed twice, once before the *.cf* file and once after. About the only thing you need to set in the "before" section is `HasGcc`; just about everything else can be set in the "after" section.

There are a large number of parameters that you can modify to change what gets built and how it gets built. An exhaustive list and explanation will not be given here; you can browse through *mit/config/README* to see a list of parameters. However, here are some notable parameters that you can set in the "after" section:

BuildXsi and **BuildXimp**
New in this release, Xlib contains support for internationalized input methods, using library- or network-based implementation methods. The implementation details internal to Xlib can vary considerably depending on the types of input methods supported.

In this release, two different implementations are supported, named *Xsi* and *Ximp*. As distributed, the default on all systems except Sony is *Xsi*. If you want to use *Ximp* instead, add this:

```
#define BuildXimp YES
```

BuildServer

This controls whether or not an X server is built. If the variable is not set to NO in the *.cf* file, then the default is to build a server. If you want to disable the server, add this:

```
#define BuildServer NO
```

BuildFonts

Compiled fonts take up a lot of disk space. In this release, the compiled form (called "pcf") can be shared across all machines of all architectures, so you may only want to build the fonts on one machine. To disable font building, add this:

```
#define BuildFonts NO
```

BuildPex

PEX is an X extension supporting 3-D graphics and the PHIGS programming interface. The PEX sources are known to cause some compilers to exceed their static symbol table sizes. If this happens to you, you can disable PEX by adding this:

```
#define BuildPex NO
```

ManSuffix

User program man pages are installed by default in subdirectory *mann* with suffix *.n*. You can change this to *man1* and *.1*, for example, by adding this:

```
#define ManSuffix 1
```

InstallLibManPages

By default, the programming library man pages (Xlib, Xt, various extensions) are installed along with all of the other man pages. The library pages constitute a considerable number of files. If you do not expect to be programming with X, or prefer using other forms of documentation, you can disable installation of the library pages by adding this:

```
#define InstallLibManPages NO
```

InstallXdmConfig and InstallXinitConfig

The *xdm* and *xinit* programs are the normal ways to run X servers. By default, the configuration files for these programs are not installed, to avoid inadvertently destroying existing configuration files. If you are not yet using *xdm* or *xinit*, or will be installing into a new destination, or do not wish to retain your old configuration files, add these:

```
#define InstallXdmConfig YES
#define InstallXinitConfig YES
```

XdmServersType

Some of the *xdm* config files are generated based on configuration parameters. One of the files controls whether an X server is started by default. By default the choice is made based on whether an X server is built as part of this distribution (the `Build-Server` parameter). If you are not building a server, but you will be running a product server on the workstation under *xdm*, you should add this:

```
#define XdmServersType ws
```

HasXdmAuth

This release supports a DES-based form of authorization called XDM-AUTHORIZATION-1. The source file *mit/lib/Xdmcp/Wraphelp.c*, which is necessary for this to compile, might not be included in your distribution due to possible export regulations; if it is not included and you are a US citizen, you should be able to obtain the file over the network. To enable building of this mechanism, add this:

```
#define HasXdmAuth YES
```

InstallFSConfig

New to this release is a network font server, *fs*. By default, the configuration files for the font server are not installed. To have them installed, add this:

```
#define InstallFSConfig YES
```

MotifBC

If you want to use the Release 5 Xlib and Xt with Motif 1.1, you will need to enable a backward compatibility flag, by adding this:

```
#define MotifBC YES
```

A.2.4 System Pitfalls

On a few systems, you are likely to have build problems unless you make some minor changes to the system. Naturally, you should exercise caution before making changes to system files, but these are our recommendations based on our experience.

On VAX Ultrix systems, you may find that *<stdlib.h>* contains declarations of `malloc`, `calloc`, and `realloc` with a return value of `void *`. You may find this causes problems when compiling with a non-ANSI-C compiler, in which case a workaround is to change the return values to `char*` in the `#else` section.

Ultrix may not provide *<locale.h>* unless you load the Internationalization subset. You will need this file to compile the distribution (or else you will need to reset a configuration parameter, see below).

On SunOS systems, you may find that statically linking (when debugging) against both Xlib and the *libc* will result in unresolved symbols to dynamic linker functions, because Xlib contains calls to `wcstombs`. Either link dynamically against *libc*, or compile and link the stub routines in *mit/util/misc/dlsym.c*.

On Sun 3's, the default is to compile library files with no special floating-point assumptions. If all of your Sun 3's have floating-point hardware, you may want to change this, for better performance of Xlib color functions. For example, in the "after" section of your *site.def* file, you might add:

```
#if defined(SunArchitecture) && defined(mc68000)
#undef LibraryCCOptions
#define SharedLibraryCCOptions -f68881 -pipe
#endif
```

On AOS, you may find that *<stdarg.h>* is missing. In that case, you should be able to copy *mit/util/misc/rt.stdarg.h* to create the file.

On some System V/386 systems, you may find when using *gcc* in ANSI mode that there are inconsistent declarations between *<memory.h>* and *<string.h>*. In that case, you may find it convenient to remove *<memory.h>* and make it a link to *<string.h>*.

On some System V/386 systems, you may need to build and install a *dbm* library before building the X server and RGB database. One can be found in *contrib/util/sdbm*.

Internationalization

This release has support for internationalization, based on the ANSI-C and POSIX locale model. On some systems, you may discover that while the locale interface is supported, only the "C" locale is actually provided in the base operating system. If you have such a system, and would like to experiment with a broader set of locales, the Xlib implementation contains support you can use, although use of this override has not really been tested. You need to add the following defines to the **StandardDefines** parameter:

```
-DX_WCHAR -DX_LOCALE
```

In most cases you will have to directly edit the *.cf* file to do this, or else you will have to know what the rest of the values are supposed to be, and add this to *site.def*:

```
#undef StandardDefines
#define StandardDefines previous-values -DX_WCHAR -DX_LOCALE
```

It is also possible to directly edit the file *mit/include/Xosdefs.h* but this is not recommended.

With this setup, you will have to be careful that the system's declaration of **wchar_t** (in *<stddef.h>*) never gets used; this might be tricky.

A.2.5 Typing "make World"

One more piece of information is required before building, at least on some systems: bootstrap flags. Look in your *.cf* file for a line of the form:

```
#define BootstrapCFlags value
```

If this line isn't in your *.cf* file, things are simple; otherwise things are only slightly more complicated. If there is more than one (for example, in *ibm.cf*, *moto.cf*, and *sony.cf*), then you need to select the right one; it should be pretty obvious by the grouping according to operating system type. Note that on A/UX you only need this value if you are using *gcc*, and that on a Sun you only need this value if you are using an earlier version of the operating system.

If you are using *x386.cf*, you will have to "compute" the value from the information given in the file. Please read *mit/server/ddx/x386/README* to see if you need to do other preparatory work.

If no value is required on your system, you can *cd* to the *mit* directory and start the build with:

```
% make World >& world.log
```

If a value is required, start the build with:

```
% make World BOOTSTRAPCFLAGS="value" >& world.log
```

You can call the output file something other than *world.log*, but do not call it *make.log* because files with this name are automatically deleted during the "cleaning" stage of the build.

Because the build can take several hours to complete, you will probably want to run it in the background, and keep a watch on the output, for example:

```
% make World >& world.log &
% tail -f world.log
```

If something goes wrong, the easiest thing is to just start over (type "make World" again) once you have corrected the problem. It is possible that a failure will corrupt the top-level *Makefile*. If that happens, simply delete the file and recreate a workable substitute with:

```
% cp Makefile.ini Makefile
```

When the build completes, examine the *world.log* file for errors. If you search for colon (:) characters, and skip the obvious compile lines, it is usually pretty easy to spot any errors.*

A.3 Installing the Release

Although it is possible to test the release before installing it, it is a lot easier to test after it has been installed. If everything is built successfully, you can install the software by typing the following as root, from the *mit* directory:

```
% make install >& install.log
```

Again, you might want to run this in the background and use *tail* to watch the progress.

---

*Searching for the colon (:) does not work particularly well on the RS/6000 because it appears in command lines when building shared libraries. Try searching for the colon followed by space.

You can install the man pages by typing the following as root, from the *mit* directory:

```
% make install.man >& man.log
```

You can install lint libraries (useful if your system does not have an ANSI-C compiler) by typing the following as root, from the *mit* directory:

```
% make install.ln >& lintlib.log
```

A.3.1 Setting Up xterm

If your */etc/termcap* and */usr/lib/terminfo* databases do not have correct entries for *xterm*, sample entries are provided in the directory *mit/clients/xterm*. System V users may need to compile and install the *terminfo* entry with the *tic* utility.

Since each *xterm* will need a separate pseudoterminal, you need a reasonable number of them for normal execution. You probably will want at least 32 on a small, multi-user system. On most systems, each *pty* has two devices, a master and a slave, which are usually named */dev/tty[pqrstu][0-f]* and */dev/pty[pqrstu][0-f]*. If you don't have at least the "p" and "q" sets configured (try typing *ls /dev/?ty??*), you should have your system administrator add them. This is commonly done by running the *MAKEDEV* script in the */dev* directory with appropriate arguments.

A.3.2 Starting Servers at System Boot

The *xdm* program is designed to be run automatically at system startup. Please read the *xdm* man page for details on setting up configuration files; reasonable sample files can be found in *mit/clients/xdm/config*. If your system uses an */etc/rc* file at boot time, you can usually enable *xdm* by placing the following at or near the end of the file:

```
if [ -f /usr/bin/X11/xdm ]; then
        /usr/bin/X11/xdm; echo -n ' xdm'
fi
```

The example here uses */usr/bin/X11*, but if you have installed into a different directory (for example, by setting **ProjectRoot**) then you need to substitute the correct directory.

If you are going to use the font server, you can also start it at boot time by adding this:

```
if [ -f /usr/bin/X11/fs ]; then
        /usr/bin/X11/fs &; echo -n ' fs'
fi
```

If you are unsure about how system boot works, or if your system does not use */etc/rc*, consult your system administrator for help.

A.4 Rebuilding the Release

You shouldn't need this right away, but eventually you are probably going to make changes to the sources, for example, by applying public patches distributed by MIT. If only C source files are changed, you should be able to rebuild just by going to the *mit* directory and typing:

```
% make >& make.log
```

If configuration files are changed, the safest thing to do is type:

```
% make Everything >& every.log
```

`Everything` is similar to `World` in that it rebuilds every *Makefile*, but unlike `World` it does not delete the existing objects, libraries, and executables, and only rebuilds what is out-of-date.

Note that in both kinds of rebuilds you do not need to supply the `BootstrapCFlags` value any more; the information is already recorded.

A.5 Building Contributed Software

The software in *contrib* is not set up to have everything built automatically. It is assumed that you will build individual pieces as you find the desire, time, and/or disk space. You need to have the MIT software built and installed before building the contributed software. To build a program or library in *contrib*, look in its directory for any special build instructions (for example, a *README* file). If there are none, and there is an *Imakefile*, *cd* to the directory and type:

```
% xmkmf —a
% make >& make.log
```

This will build a *Makefile* in the directory and all subdirectories, and then build the software. If the build is successful, you should be able to install it using the same commands used for the *mit* software:

```
% make install >& install.log
% make install.man >& man.log
```

A.6 Filing Bug Reports

If you find a reproducible bug in software in the *mit* directory, or find bugs in the *mit* documentation, please send a bug report to MIT using the form in the file *mit/bug-report* and the destination address:

    xbugs@expo.lcs.mit.edu

Please try to provide all of the information requested on the form if it is applicable; the little extra time you spend on the report will make it much easier for us to reproduce, find, and fix the bug. Receipt of bug reports is generally acknowledged, but sometimes it can be delayed by a few weeks.

Bugs in *contrib* software should not be reported to MIT. Consult the documentation for the individual software to see where (if anywhere) to report the bug.

A.7 Public Fixes

We occasionally put out patches to the MIT software, to fix any serious problems that are discovered. Such fixes (if any) can be found on *export.lcs.mit.edu*, in the directory *pub/R5/fixes*, using anonymous *ftp*. Fixes are applied using the *patch* program; a copy of it is included in the directory *mit/util/patch*.

For those without *ftp* access, individual fixes can be obtained by electronic mail by sending a message to:

    xstuff@expo.lcs.mit.edu

(Note that the host here is "expo," not "export.") In the usual case, the message should have a subject line and no body, or a single-line body and no subject, in either case the line should look like:

    send fixes number

where *number* is a decimal number, starting from one. To get a summary of available fixes, make the line:

    index fixes

If you need help, make the line:

    help

Some mailers produce mail headers that are unusable for extracting return addresses. If you use such a mailer, you won't get any response. If you happen to know an explicit return path, you can include one in the body of your message, and the daemon will use it, for example:

    path *user%host.bitnet@mitvma.mit.edu*

or:

    path *host1!host2!user@uunet.uu.net*

A.8 What's New, What's Changed

In this section we briefly describe some of the more significant new features of Release 5.

A.8.1 New Standards

The following standards are new in Release 5:

X Font Service Protocol

> Instead of forcing each X server to read all fonts from the filesystem, the X Font Server Protocol makes it possible to manage fonts separately from the X server, directing the X server to request fonts via this new Consortium standard network protocol from a font server. In addition, for fonts which take a long time to open, this allows the X server to continue with other clients while the font server services the font requests.

XLFD changes for scalable fonts

> The X Logical Font Description standard has been compatibly enhanced to allow clients to specify and use scalable fonts.

X Input Device Extension

> This extension has been promoted from Draft Standard to full Consortium Standard with this release.

Inter-Client Communications Conventions

> This standard has been updated to cover the new X Device Color Characterization Conventions for device-independent color support in Xlib.

A.8.2 Clients

Most clients participate in the WM_DELETE_WINDOW protocol. The following is a list of client changes:

- New clients: *editres, viewres, xconsole, xcmsdb.*

- New demos: *beach_ball, auto_box, gpc, xcmstest, xgas, x11perf.*

- *Xlswins* has been removed; it is replaced by *xwininfo -tree.*

Release Notes

- Moved to contrib: *muncher, plaid*.

- Completely new implementation: *bitmap* and *xmag*.

Other noteworthy changes include the following:

editres   *editres* is a tool that allows users and application developers to view the full widget hierarchy of any X Toolkit client that speaks the Editres protocol. In addition, *editres* will help the user construct resource specifications, allow the user to apply the resource to the application and view the results dynamically. Once the user is happy with a resource specification, *editres* will append the resource string to the user's resources file.

xdm   *xdm* can now display a menu of hosts for XDMCP-capable terminals using the new *chooser* client. This is useful for X terminals that do not themselves offer such a menu. XDMCP works with STREAMS. A new setup program is invoked by *xdm* prior to putting up the login window; this program can be used to run *xsetroot, xcmsdb*, and to do any other custom initialization required.

xterm   Cuts of wrapped lines are now treated as a single line. Cuts of multi-page regions now work and highlight correctly. Pasting large amounts of data into *xterm* now works (on systems with properly-working pty implementations). New arguments have been added to the send-signal action: quit, alarm. The `titleInhibit` resource has been modified to also inhibit the escape sequence which switches to the alternate screen. Two new items have been added to the VT Fonts menu: 5x7 (Tiny) and 10x20 (Huge). The following resources have been added: `resizeGravity`, `bellSuppressTime`, `appcursorDefault`, `appkeypadDefault`, `ginTerminator`, `auto-Wrap`. The *Xterm Control Sequences* document is up-to-date. *Xterm* is installed securely when made setuid on SunOS 4.1.1 with shared libraries.

xmh   *xmh* now uses the `MH` environment variable, if set. *xmh* now supports checking for mail in multiple maildrops. Enhanced participation in WM_PROTOCOLS has been added. New resources have been added, including: `checkpoint-Interval`, `checkpointNameFormat`, `mailInterval`, `rescan-Interval`, `showOnInc`, `noMailBitmap`, `newMailBitmap`, `new-MailIconBitmap`, and `noMailIconBitmap`. New actions have been added: XmhWMProtocols, XmhShellCommand, XmhCheckForNewMail, Xmh-ViewMarkDelete. Better recovery from unexpected inconsistencies with the filesystem has been implemented. Better POP support has been added. See the file *mit/clients/xmh/CHANGES* for more details.

oclock   *oclock* has a new `–transparent` option.

xload   *xload* is secure on SunOS 4.1.1 with shared libraries.

xditview   *xditview* now supports *pic*, scalable fonts, settable device resolution, and now has a better user interface.

A.8.3 Libraries in General

All of the useful libraries now use function prototypes by default for systems which support them. SunOS shared libraries now use much less swap space than in R4. In addition, System V Release 4 and AIX 3.1 shared libraries are also supported now. Configuring new shared library systems should be much easier than before.

A.8.4 Xlib Manual

The Xlib manual has been reorganized for Release 5. Unfortunately, this may cause considerable confusion for a while when people quote section numbers without reference to the release. However, we feel that the new organization is a considerable improvement.

A.8.5 Athena Widget Set

Many minor bugs have been fixed. The Xaw examples have been moved to *contrib*. However, please note that the Athena Widgets have been and continue to be low on our priority list, so many bugs remain (particularly in the Text widget) and many requests for enhancements have not been implemented. Because some incompatible changes have been made, the shared library major version number on Suns has been incremented.

`Header Files` Function prototypes have been added to the public interfaces.

`AsciiSrc` No warning message is printed when the file cannot be written to; the return value should be enough info. `GetValues` on the string resource was failing when "useStringInPlace" was set to true; fixed. A memory leak when freeing pieces in a source of type "ascii String" has been plugged. The buffer is now updated whenever the "string" resource is set using `XtSetValues`. If the type is file then the file is read in again.

`Box` *Box.h* now includes *<X11/Xmu/Converters.h>* for the orientation resources.

`Clock` Changed to be a subclass of Simple instead of Core.

`Command` A bug in changing the shape style back to Rectangular has been fixed.

`Dialog` The Icon resource type has changed from `Pixmap` to `Bitmap`.

`Form` The geometry handler now will now disallow geometry management requests that will force the child outside the Form's window. Edge-Type names have been changed to have prefix `Xaw` instead of `Xt`, but the old definitions are still around with a #define. The string-to-widget converter no longer caches resources.

`Logo`	Changed to be a subclass of Simple instead of Core. Reverse video now works correctly.
`Mailbox`	Changed to be a subclass of Simple instead of Core. Reverse video now works correctly.
`MenuButton`	The MenuButton widget no longer places a server grab on itself. Instead, **PopupMenu** is registered as a grab action. As a result of this, clients which popped up menus without using **XtMenuPopup** or **MenuPopup** or **PopupMenu** in the menu button translations will fail to have a grab active. They should make a call to **XtRegisterGrabAction** on the appropriate action in the application initialization routine, or use a different translation.
`Paned`	*Paned.h* now includes *<X11/Xmu/Converters.h>* for the orientation resources. A bug that caused **XtGeometryYes** returns to have bogus values, and caused panes to get random sizes, has been fixed.
`Panner`	This widget is new in R5.
`Porthole`	This widget is new in R5.
`Repeater`	This widget is new in R5.
`Scrollbar`	Changed to be a subclass of Simple instead of Core. The type of thumb resource has changes from **Pixmap** to **Bitmap**. However, if applications provide the resource conversion, the **SetValues** method can still handle pixmaps of correct depth.
`Simple`	A color cursor converter has been added, as well as three new resource types: **XtNpointerColor**, **XtNpointerColorBackground**, and **XtNcursorName**.
`SmeBSB`	The Right bitmaps are now painted in the correct location. Right and Left Bitmaps can be specified in resource files and at startup time.
`Text`	If there is no current selection the selection extends from the insert point, rather than some random location. Forward (Backward) Paragraph works at the paragraph boundaries now. Selecting a word now transitions correctly at both endpoints. An infinite loop when using fill paragraph in a read-only text widget has been found and fixed. When the "resize" resource is set, the text will start up with exactly enough space to contain the text in the widget. A bug that could cause an infinite loop when Meta-Q was used to invoke the form-paragraph function on a read-only text widget has been fixed. Problems dealing with exposure events have been fixed. In *TextP.h*, the names of the following symbolic constants have had the prefix Xaw added to them: **XawLF**, **XawCR**, **XawTAB**, **XawBS**, **XawSP**, **XawDEL**, and **XawBSLASH**.
`Toggle`	The widget state is preserved across changes in sensitivity. A string-to-widget converter is registered for radio groups.
`Tree`	This widget is new in R5.

Vendor	Support has been added for the *editres* protocol. All applications using the Athena Widgets are automatically editable with *editres*. A bug that cause Shell to ignore all but the first child has been fixed.
Viewport	`XawPannerReport` support has been added.

A.9 Acknowledgements

The MIT Release 5 distribution is brought to you by the MIT X Consortium. A cast of thousands, literally, have made this release possible. We cannot possibly acknowledge them all here. The names of all people who made it a reality will be found in the individual documents and source files. We greatly appreciate the work that everyone has put into this release.

Hoping you enjoy Release 5,

Donna Converse
Stephen Gildea
Susan Hardy
Jay Hersh
Keith Packard
David Sternlicht
Bob Scheifler
Ralph Swick

(R5 Survival Club)

Release Notes

B

ICCCM Changes

The Inter-Client Communication Conventions Manual, *or ICCCM, describes conventions for the communication between X clients, including client-to-client, client-to-window manager, and client-to-session manager communcation. The ICCCM is printed as Appendix L of Volume Zero,* X Protocol Reference Manual. *In X11R5, a section has been added to the ICCCM which describes the contents and format of root window properties used to communicate the color characterization of a screen with clients that use device-independent color. This new section is printed in this appendix. It is excerpted from the X Consortium document,* Inter-Client Communication Conventions Manual, Version 1.1, MIT X Consortium Standard, X Version 11, Release 5.

In This Chapter:

The following section is new in the X11R5 ICCCM document. It documents the X Device Color Characterization Conventions, or XDCCC.

B.1 Device Color Characterization

This is Section 7 of the X11R5 ICCCM. It replaces Section L.7 of the X11R4 document printed in Volume Zero. The previous Section L.7 had a title, but had not been written in X11R4, and has been removed in X11R5.

The X protocol allows colors to be specified by explicit RGB value or by name. RGB values provide a mechanism for accessing the full capabilities of the display device. However, this is at the expense of having the color perceived by the user remain unknowable through the protocol. Color names were originally designed to provide access to a device-independent color information back database by having the server vendor tune the definitions of the colors in that textual database. Unfortunately, this still does not provide the client any way of using an existing device-independent color, nor for the client to receive device-independent color information back about colors which it has selected.

Furthermore, the client must be able to discover which set of colors are displayable by the device (the *device gamut*), both to allow colors to be intelligently modified to fit within the device capabilities (*gamut compression*), and to enable the user interface to display a representation of the reachable color space to the user (*gamut display*).

So, a system is needed which will provide full access to device-independent color spaces for X clients. This system should use a standard mechanism for naming the colors, be able to provide names for existing colors, and provide means by which unreachable colors can be modified to fall within the device gamut.

We are fortunate in this area to have a seminal work, the 1931 CIE color standard, which is nearly universally agreed upon as adequate for describing colors on CRT devices. This standard uses a tri-stimulus model called CIE XYZ in which each perceivable color is specified as a triplet of numbers. Other appropriate device-independent color models do exist, but most of them are directly traceable back to this original work.

X device color characterization provides device-independent color spaces to X clients. It does this by providing the barest possible amount of information to the client, which allows the client to construct a mapping between CIE XYZ and the regular X RGB color descriptions.

Device color characterization is defined by the name and contents of two window properties which, together, permit converting between CIE XYZ space and linear RGB device space (such as standard CRTs). Linear RGB devices require just two pieces of information to completely characterize them:

- A 3×3 matrix M (and it's inverse, M^{-1}) which convert between XYZ and RGB intensity ($RGB_{intensity}$):

$$RGB_{intensity} = M \times XYZ$$

$$XYZ = M^{-1} \times RGB_{intensity}$$

- A way of mapping between RGB intensity and RGB protocol value. XDCCC supports two mechanisms which will be outlined below.

If other device types are eventually necessary, additional properties will be required to describe them.

B.1.1 XYZ → RGB Conversion Matrices

Because of the limited dynamic range of both XYZ and RGB intensity, these matrices will be encoded using a fixed point representation of a 32-bit 2s complement number scaled by 2^{27}, giving a range of −16 to 16−ε, where ε = 2^{-37}.

These matrices will be packed into an 18 element list of 32 bit values, XYZ → RGB matrix first, in row major order and stored in the XDCCC_LINEAR_RGB_MATRICES properties (format = 32) on the root window of each screen, using values appropriate for that screen. This will be encoded as shown in Table B-1.

Table B-1. XDCCC_LINEAR_RGB_MATRICES Property Contents

Field	Type
$M_{0,0}$	INT32
$M_{0,1}$	INT32
...	
$M_{3,3}$	INT32
$M^{-1}_{0,0}$	INT32
$M^{-1}_{0,1}$	INT32
...	
$M^{-1}_{3,3}$	INT32

B.1.2 Intensity → RGB Value Conversion

XDCCC provides two representations for describing the conversion between RGB intensity and the actual X protocol RGB values:

• RGB value/RGB intensity level pairs for type 0 correction.

• RGB intensity ramp for type 1 correction.

In both cases, the relevant data will be stored in the XDCCC_LINEAR_RGB_CORRECTION properties on the root window of each screen, using values appropriate for that screen, in whatever format provides adequate resolution. Each property can consist of multiple entries concatenated together, if different visuals for the screen require different conversion data. An entry with a VisualID of 0 specifies data for all visuals of the screen that are not otherwise explicitly listed.

The first representation is an array of RGB value/intensity level pairs, with the RGB values in strictly increasing order. When converting, the client must linearly interpolate between adjacent entries in the table to compute the desired value. This is to allow the server to perform gamma correction itself and encode that fact in a short 2-element correction table. The intensity will be encoded as an unsigned number to be interpreted as a value between 0 and 1 (inclusive). The precision of this value will depend on the format of the property in which it is stored (8, 16, or 32 bits). For 16- and 32-bit formats, the RGB value will simply be the value stored in the property. When stored in 8-bit format, the RGB value can be computed from the value in the property by:

$$RGB_{value} = \frac{Property\ Value \times 65535}{255}$$

Because the three electron guns in the device may not be exactly alike in response characteristics, it is necessary to allow for three separate tables, one each for red, green, and blue. So, each table will be preceded by the number of entries in that table, and the set of tables will be preceded by the number of tables. When three tables are provided, they will be in red–green–blue order. This will be encoded as shown in Table B-2.

Table B-2. XDCCC_LINEAR_RGB_CORRECTION Property Contents for Type 0 Correction

Field	Type	Comments
VisualID0	CARD	Most significant portion of VisualID.
VisualID1	CARD	(Exists iff property format is 8.)
VisualID2	CARD	(Exists iff property format is 8.)
VisualID3	CARD	Least significant (exists iff property format is 8 or 16).
type	CARD	0 for this type of correction.
count	CARD	Number of tables following (either 1 or 3).
length	CARD	Number of pairs minus 1 following in this table.
value	CARD	X Protocol RGB value.
intensity	CARD	Interpret as a number 0 <= intensity <= 1.kk
...	...	Total of *length+1* pairs of value/intensity values
lengthg	CARD	Number of pairs minus 1 following in this table (iff *count* is 3).

Field	Type	Comments
value	CARD	X Protocol RGB value.
intensity	CARD	Interpret as a number 0 <= intensity <= 1.
. . .	. . .	Total of *lengthg+1* pairs of value/intensity values.
lengthb	CARD	number of pairs minus 1 following in this table (iff *count* is 3).
value	CARD	X Protocol RGB value.
intensity	CARD	Interpret as a number 0 <= intensity <= 1.
. . .	. . .	Total of *lengthb+1* pairs of value/intensity values.

Note that the VisualID is stored in 4, 2, or 1 pieces, depending on whether the property format is 8, 16, or 32, respectively. The VisualID is always stored with the most-significant piece first. Note that the length fields are stored as one less than the actual length, so that 256 entries can be stored in format 8.

The second representation is a simple array of intensities for a linear subset of RGB values. The expected size of this table is the bits-per-rgb-value of the screen, but it can be any length. This is similar to the first mechanism, except that the RGB value numbers are implicitly defined by the index in the array (indices start at 0):

$$RGB_{value} = \frac{Array\ Index \times 65535}{Array\ Size - 1}$$

When converting, the client may linearly interpolate between entries in this table. The intensity values will be encoded just as in the first representation. This will be encoded as shown in Table B-3.

Table B-3. XDCCC_LINEAR_RGB_CORRECTION Property Contents for Type 1 Correction

Field	Type	Comments
VisualID0	CARD	Most significant portion of VisualID.
VisualID1	CARD	(Exists iff property format is 8).
VisualID2	CARD	(Exists iff property format is 8)
VisualID3	CARD	Least significant (exists iff property format is 8 or 16).
type	CARD	1 for this type of correction.
count	CARD	Number of tables following (either 1 or 3).
length	CARD	Number of elements minus 1 following in this table.
intensity	CARD	Interpret as a number 0 <= intensity <= 1.
. . .	. . .	Total of *length+1* intensity elements.
lengthg	CARD	Number of elements minus 1 following in this table (iff *count* is 3).
intensity	CARD	Interpret as a number 0 <= intensity <= 1.
. . .	. . .	Total of *lengthg+1* intensity elements.
lengthb	CARD	Number of elements minus 1 following in this table (iff *count* is 3).
intensity	CARD	Interpret as a number 0 <= intensity <= 1.
. . .	. . .	Total of *lengthb+1* intensity elements.

C

XLFD Changes

The X Logical Font Description Conventions, *or XLFD, is a document that defines conventions for the naming of fonts. It is printed as Appendix M of Volume Zero,* X Protocol Reference Manual. *In X11R5, two sections have been added to the XLFD to describe the naming of scalable fonts. These new sections are printed in this appendix. They are excerpted from the X Consortium document,* X Logical Font Description Conventions, Version 1.4, MIT X Consortium Standard, X Version 11, Release 5.

In This Chapter:

The sections that follow have been added in the X11R5 *X Logical Font Description* document.

C.1 Support Scalable Fonts

This paragraph has been added to Section 1, Requirements and Goals, in the X11R5 XLFD document. It falls between Section M.1.2 and Section M.1.3 of the X11R4 document as printed in Volume Zero.

If a font source can be scaled to arbitrary size, it should be possible for an application to determine that fact from the font name, and the application should be able to construct a font name for any specific size.

C.2 Scalable Fonts

This is Section 3 from the X11R5 XLFD document. It falls between Section M.2 and Section M.3 of the X11R4 document as printed in Volume Zero.

The XLFD is designed to support scalable fonts. A scalable font is a font source from which instances of arbitrary size can be derived. A scalable font source might be one or more outlines together with zero or more hand-tuned bitmap fonts at specific sizes and resolutions, or it might be a programmatic description together with zero or more bitmap fonts, or some other format (perhaps even just a single bitmap font).

The following definitions are useful for discussing scalable fonts:

Well-formed XLFD pattern
> A pattern string containing 14 hyphens, one of which is the first character of the pattern. Wildcard characters are permitted in the fields of a well-formed XLFD pattern.

Scalable font name
> A well-formed XLFD pattern containing no wildcards and containing the digit "0" in the PIXEL_SIZE, POINT_SIZE, and AVERAGE_WIDTH fields.

Scalable fields

The XLFD fields PIXEL_SIZE, POINT_SIZE, RESOLUTION_X, RESOLUTION_Y, and AVERAGE_WIDTH.

Derived instance

The result of replacing the scalable fields of a font name with values to yield a font name that could actually be produced from the font source. A scaling engine is permitted, but not required, to interpret the scalable fields in font names to support anamorphic scaling (i.e., scaling by unequal amounts in the x and y dimensions).

Global list

The list of names that would be returned by an X server for a **ListFonts** protocol request on the pattern "*" if there were no protocol restrictions on the total number of names returned.

The global list consists of font names derived from font sources. If a single font source can support multiple character sets (specified in the CHARSET_REGISTRY and CHARSET_ENCODING fields), each such character set should be used to form a separate font name in the list. For a non-scalable font source, the simple font name for each character set is included in the global list. For a scalable font source, a scalable font name for each character set is included in the list. In addition to the scalable font name, specific derived instance names may also be included in the list. The relative order of derived instances with respect to the scalable font name is not constrained. Finally, font name aliases may also be included in the list. The relative order of aliases with respect to the "real" font name is not constrained.

The values of the RESOLUTION_X and RESOLUTION_Y fields of a scalable font name are implementation-dependent, but to maximize backward compatibility they should be reasonable non-zero values, for example, a resolution close to that provided by the screen (in a single-screen server). Since some existing applications rely on seeing a collection of point and pixel sizes, server vendors are strongly encouraged in the near term to provide a mechanism for including, for each scalable font name, a set of specific derived instance names. For font sources that contain a collection of hand-tuned bitmap fonts, including names of these instances in the global list is recommended and sufficient.

The X protocol request **OpenFont** on a scalable font name returns a font corresponding to an implementation-dependent derived instance of that font name.

The X protocol request **ListFonts** on a well-formed XLFD pattern behaves as follows:

- Start with the global list.

- If the font pattern has scalable fields that are not wildcarded, then substitute each such field into the corresponding field in each scalable font name in the list.

- For each resulting font name, if the remaining scalable fields cannot be replaced with values to produce a derived instance, remove the font name from the list.

- Now take the modified list, and perform a simple pattern match against the pattern argument. **ListFonts** returns the resulting list.

For example, given the global list:

-Linotype-Times-Bold-I-Normal- -0-0-100-100-P-0-ISO8859-1
-Linotype-Times-Bold-R-Normal- -0-0-100-100-P-0-ISO8859-1
-Linotype-Times-Medium-I-Normal- -0-0-100-100-P-0-ISO8859-1
-Linotype-Times-Medium-R-Normal- -0-0-100-100-P-0-ISO8859-1

a **ListFonts** request with the pattern:

-*-Times-*-R-Normal--*-120-100-100-P-*-ISO8859-1

would return:

-Linotype-Times-Bold-R-Normal- -0-120-100-100-P-0-ISO8859-1
-Linotype-Times-Medium-R-Normal- -0-120-100-100-P-0-ISO8859-1

ListFonts on a pattern containing wildcards that is not well-formed is only required to return the list obtained by performing a simple pattern match against the global list. X servers are permitted, but not required, to use a more sophisticated matching algorithm.

Index

Cardinal *, 139
catalogues, 13
CCC, **29**, 33
color specifications, converting, 189, 322
default, 34
getting default for a screen, **193, 326**
of colormap, 34, 185, 318
.cf files, 326
character set, 45
character width, versus string width, 53
characters, accented, displaying, 41
unconvertible, 63
charset, 45
Chinese text, 42, 74
Chroma, color space, 24, 34
finding maximum Value for, 212, 345
CIELab, gamut-querying functions for, 35
CIELuv, gamut-querying functions for, 35
class, and portability, 138
client_data, 98
clients, new features, 335
client-side, color name database, 28
client-to-client, internationalization, 57
client-to-window-manager, internationalization, 57
Clock widget, 337
codeset, 43, 45
collation, 44
color, 23, 35
aliases, 28
conversion, 33-34
device-independent, 4, 23-36
distinguishing, 265-266, 398-399
naming, 26-28
new features, 23
reversing foreground and background, 100
specifying, 26-27, 189, 322
strings, 27

values, 194, 198-199, 327, 331-332;
obtaining, 31
(see also device dependent/independent color; Xcms.)
color cell, setting color of, 31, 205, 207, 338, 340
color conversion context, (see CCC)
color spaces, 24-25, 27, 29
color, 191, 324
colorimetry, **24**
colormap cells, distinguishing, 266, 399
querying, 30
colormaps, functions, 30
obtaining CCC of, 34, 185, 318
specifying, 93
Command widget, 337
composed text, 79, 106
compound text, 47, 57
concatenating strings, 47
-config configuration_file, 157, 290
configuration files, 325, 328
font server, installing, 329
configuration parameters, setting, 325
const keyword, 136
context dependencies, 53
contributed software, building, 333
convex.cf, 326
COnvexOS, .cf file, 326
-cpp, 280, 413
cray.cf, 326
cursor position, moving, 101-102
customizations, resources, 123
specifying multiple, 123

D

-D option (xrdb), 281, 414
databases, (see resource databases)
dates, displaying in internationalized applications, 41, 44
decimal separators, 44
DECnet, font servers, naming, 14
derived instances, 16-17

defining, 135
initialization procedure, registering, 258, 391
initializer functions, calling, 259,
  392
input contexts, and input methods,
  90
  and windows, 91
  attributes, 88, 90-95;
    obtaining, 234, 367;
    setting, 424
  choosing interaction styles, 86
  creating, 77, 86, 221, 354
  destroying, 86, 225, 358
  focus, 78, 90, 433
  functions, 85
  geometry negotiation, 93
  getting input method of, 239, 372
  resetting, 89, 248, 381, 442
  utility functions, 90
input focus, setting, 78, 423
input manager, 75
input methods, 90
  and input contexts, 90
  and input servers, 75
  and line spacing, 94
  and text internationalization, 69
  attributes, 84
  closing, 82, 181, 314
  colormaps, specifying, 93
  editing the pre-edit string, 99
  geometry, 92
  getting; display of, 226, 359;
    information, 237, 370;
    locale of, 241, 374
  internationalization, 74
  obtaining multi-byte input from,
    106, 246, 379
  obtaining wide-character input
    from, 440
  opening, 77, 82, 276, 409
  overriding default, 83
  returning display associated with,
    90
  size, querying for, 95
  specifying pixels for, 94
  user interaction with, 76
  wide-character input, obtaining
    from, 106
input servers, 75
input streams, and multi-byte
  strings, 48

InstallFSConfig, 329
InstallLibManPages, 328
InstallXdmConfig, 328
InstallXinitConfig, 328
interaction styles, 76
  choosing, 86
INTERACTIVE, .cf file, 326
interclient communication, internationalized, 60
Inter-Client Communication
  Conventions, new features,
  335
Inter-Client Communication
  Conventions Manual
  (ICCCM), 29
internationalization, 5, 39-69
  and interclient communication,
    60
  and string encoding, 56
  and the X Toolkit, 66
  and X11R5, 48
  new features, 40
  of strings, 41
  overview, 41
  programs, 39, 45
  strings, 47
  summary, 69
  text; drawing, 50, 54;
    input, 73-116;
    output, 50
  with ANSI-C, 43
IRIXC, .cf file, 326
ISO8859-1 character set, 46

J

Japanese text, 42, 46, 50, 133,
  146

K

Kanji text, 133, 146
keyboard input, Asian, 42
keysyms names, 138
Korean text, 42, 133, 146

Index

nested, argument lists, 82
function prototypes, 136
nested variable argument lists,
allocating, 434
networked font service, (see font
service)
new, (as structure name), and portability, 138
NEW-OS, .cf file, 326
-nocpp, 280, 413
numeric color specification, 27

O

oclock, 146, 336
off-the-spot interaction style, 77
outline fonts, 12, **15**
output streams, and multi-byte
strings, 48
overspecified font names, 18
over-the-spot interaction style,
77

P

Paned widget, 338
Panner widget, 133, 141, 144,
160, **293**
destroying, 164, 297
parameters, list of, 327
setting configuration, 325
pcf, 133, 146, 328
pegasus.cf, 326
PEX, 6, 328
PHIGS, 5
PHIGS-PLUS, 5
PHIGS-SI, 5
pixels, distinguishing, 266, 399
specifying for input methods, 94
PIXEL_SIZE, 16
pixmaps, creating from a file, 267,
400
plaid, 146, 335
POINT_SIZE, 16
port numbers, 14
-port, 157, 290
portability, and header files, 134
and X11R5, 134
Portable Compiled Fonts, 133,
146

Porthole widget, 133, 141, **165,**
298
POSIX, and X11R5, 133-134
header files, 135
_POSIX_SOURCE, 135
Preedit, 77
attributes, 92
callbacks, 94, 98-99
geometry management, 78,
95-97
sub-attributes, querying, 89
pre-edit string, editing, 99
ProjectRoot, 326
protocols, authorization, 133, 145
public fixes, 334

Q

quarks, and strings, 120, 128
supporting names in encoding,
64
-query, 191, 280, 324, 413
querying, colormap cells, 30
device gamut, 34-35
display databases, 119
scalable fonts, 19
-quiet, 280, 413

R

rectangles, input context attributes, 92
registering language procedures,
66
-remove, 191, 281, 324, 414
Repeater widget, 133, 141, **168,**
301
RESOLUTION_X, 16
RESOLUTION_Y, 16
resource databases, ? wildcard,
120
and displays, 119, 128, 421
combining contents of, 127
enumerating entries, 128, 417
finding locale of, 64
localization of, 63
merging contents of, 119
retrieving, 64, 128, 419
returning locale of, 119, 129, 420

screen specific, 124
storing, 64
X Toolkit, 129
resource files, customized, 123
including files in, 122
syntax, 120-122
resource management, 6,
119-130
**resource manager functions
(Xrm)**, string encoding and
locale changes, 64
resource names, and localization,
63
resource properties, server,
obtaining, 283, 416, 422
resource strings, screen specific,
124
RESOURCE_MANAGER, 124
resources, and specifying locales,
66
specifying translation tables as,
126
widget, 270, 403
widget, obtaining, 271, 404
-retain, 281, 414
RGB, 24
RGBi, 27
right-to-left text, 53
rindex, 135
RISCOS, .cf file, 326
root window, interaction style, 77
properties, 23

S

%S, 123
scalable fields, 16
scalable fonts, 3, 11-20, **15**
and scalable fields, 16
average width, 16, 18
backwards compatibility, 16
derived instances, 16-17
finding, 15, 18
in complex applications, 18
in simple applications, 18
loading, 19
naming, 16
overspecified names, 18
pixel size, 16
point size, 16

querying, 19
recognizing, 18
resolution, 16
scaling, 19
underspecified names, 17
well-formed names, 16
scaling fonts, 15
screen, and input methods, 76
characterization, 29
getting default CCC for, 193, 326
setting defaults for, 125
-screen, 280, 413
SCREEN_RESOURCES, setting
resources in, 124
screens, 280, 413
Scrollbar widget, 338
server, building, 328
disabling, 328
resource properties, obtaining,
283, 416, 422
ServerVendor, 57
setlocale, 41, **43**, 108
systems that don't support, 50
sgi.cf, 326
shift sequences, 46
Simple widget, 338
site.def, 326
SmeBSB, 338
snf, 133
sony.cf, 326
standard selection target types,
260, 393
standards, new, 335
state-dependent encodings, and
multi-byte strings, 47
Status area, 76
callbacks, 94, 98
displaying strings and bitmaps in,
103
geometry management, 78
negotiating geometries, 95-97
sub-attributes, querying, 89
Status area callbacks, 78
stdarg.h, 134
STDC, 134
strcat, 48
strchr, defining, 135
strcmp, 48
strcpy, 48
strftime, 44
string constants, X Toolkit, 139

string encodings, 56
  in the X Toolkit, 66
  used by XLib functions, 57
string lists, and text properties, 60
string width, versus character
    width, 53
strings, comparison routines, 48
  Compound Text, 47
  concatenating, 47
  conversion functions, 142
  converting from one locale to
    another, 57
  converting to various types, 262,
    395
  converting to widgets, 268, 401
  internationalized, 41, 45, 47
  multi-byte; (see multi-byte
    strings)
  unconvertible characters in, 63
  wide-character; (see wide-char-
    acter strings)
strlen, 48
strncmp, 48
strptime, 44
strrchr, defining, 135
Success value, 61
sun.cf, 326
SUN-DES-1, 133, 145
SunOS, .cf file, 326
  static linking, 329
SVR4, 138
symbolic link trees, 324
symbols, system-specific, 138
-symbols, 280, 413
system, startup, 332
system files, making changes to,
    329
system-specific symbols, 138
SYSV, 138

                    T

%T, 123
target types, converting to stan-
    dard selection, 260, 393
TCP/IP, font servers, naming, 13
TekHVC, 24, 35
  Chroma, 24
  coordinates, obtaining, 215, 348
  diagram of color solid, 25

finding maximum Chroma for,
    211, 344
finding the maximum Value for,
    212, 345
Hue, 24
returning boundaries of, 214, 347
Value, 24
text, and internationalized inter-
    client communication, 60
  composed, 106
  conversion,
    returning default string used for,
      224, 357
    to Compound Text encoding,
      54, 61
    to STRING encoding, 61
  drawing, 54, 242, 375, 435
  escapement, obtaining, 53, 249,
    382, 443
  events, computing, 250, 383, 444
  in internationalized programs, 45
  leaving unconverted, 61
  multi-byte, drawing, 243-244,
    376-377
  strings, obtaining information for,
    254, 387, 448
  wide-character, drawing,
    436-437
text events, computing, 54
text input, 73-116, 106
  (see also input methods; interna-
    tionalization, text input; wide-
    character input; multi-byte
    input)
text lists, converting to text proper-
    ties, 60, 252, 385, 439, 446
text properties, converting to text
    lists, 60, 252, 385, 439, 450
text strings, obtaining information
    for, 60
Text widget, 338
3-D structured graphics, 5
time, displaying in international-
    ized applications, 41, 44
time function, defining, 135
Toggle, 338
-top option, 176, 309
translation tables, encoding, 66
  overriding items in, 119
  specifying as resources, 126
-transparent option, 146

Tree widget, 133, 141, **172, 305**
-tree option, 146

U

-U option (xrdb), 281, 414
Ultrix, build problems, 329
.cf file, 326
ultrix.cf, 326
underlining, 101
underspecified font names, 17
UNICOS, .cf file, 326
UNIOS-B, .cf file, 326
UNIX System C/386, .cf file, 326
USG, 138
UTek, .cf file, 326
UUCP, obtaining X11R5 from, iv

V

Value, finding maximum Chroma
for, 211, 344
Value color space, 24, 34
variable argument lists, in C, 137
nested, allocating, 434
-variable option, 176, 309
Vendor widget, 338
-vertical option, 176, 309
Viewport widget, 339
viewres, 143, 146, **176, 309**

W

wchar_t, 47
well-formed font names, 16
wide-character input, obtaining,
106, 440
wide-character strings, 47
drawing, 55
freeing, 61
wide-character type, 47
widget node functions, 143
widget nodes, initializing arrays
of, 273, 406
looking up by name, 275, 408
widgets, 337
converting strings to, 268, 401
determining number of resources
inherited, 270, 403

inverting, 153, 286
obtaining resource lists of, 271,
404
reshaping, 269, 402
wildcards, 119
and resource component names,
120
in scalable fonts, 16
window managers, communicating with, 60
windows, multiple, and input
focus, 54, 78
root; (see root window)
**WM_DELETE_WINDOW proto-
col,** 146

X

X Color Management System,
(see Xcms)
X Device Color Characterization
Conventions (XDCCC), 23,
29, **29**
X Font Service Protocol, 11, **12,**
335
X Input Context (XIC), 73
X Input Device Extension, new
features, 335
X Input Method (XIM), 73
X Logical Font Description
(XLFD), 4, 12, 15
X Toolkit, and internationalization,
66
and locale dependencies, 66
and string encoding, 66
building resource databases, 129
changes in X11R5, 139
locale, establishing, 66
string constants, 139
X Window System, font server,
157, 290
X11 Input Device Extension, 133,
144
X11/Intrinsic.h, 139
x11perf, 335
X11R5, and ANSI-C standards,
133-134
and Athena widgets, 141
and POSIX standards, 133-134
and Xmu, 141

Index

Index

About the Author

David Flanagan is a consulting programmer and technical writer. He has worked on a number of educational software projects, most recently at MIT's Project Athena where he specialized in user interface design and X Toolkit widget writing. He has been programming with the Motif widgets since their pre-release days and has also been involved in debugging those widgets. David holds an S.B. degree in Computer Science and Engineering from the Massachusetts Institute of Technology.

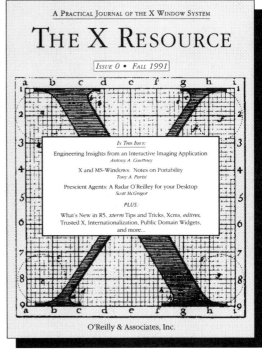

XrmCombineDatabase

Name

XrmCombineDatabase — combine the contents of two resource databases.

Synopsis

```
void XrmCombineDatabase(source_db, target_db, override)
    XrmDatabase source_db;
    XrmDatabase *target_db;
    Bool override;
```

Arguments

source_db   Specifies the resource database that is to be merged into the target database.

target_db   Specifies the address of the resource database with which the resource file is to be combined.

override   Specifies whether resources from *source_db* should override matching resources in *target_db*.

Availablity

Release 5 and later.

Description

XrmCombineDatabase merges the contents of one database into another. If the same resource specifier is used for an entry in both databases, the entry in *source_db* will replace the entry in *target_db* if *override* is True; otherwise, the entry in from *source_db* is discarded.

If *target_db* points to a NULL database, *XrmCombineDatabase* simply stores *source_db* at the location pointed to by *target_db*. Otherwise, *source_db* is destroyed by the merge, and the database pointed to by *target_db* is not destroyed.

The database entries are merged without changing values or types, regardless of the locales of the databases. The locale of the target database is not modified.

Related Commands

XrmCombineFileDatabase, XrmMergeDatabases

XrmCombineFileDatabase

Name

XrmCombineFileDatabase — combine the contents of a resource file and a resource database.

Synopsis

```
Status XrmCombineFileDatabase(filename, target_db, override)
    char *filename;
    XrmDatabase *target_db;
    Bool override;
```

Arguments

filename   Specifies the name of the resource file.

target_db   Specifies the address of the resource database with which the resource file is
             to be combined.

override   Specifies whether resources from the file should override matching resources
             in the database.

Availablity

Release 5 and later.

Description

XrmCombineFileDatabase merges the contents of a resource file into a database. If the
same resource specifier is used for an entry in both the file and the database, the entry in the file
will replace the entry in the database if override is True; otherwise, the entry in the file is
discarded.

If target_db points to a NULL database, XrmCombineFileDatabase creates a new
database, reads the file into it and stores this new database at the location pointed to by target_db. Otherwise, the database pointed to by target_db is not destroyed by the merge.

If the file cannot be read a zero status is returned; otherwise a nonzero status is returned.

The file is parsed in the current locale. The database entries are merged without changing values or types, regardless of the locale of the database, and the locale of the target database is not
modified.

Related Commands

XrmCombineDatabase, XrmMergeDatabases

Name

XtAllocateGC — obtain a shareable GC with modifiable fields.

Synopsis

```
GC XtAllocateGC(object, depth, value_mask, values, dynamic_mask,
        dont_care_mask)
    Widget object;
    Cardinal depth;
    XtGCMask value_mask;
    XtGCValues *values;
    XtGCMask dynamic_mask;
    XtGCMask dont_care_mask;
```

Inputs

object   Specifies an object; may be of class Object or any subclass thereof.

depth   Specifies the depth for which the returned GC is valid, or 0.

value_mask   Specifies the fields of the GC which must have fixed values.

values   Specifies the values for the fields in *value_mask*.

dynamic_mask
                 Specifies fields of the GC which may be modified.

dont_care_mask
                 Specifies fields of the GC which will never be used.

Returns

A GC with fields as specified in *value_mask* and *values*.

Availability

Release 5 and later.

Description

XtAllocateGC() returns a sharable GC with values as specified in *values* for each field
set in *value_mask*. The GC is valid for the screen of the specified object (the screen of the
nearest widget ancestor if the specified object is not itself a widget) and for drawable depth
depth. If *depth* is 0, the depth is taken from the XtNdepth resource of the object (or from
its nearest widget ancestor). The *dynamic_mask* and *dont_care_mask* arguments specify more information about the intended usage of the GC which influences how the GC may be
shared. These arguments are explained below.

When returned, the GC may already be in use by other widgets, and it may be passed to other
widgets in the future. For this reason, none of the fields specified in *value_mask* should ever
be modified. The *dynamic_mask* argument specifies fields of the GC that may be modified
by the widget. Because this is a shared GC, other widgets may also modify those fields, and a
widget cannot rely on them to remain unchanged. For this reason, these fields must be explicitly set prior to every use.

The *dont_care_mask* argument specifies fields of the GC that the widget does not care about (ie. fields that will never be used by any of the graphic functions called with this GC). The returned GC may have any values for these fields.

GC fields that are not specified in *value_mask*, *dynamic_mask*, or *dont_care_mask* will always have their default values in the returned GC. If a field is specified in both *value_mask*, and in *dynamic_mask*, then the field is modifiable, but will also be initialized to the appropriate value specified in *values*. If a field is set in *dont_care_mask* and is also set in one of the other masks, the *dont_care_mask* is ignored for that field.

Usage

XtAllocateGC() is a generalization of XtGetGC(). Calling XtAllocateGC() with *depth*, *dynamic_mask*, and *dont_care_mask* all 0 is equivalent to calling XtGetGC() with the remaining arguments.

There are several common situations in which a modifiable GC is necessary. If you are drawing complex text with XDrawText(), the font field of your GC will be automatically changed to each of the font values in your text description. Also, if you use clip masks to protect or speed up drawing in a widget's expose method, you will need to modify the clipping fields of the GC. Using XtAllocateGC() with a *dynamic_mask* argument means that you can share a GC, with other instances of the same widget, at least, instead of allocating a private GC with XCreateGC().

Furthermore, specifying a *dont_care_mask* when allocating a shared GC can make that GC much more sharable. For example, if a widget draws text with XDrawString() only, then it is only interested in the font and foreground fields of a GC. If it allocates its GC and specifies that it doesn't care about the background field, then it can share its GC with another widget that uses the same font and foreground, but draws with XDrawImageString() and so *does* care about the background field. This kind of sharing is not possible with XtGetGC().

Note that XtAllocateGC() is new in Release 5. If you use it in a widget, you will loose portability to Release 4. If you have a Release 4 widget that uses a private GC, you may be able to add conditional compilation directives to make it use the more efficient XtAllocate-GC() when compiled with X11R5.

When done with a GC obtained with XtAllocateGC(), it should be freed with Xt-ReleaseGC().

Structures

The XtGCMask type is simply an unsigned long:

```
typedef unsigned long  XtGCMask; /* Mask of values that are used by widget*/
```

Each of the symbols in the table below sets a single bit in an XtGCMask. The *value_mask*, *dynamic_mask*, and *dont_care_mask* arguments are formed by combining these symbols with the bitwise OR operator (|):

GCArcMode	GCFillRule	GCLineWidth
GCBackground	GCFillStyle	GCPlaneMask
GCCapStyle	GCFont	GCStipple

GCClipMask	GCForeground	GCSubwindowMode
GCClipXOrigin	GCFunction	GCTile
GCClipYOrigin	GCGraphicsExposures	GCTileStipXOrigin
GCDashList	GCJoinStyle	GCTileStipYOrigin
GCDashOffset	GCLineStyle	

The XGCValues structure has one field for each of the GC fields:

```
typedef struct {
    int function;                   /* logical operation */
    unsigned long plane_mask;       /* plane mask */
    unsigned long foreground;       /* foreground pixel */
    unsigned long background;       /* background pixel */
    int line_width;                 /* line width */
    int line_style;                 /* LineSolid, LineOnOffDash,
                                       LineDoubleDash */
    int cap_style;                  /* CapNotLast, CapButt,
                                       CapRound, CapProjecting */
    int join_style;                 /* JoinMiter, JoinRound, JoinBevel */
    int fill_style;                 /* FillSolid, FillTiled,
                                       FillStippled, FillOpaqueStippled */
    int fill_rule;                  /* EvenOddRule, WindingRule */
    int arc_mode;                   /* ArcChord, ArcPieSlice */
    Pixmap tile;                    /* tile pixmap for tiling operations */
    Pixmap stipple;                 /* stipple 1 plane pixmap for stipping */
    int ts_x_origin;                /* offset for tile or
    int ts_y_origin;                 * stipple operations */
    Font font;                      /* default text font for text operations */
    int subwindow_mode;             /* ClipByChildren, IncludeInferiors */
    Bool graphics_exposures;        /* should exposures be generated? */
    int clip_x_origin;              /* origin for clipping */
    int clip_y_origin;
    Pixmap clip_mask;               /* bitmap clipping; other calls for rects */
    int dash_offset;                /* patterned/dashed line information */
    char dashes;
} XGCValues;
```

See Also
XtGetGC, XtReleaseGC.

Name

XtScreenDatabase — obtain the resource database for a screen.

Synopsis

```
XrmDatabase XtScreenDatabase(screen)
    Screen *screen;
```

Arguments

screen   Specifies the screen for which the database should be obtained.

Availablity

Release 5 and later.

Description

XtScreenDatabase returns the fully merged resource database for the the specified screen. If that database has not already been built (by XtDisplayInitialize, for example), Xt-ScreenDatabase builds it. If the specified screen does not belong to a display initialized by XtDisplayInitialize, the results are undefined.

XtAppInitialize, XtGetResourceList, and XtGetSubresources provide a more manageable approach to obtaining resources.

Related Commands

XtDatabase